QUANTUM
GOD

How Life Really Works

Michelle Langenberg

BALBOA.
PRESS
A DIVISION OF HAY HOUSE

Author Credits
Langenberg contributed to *Chicken Soup* and *The Formalist* and is author of *The Painted Bible; Portraits of a Poet; Wherever We Are . . . Unity; You Won't Always Be Little, Tad,* the manuscript, *Integrative Health Guide,* and two screenplays looking for a producer.

Balboa Press books may be ordered through booksellers or by contacting:

Balboa Press
A Division of Hay House
1663 Liberty Drive
Bloomington, IN 47403
www.balboapress.com
1-(877) 407-4847

Because of the dynamic nature of the Internet, any web addresses or links contained in this book may have changed since publication and may no longer be valid. The views expressed in this work are solely those of the author and do not necessarily reflect the views of the publisher, and the publisher hereby disclaims any responsibility for them.

The author of this book does not dispense medical advice or prescribe the use of any technique as a form of treatment for physical, emotional, or medical problems without the advice of a physician, either directly or indirectly. The intent of the author is only to offer information of a general nature to help you in your quest for emotional and spiritual well-being. In the event you use any of the information in this book for yourself, which is your constitutional right, the author and the publisher assume no responsibility for your actions.

Any people depicted in stock imagery provided by Thinkstock are models, and such images are being used for illustrative purposes only. Certain stock imagery © Thinkstock.

ISBN: 978-1-4525-7128-7 (sc)
ISBN: 978-1-4525-7130-0 (hc)
ISBN: 978-1-4525-7129-4 (e)

Library of Congress Control Number: 2013905501

Printed in the United States of America.

Balboa Press rev. date: 07/08/2013

*I am called
by many names.
Speak any word
and it is I
and yet, My Self
is greater than
the all of All,
that which you call*
God.

The Tao can't be perceived,
smaller than an electron,
it contains uncountable galaxies . . .

The Tao is called the Great Mother:
empty yet inexhaustible,
it gives birth to infinite worlds.
It is always present within you.
You can use it any way you want.

Tao Te Ching
Lao-Tsu[1]

"Science can never rule out the theory that
the universe was made by an all-powerful God."

Brian Greene
Late Night with David Letterman
March 22, 2005

Acknowledgments

Cover photo credit: Lagoon Nebula, M 8, Messier 8
Original image by ESA/Hubble & NASA
Mark Jarman's poetry is courtesy of Sarabande Books
"It's All in Your Outlook" illustration credit: Matt Ulmer
"One with Everything" illustration credit: Kelsey Winscott
"Chakra Tree" photo credit: John Langenberg

I am most grateful to the following people for their endless patience and assistance:

Deborah Shouse for advising me to make *Quantum God* the tale of my own journey, Beverly Karol Turner-Allen for her unlooked-for and unflagging support, Gene Mitchell and Dennis Wiggins who so willingly read, re-read, and commented on my manuscript, the Johnson County, Kansas reference librarians, Matt Ulmer for sharing his expertise and his treatise, *Handbook of Meridian Therapy and More*, and Reagan Brewer for printing numerous working copies of *Quantum God* and other manuscripts.

These join a wealth of people who have encouraged and upheld me, a list that would fill a book in itself and includes my mother and children, sisters and brothers, fellow writers and teachers. So many angels walk this earth, sharing kindnesses as naturally as the sun shares its warmth.

Foreword

It was cold, snowy day in Kansas City. The schools had been shut down and it wasn't safe to drive on the icy streets. I was homebound and not particularly pleased about it until I found the perfect companion for such a day. It was Michelle Langenberg's book, *Quantum God: How Life Really Works*. From the very first page it captivated me with the mysterious intricacies of existence. Langenberg has a brilliance that goes way beyond "text-book" information and leads the reader into the realm of deep intuitive resonance. She weaves simplicity and complexity together in such a way that the point she makes is stimulating yet easily understood.

If you want to peek behind the curtain, discover what life is truly all about, and be introduced to a new and deeper understanding of God, this book is a must-read.

Duke Tufty, CEO and Senior Minister
Unity Temple on the Plaza

Table of Contents

Part Two

Appendix

Preface

"No man cometh unto the Father, but by me."

No one comes into rhythm with the breathing life of
all, the sound and atmosphere that created the cosmos,
except through the breathing, sound, and atmosphere,
of another embodied "I" connected to the ultimate "I
Am." . . . Through attunement with Jesus' breathing,
atmosphere, and way of prayer, they will be led to
experience what he experiences.

Neil Douglas-Klotz
The Hidden Gospel

W hat is God? Who, what, where, when and why is God? When I was
young, we walked to whatever church was closest to our house—
Presbyterian, Baptist, Methodist—and we made the trek every Sunday. As
a teenager, my best friend was a Jewish girl, and I worried about the "fact"
that our religion was condemning her to hell, along with all the other Jews,
Buddhists, Hindus, Baha'is, American Indians, pagans and pygmies, atheists
and, as far as I knew, the Eskimos, too. Surely something was wrong with this
picture. Or something was wrong with the person we claimed as our God.

I was told I needed to be "saved," and that rankled, too. Our mortal
quandary was explained to me this way: God is perfect, we are not; therefore,
we need Jesus as an intermediary, like a bridge between this perfect Being and
human beings, who are sinful merely because we are born into life on Earth.
This made no sense to me; not from my viewpoint as a child, nor as a parent,
friend, or the product of a Creator in whose image we were made.

What good is God if God isn't good? The first thing many of us learned
in Sunday School was "God is Love." What's going on here? If God is
unconditional Love, why would He play favorites and banish anyone or
anything to everlasting isolation in a hell worse than any we on Earth can
conceive? For heaven's sake, this hardly sounded like Love with a capital "L."
Our Old Testament concept of God as a cosmic tyrant swayed by whims and

motivated by anger reminded me of the impulsive, preferential, and completely selfish Greek and Roman gods who caused havoc in the lives of their innocent worshippers.

The exclusive divinity of Jesus—our *brother*—troubled me, too, until I learned what happened at the Constantine formation of the "official" Bible in Nicea (325 CE): 1,100 documents arbitrarily thrown out and the decision to denote Jesus as immaculately conceived and divine, thus supplying the Church with the means to support itself by requiring fees as liaison between (this old theme again) perfect God and sinful mortals! This decision smacked of corporate cover-up, usury, and downright falsifying. Jesus had the chance to precipitate a political revolt, as Judas hoped he would, and become King of the (Mediterranean) World. Instead, he opted for life as an itinerant preacher who kept company with "the dregs of society." His prime message seemed to be "love all" and "death is not the end" and "what I have done, so can you."

Yes, it is reported that Jesus said, "No one comes to the Father but through me," and yet as a student of classical Greek and Latin, I had a good idea of the pitfalls involved in translating a foreign language used by an ancient people whose culture, idioms, and teaching methods differ greatly from even King James' seventeenth-century interpreters. I also knew that Biblical scholars have found 20,000 mistakes in our version of the Bible; although the Bible was divinely inspired, it is not free from the egos of its writers or imperfections of later scribes and interpreters.

And various versions of the Bible witness to the fact that the *way* it is translated makes a difference in *how* it reads. In his book, *The Hidden Gospel*, Neil Douglas-Klotz provides alternate translations of key verses that illuminate the messages behind Jesus' words. In fact, the Aramaic scholar translates the key Christian verse, John 14:6, "I am the way, the truth and the life" as the light of the sacred force, free and in harmony with the universe, that uncovers a path; and "No man cometh unto the Father, but by me" as "No one comes into rhythm with that which created the cosmos except through the breathing, sound, and atmosphere, of 'I Am.' This statement is valid for those who hold Jesus as their guide, or for one who matches Jesus' breathing, aura, and way of prayer."[2]

And the Bibles we use today—on what documents were they based: the original scrolls written in Hebrew and Aramaic and Greek? No. Even if we did possess the original documents compiled by Moses and the writers of the New Testament (few of whom were *actual* eyewitness disciples of Christ), the question then becomes: Are these the true scriptures, or are they copies "doctored" by the Essenes in case they fell into the hands of the early churches' enemies? Imagine what would have happened if the Romans seized a group's scriptures in which Pontius Pilate was named as the responsible party for ordering the crucifixion of Christ? (For *only* the Romans had the authority to crucify anyone.) The whole lot would have found themselves suspended from crosses before they had time to cry, "Lord, have mercy!" And even if our documents were the original gospels handwritten by Matthew, Mark, Luke and John, any translation between two languages, two cultures, and 2,000 years (not to mention the personal viewpoints of the translators and errata of scribes) would be bound to contain distortions.

For example, even so small a matter as a misplaced comma can make a tremendous difference in the outcome of the message, as in "Woman without her man is nothing," which can be punctuated as

"Woman, without her man, is nothing,"
or, in a complete turnaround in meaning, as
"Woman! Without her, man is nothing."

And that example is one simple string of contemporary, non-idiomatic words in a language familiar to most of us.

These religious prickles—including the immaculate conception of Mary,[3] which surely John would have mentioned, were it true—grated against my soul, along with the largest wound of all, the fact that over the past millennium, those wearing the banner of Christ (who commanded us to love God and neighbor, self and *enemy*) have taken it upon themselves to ostracize, upbraid, torture and/or slaughter "heathens" who believe differently, and all *in God's name.*

In a series of letters between Albert Einstein and Niels Bohr, two of the greatest physicists of the twentieth century, Einstein wrote, "God does not play dice with the universe," and Bohr immediately wrote Einstein to "stop telling God what to do."[4] The fact is, we cannot hope to know God if we believe we already know what God is like. Thich Nhat Hanh, the well-known Vietnamese monk and Nobel Peace Prize Laureate, has said that Buddha was not opposed to God, but to any *concepts* of God that hinder us from self-development and "touching ultimate reality."[5]

In my search, I made two outstanding discoveries: First, that several of the same "eternal truths" ran through every race, every creed, like the Golden Rule. The life-guides of our civilization—Christianity, Judaism, Taoism, Buddhism, Hinduism, Shintoism, Islam (which literally means "surrender"[6]), pantheism, Wicca, and tribal traditions—comprise basic truths, but the simple, *original* messages have been deeply buried through ages of oral transmissions, deletions, and translations.

I also discovered that ancient peoples as diverse as the Indians in Asia to the Indians of North America held profound insights into the workings of Nature long before our "modern" physical sciences. Such were the stimuli for and some of the solutions to my ongoing search for the Truth . . . about God and our relation to God, about the man called Yeshua, truths contained in the Kabbalah and in other world religions and philosophies, the way science and spirituality support each other, and the life-affirming doors that have been all but hidden behind dogma—in short, Quantum God, and how life really works.

May this book be one such doorway, and to all who enter in, blessed be.
Michelle Langenberg

One

Will you have the soup?

If thou canst believe, all things are possible.

Mark 9:23 (KJV)

In the image of God...

Once upon a time—Star Date 29 December, 1966—I watched in wonder as crew members of the *Enterprise* beamed down to an uncharted planet for "Shore Leave" where Dr. McCoy caught sight of a white rabbit chasing Alice, a Samurai warrior attacked Lieutenant Sulu, and Captain Kirk met an old flame, who looked just as he remembered her. Before the *Star Trek* episode ended, Kirk and his crew discovered the planet itself was making their thoughts, their fantasies, and their fears come to life. Gene Roddenberry had, in fact, attended many channelings of the divine "Council of Nine" and heard their message: "The Earth was created to be a paradise."[7]

What if we *do* live on such a magical planet? One summer afternoon, my mom and I went to watch a city parade. She loves parades. I don't. Not as a child, and not as an adult. That day I was hot and hungry and kept thinking, "I want a cigarette and a piece of gum." A couple of hours passed, along with most of the parade. As the stream was winding down, Mom and I began walking back to my car. After a half block or so, at the tail-end of the parade, a few stragglers passed us. They were tossing out goodies, and I caught two pieces of gum.

Those two pieces of gum may seem trivial, but they transformed the outing into a magical adventure. There they were, products of the Law of Manifestation, lying in my hot little hand. I laughed for the joy of it—a wish come true!

What if each of us is our own genie, except that we don't need any *thing*, like a transporter or Aladdin's magic lamp, because the magic is already inside us? Christian and Jewish scriptures say that we humans were "made in the image of God." But in Sanskrit, God is *neti, neti*: "Not this, not that." Not *things*.[8] Our likeness to God refers to our capability of creating as God does.

> Because your Creator creates only like Himself, you are like Him. You are like Him Who is all power and glory, and are therefore as unlimited as He is.
>
> *A Course in Miracles (ACIM)*

So why do we worship Jesus or Buddha (or rock stars and sports celebrities)? Because we think we can never be like them. But we are. The Church has separated the human "us" from our birthright, the divine "Us." And why not? Any business requires a group of people who needs its products or services. Where would cobblers be if we were all hobbits? Where would hospitals be if everyone believed in our inherent ability to possess complete good health? What would happen to many churches if everyone believed in our inherent goodness, because we have been created in the likeness and goodness of God?

We haven't fully grasped the implication of "in God's image." We haven't claimed the role of *creator* as our own. The truth is that *the Divine is what we are*, and we are *always* creating, whether or not we realize what we're doing.

Always creating . . . even miracles? What if miracles are the way life is meant to work all the time, but our disagreements, denials, and tenacious clinging to half-truths throw a giant wrench into what was supposed to be a divinely running operation?

Try It Yourself

Using Einstein's equation, $E = mc^2$, to figure out how powerful you are, multiply the speed of light by itself and then multiply that figure by what you weigh.

Example:

```
        186,282
     x 186,282 (miles per second = how fast light travels)
 34,700,983,524
            x 47 (my approximate weight in kilograms)
 1,631,946,225,628 my potential creative power in kilograms
```

Living in the Shadowlands

Plato used an analogy suggesting most people live in a cave, sitting with our backs to the mouth of the opening. Outside the cavern shines the light of true reality, but on the inside we only notice the shadows cast on the stone walls. Then we base our science and philosophy on those shadows.[9]

This sounds a little like the veils of the Hindus. The Hindus believe we abide in *maya*. Maya, however, is not our *world* but the *belief* that the illusions we see is the true realm of existence. Over the last century, science has been playing catch-up in trying to understand how to move past the shadows and dispel the illusions by more fully comprehending the system we're living in.

> What we call reality consists of a few iron posts of observation between which we fill in an elaborate papier-mache of imagination and theory.
>
> John Archibald Wheeler
> *Quantum Theory and Measurement*

In the *Twilight Zone* of my childhood, Rod Serling told us each week that we unlock the door to new dimensions of the mind with imagination. The door is unlocked not with a key, but with a new thought, an open mind.

Albert Einstein compared our universe to the movies we watch in theatres. The ancients already knew this; the Sanskrit word for "creation" is *srishti*, which means "projection."[10] And don't we love movies? The *Matrix* movies portray the majority of humans asleep, with each person merely dreaming of living in the world. This theme is also hinted at in the Bible: "And the Lord God caused a deep sleep to fall on Adam, and he slept." *But no verse following this passage ever mentions that Adam woke up.*[11]

Like Neo, are we all asleep? A Taoist parable tells about a man who dreamed he was a butterfly. Upon waking, he asked himself, "Am I a man who dreamed he was a butterfly, or a butterfly dreaming it is a man?"[12] Mystics through the ages have agreed that we are indeed asleep—and many of us are living in a nightmare.

I agree! I want to wake up, or at least learn how to direct my own dream.

> The central text of the *Zohar* exclaims, "You beings on earth who are in deep slumber, awaken!"
>
> Rabbi David Cooper
> *God is a Verb: Kabbalah and the Practice of Mystical Judaism*

Belief Systems on the Go

Imagine two people walking side by side down a winding path. If we ask them to describe their journey, one might say it was heaven while the other claimed it was hell, and they'd both be right.[13] Our belief systems envelop each of us and go with us wherever we go.

I have been like the second traveler, and I don't travel light. As a treble Cancer, my home goes with me. In my little four-cylinder Saturn I carry food and drink; books and word puzzles; notebooks for teachers' meetings and church; a blanket, pillow, and extra change of clothes; recycled bags for groceries (which I forget to take into the store); art portfolio and resumes; lipstick, earrings, and perfume; a dog leash and fold-out chair; petty cash, a suitcase of teaching materials, and books to give away. If I lug all this material stuff everywhere I go, what emotions and memories and self-condemnation am I also hauling around? For too long I failed to realize the door to my take-along hell was locked on the inside, and that I myself held the key in hand. No, make that "in *mind*." It's as if I had been living in the C.S. Lewis story where people have damned themselves to hell, and nothing other than their own choice prevents them from entering heaven.

So what is the truth about how life works? Can anything be absolutely true? In scientists', theologians', and parents' search for truth, they have found that there are constants the world goes by, physical laws that are always true:

Toddlers like playing with the boxes their gifts come in.
It rains after you wash your car.
Gravity always holds true . . . uh, except for the yogis who levitate.
The shortest distance is a straight line between two points . . . except for a swami who, a man from India once told me, vanished and reappeared the next instant a hundred yards away from where he and his family were standing.

The World of Quantumstuff

Can levitation and teleportation be true? Yes. What scientists call quantum entanglement makes teleportation possible.

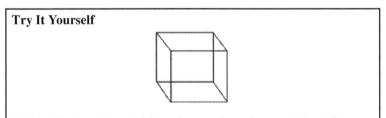

Try It Yourself

This is a Necker Cube, which can be seen from above or below. If you see the cube facing first down to the right and then up to the left, you have participated in a "quantum leap" or "quantum jump." Your mind has jumped between one possibility and another without passing any point in between.

All sorts of weird things can happen when we learn that atoms are filled with "quantumstuff," which acts like a cloud of possibilities.[14] From this nebulous, almost-real stuff the magic arises. What it comes down to is, we *are* each a genie. A magician. A creator.

When we get down to the subatomic level, the solid world we live in also consists . . . of almost nothing and that whenever we do find something it turns out not to be actually something, but only the probability that there may be something there. One way or another, this is a deeply misleading universe.

Douglas Adams
The Salmon of Doubt: Hitchhiking the Galaxy One Last Time

The *whole world* is made from almost-real stuff? Clouds of "maybe" and "probability?" Wait a minute. That sounds like the Twilight Zone. I'm touching this paper. The chair I'm sitting in is holding me up. I'm flesh and blood, not supernatural.

But honestly, I also know that my physical senses *do* lie to me. The Earth does *seem* to be flat, doesn't it? And sometimes I know who's calling before I pick up the phone. Maybe I'd better move beyond my five senses and take a look at the quantum world.

To understand what the quantum world is like, find a photograph on the Internet. It looks like a product the ad agency is trying to sell you, but if you look very closely, you'll see that the screen picture is made up of a bunch of colored dots. When you zoom in even closer, even the pixels look different. They seem boxy and meaningless, while the larger picture, taken as a whole, looks smooth and realistic.

The macrocosmic world is like that photo, but instead of pixels it's made of quanta, little cloudbursts of energy whose essence is more like a *thought* than a *thing*. Photons are the quanta in a light beam; electrons are a kind of quanta in atoms. *Everything* is composed of quanta, and all processes are governed by the rules of quantum theory.

Everything is composed of little magical packets of potential called quanta.[15] Although human beings are slow-moving macrocosms in relation to subatomic particles, *we are composed of quanta and what quanta can do, we can also do.*[16] And quanta, as we shall see in Chapter Four, *can* do mind-boggling things.

The new physics shows that humans are capable of much more than we ever thought. Even Jesus said that the things he had done, so shall we do, and more (John 14:12). We possess abilities we've reserved for the Divine, the Christs and Buddhas, the avatars and swamis. In fact, the word "Christ" is historically merely a term given to "enlightened" people, including early Hebrew kings.[17]

> It is better that we know we are God and give up this fool's search after Him; and knowing that we are God we become happy and contented. Give up all these mad pursuits, and then play your part in the universe, as an actor on the stage . . . [And] this very world becomes heaven, which formerly was hell.
>
> Vivekananda, "Practical Vedanta"

My son, Sean, and I have trouble when we visit a restaurant. He can't decide on the best item to order, and I know chances are good that I'll pick something I won't like and then feel bad about having to *pay* for food I didn't enjoy eating. But if the soup's homemade, it's a sure bet for both of us and a big tip for the wait staff.

FROM QUANTUM SOUP,
EVERYTHING WE TOUCH TURNS TO MATTER

When we turn our backs, "reality" is the quantum soup of potentialities.
But then we look and everything we see, everything we touch turns to matter.

How does quantumstuff work? The world is like "quantum soup," and it stays soupy until our attention freezes it into subatomic particles, turning it into ordinary reality. That means, as both physicists and Rod Serling have noted, imagination is the key that transforms potential ingredients into the meal, city, planet, and universe.

It's time to use our imagination, like rubbing a genie's lamp or putting on a magician's cape, and consciously use the laws of quantum physics. The concepts below have progressed from *theoretical* spiritual ideas to scientifically *proven* ideas:

- We are all connected.
- Everything, including all "living" and "non-living" matter, vibrates at a specific frequency.

- Anything physical begins as a mental concept.
- Our thoughts, feelings, and actions affect everything in existence.
- Time does not absolutely move in only one direction.
- There is something beyond what we can see, hear, touch and taste.
- Heredity, karma, conditioning—none of these are unchangeable limitations.
- Light behaves like both a wave and a particle, and so does everything else.
- We are energy systems—frozen light—using a fraction of our potential.
- We have access to the wisdom of the ages.
- We are co-creators of our lives and our world.

These and the principles that follow can rouse us from the nightmare many of us are co-creating. In our present age, science and spirituality are brother and sister philosophies working hand-in-hand to wake us up.

> Electrons can dance between parallel states. They can disappear, reappear some place else, they can be two places at the same time . . . But the killer question is, electrons can dance between parallel universes, and if electrons can do it, why can't we?
>
> Michio Kaku
> *Prophets of Science: Philip K. Dick*
> (aired on the Science Channel, 11/20/11)

Two

Physically, we are both transmitters and receivers.

A tree beside the wall stands bare,
But a leaf that lingered brown,
Disturbed, I doubt not, by my thought
Comes softly rattling down.

Robert Frost
"A Late Walk"

Good Vibrations

After nearly twenty-five years of marriage, my husband and I sold the home where we'd raised our children and moved to Oregon. After a year, we returned to the Midwest; our marriage was eroding and we were both suffering from deep depression. We needed to buy a house quickly, but the market was terrible. We found shoddy houses in our price range. Even the homes we couldn't afford had old furnaces, cracked foundations, leaky roofs. Each one we looked at was too old, too far from work, too something or other. Finally my dream house went on the market. It was beyond our price range, I knew, but there was no cost for looking. "There's an Open House on Lamar this Sunday," I told John. "Can we go?"

We did, and oh, the Arts and Crafts bungalow struck a chord deep inside me. Appreciating the craftsmanship of the home, I ran a hand lovingly over a varnished window casing, a hand-sanded post, a beveled glass pane. John picked up on my feelings but reacted in a totally different manner.

By the time we walked down the front steps, John was fuming. I felt his frustration and the anger it had engendered and, as usual, I became defensive. However, I'd lately been "practicing peace" and paused a moment to calm down. Before getting into the car, I took a deep breath and formed the intention of radiating peace instead of engaging in strife. This commitment made all the difference; a gentle word to John led to untangling the misunderstanding—that home was not an option. Together we drove on to the next Open House.

The Beach Boys sang about good vibrations. Did they mean that humans are walking guitar strings? It may sound strange, but vibrations make sense when we stop to think about how, when we're stressed out and feeling bad, everything goes wrong. "Heavy" matters "weigh" on us. During an argument, the tension is "thick enough to cut with a knife." And when we're feeling cheerful or when we've fallen in love, everything looks brighter, everyone acts more kindly, and life is good. We feel "drawn" to some place or person, "lighthearted," or even "spacey," as if we're walking on air. We feel repulsed by certain personalities, "drained" by others, and attracted to people with "magnetic" personalities.

We talk about being "on the same wavelength" when we feel a rapport with someone because we have matching vibrations at that time. Rapport is an example of resonance, which means, literally, to "echo." Resonance is "like attracting like." Resonating people feed energy to one another in "sympathetic vibrations," which is how they're liable to come up with some really good ideas and finish one another's sentences. It drives my children crazy when I expect them to finish my thought, but when my mother or friend, Roxie, and I are talking together, that *Gilmore Girls* sort of dialogue comes naturally, right down to saying the same words at the same time.

We Reap What We Sow

Everything physical—everything made of matter—is actually vibrating energy. That is what Albert Einstein's famous equation, $E = mc^2$ (or rather its algebraic reversal, $E/c \times c = m$) means. Matter is slowed-down, smushed together, "crystallized" light. Condensed.

Condensed energy is easy to understand when we think about the cycle of physical life: A spinach plant absorbs sunshine (energy) and turns it into new plant growth (matter). We then eat the spinach, as Popeye did, and the matter turns into calories (energy). In fact, with enough energy (pressure) and a handful of chimney soot, we can turn ashes into diamonds.[18]

> $E = mc^2$ is "the alchemy that turns sunlight into children."
>
> K.C. Cole
> Prize-winning science columnist for the *Los Angeles Times*
> *Mind Over Matter*

Like transceivers, our brains process energy.[19] Every thought is an electromagnetic wave, and each thought travels at its own unique frequency. Thoughts—especially emotionally driven thoughts—combine with other thoughts vibrating at the same frequency. All living creatures constantly emit physical, emotional, and mental vibrational waves, and *we receive at the frequency at which we are vibrating.* We are walking, talking transformers, less like radios than like interactive X-boxes. We are creating and acting in the sitcoms or dramas of our daily life.[20]

A person who once wins the lottery is liable to win yet a second time. Why? Because that person feels lucky, and feeling lucky attracts more "good luck." If we want something good to come into our lives, we must, by the universal/quantum law of "sympathetic resonance," be vibrating at the higher pitch at which the good event is vibrating. This is the scientific basis for "As ye sow, so shall ye reap."

For more than thirty years, Princeton has conducted studies using human operators and a machine called a random event generator (REG). Princeton's experiments have shown that humans influence the behavior of mechanical, electronic, optical, acoustical, and fluid devices. Without any physical interaction with the human beings, the machines are caused to deviate in their random outputs according to *human intention. Human consciousness manipulates the machines.* The operators can be thousands of miles away and can even be exerting their influence *after* the actual operation of the machines. The premise of the Princeton Engineering Anomalies Research (PEAR) is that "consciousness exchanges information with its environment," and has "some control over its reality."

Anyone can recreate the REG findings with a computer game. "Bookworm" uses Scrabble-like tiles that fall down into columns. The goal is to link letters and form words. The intriguing thing is, this game functions according to quantum rules. The more often any certain word is formed, the more often the random letters fall so that word can again be formed. Stranger still is that I can often *will* a particular letter to fall, so as to complete the spelling of the word I have in mind. Bookworm is a fascinating man-on-the-street (or woman-in-the-chair) illustration of quantum mechanics at work in our everyday world. Bookworm proves how effective human will and repetition can be.

The technological applications of the REG experiments affect everything from aircraft cockpits and missile silos to surgical facilities and disaster control; that is, human creativity and the interconnectedness of our universe applies to medicine, management, manufacturing, communications, education—anywhere human beings work and live and interact with any sort of matter, living or (so-called) non-living.[21]

Stones that Feel Love

Non-humans are conscious beings? Yes. Time-lapse photography has shown that plants not only move toward sunlight (pleasure) and away from fire (pain) and respond to affection as do human beings, but they also react to human thoughts.[22] Cleve Backster, the creator of polygraph scoring techniques in the 1960s, has performed thousands of experiments with plants. His first lie detector experiment proved that a dracena cane plant responded to his *thought* of him burning one of the plant's leaves.

In an interview Backster said, "I didn't verbalize, I didn't touch the plant, I didn't touch the equipment. The only new thing that could have been a stimulus for the plant was the mental image. Yet the plant went wild. The pen jumped right off the top of the chart." With *no time lapse* between his thought of burning the leaf and the plant's reaction, the plant responded to Backster's intention. The houseplant also knew when Backster didn't really mean to follow through: When he again thought of burning the leaf without *intending* to harm the plant, the polygraph needle didn't move.[23]

All right, plants are alive and have the ability to think and to feel. That's no news to me; I regularly encourage and sing to my plants. But isn't consciousness limited to the living? No, the physicists say; *non*-living things are conscious beings. Physicist David Bohm maintained that electrons possess a "proto-intelligence." Subatomic particles appear to be making decisions all the time.[24] I believe it, too. I've always named my cars and sweet-talked them, because they respond to my energy (as we'll see in Chapter Eleven).

> Even stones have a love, a love that seeks the ground.
> Meister Eckhart

So every *thing* is alive? Yogananda thought so. He believed that all things, including solids, liquids, gases, electricity, all beings, gods, men, animals, plants, and bacteria, are forms of consciousness.[25] And modern science bears him out.

The How of Our Lives

If everyone and everything is conscious energy, then it follows that

1. Everything we ingest has an affect on our energy system, whether it be food, drink, drug, attitude or idea, and
2. *How* we do something affects what we end up with, because the energy involved in our action attaches itself to the product of the action. Everything we do is *infused* with the energy we used in doing it.[26] Beneficial or not. For example, the frenetic energy of worry begets more things to worry about, and a strongly felt fear may help to manifest exactly what we had feared.

In Viktor Frankl's words, "The fear is the mother of the event."[27] Whether we're feeling happy or angry, peaceful or fearful, in the likeness of Quantum God we create what we experience individually and in groups, so *we want to strive for the best feeling we can manage at any given moment.*

Three

Individually and en masse, we shape the events of our lives.

Not once in the dim past, but continuously by conscious mind is the miracle of the Creation wrought.

Sir Arthur Eddington [28]

The Participatory Universe

Theoretical physicist Frank Oppenheimer often told people that ours is not the *real* world. "It's a world we made up," he would say.[29] His colleague, John Wheeler, used to tell a joke about three umpires arguing on the ball field. The first shouts, "I calls 'em as I sees 'em."

"Not me," replies the second umpire. "I calls 'em as they really are."

The third official sums up his authority when he boasts, "They ain't nothin' until I calls 'em."[30]

Wheeler, who coined the terms "black hole" and "quantum foam," believed we all jointly create the things in our life. "Useful as it is under everyday circumstances to say that the world exists 'out there' independent of us," he wrote in an article appropriately titled "Law Without Law," "that view can no longer be upheld. There is a strange sense in which this is a 'participatory universe'."[31] Wheeler maintained that our physical world is materialized through observation (our attention). We participate in Creation, quantum studies have shown, because *we affect whatever we see or measure (or think or feel).*

> The fact that we affect what we "touch" has a very important modern-day application, especially for financial institutions. Quantum key distribution (QKD) allows information to be transmitted over the internet securely. If a hacker tries to "peek," the photon information is disturbed and the sender and recipient both *know* there's a hacker lurking in the vicinity, trying to intercept their message.
>
> American Association for the Advancement for Science
> http://news.sciencemag.org/sciencenow/2010/04/quantum-cryptography-hits-the-fa.html

Quantum mechanics has given rise to the electron microscope, the transistor, the computer, the superconductor and the laser, CDs and DVDs, mp3s, and cell phones. Mozart, Alexander Graham Bell, and Galileo would be astounded at our modern, magical contraptions. But the real magic is not in the machines, it's in the creators—us! This is one of the messages Jesus tried to leave for us when he said, "Is it not written in your law, 'I said, Ye are gods'?" (John 10:34) And what do gods do? They create stuff.

First Jesus and now a respected scientist telling me I'm responsible for my life. Okay. I'd like to know how observing and creating happen, because if I *have* been creating my life, I've been doing a *great* job with a *poor* outcome. Where does "Abracadabra," which means "I am creating as I speak," come in?[32]

I want to learn how to use my magic!

Controlling the Motion of the Atoms

Occasionally influencing a computer game is one thing, but can we control the very atoms that make up matter? Physicist Erwin Schrödinger believed it was the conscious mind that controls the "motion of the atoms."[33] Lahiri Mahasaya would have agreed. Lahiri was a Christ-like man living in India who cured the ill and materialized food and shelter—even a palace in the mountains. Lahiri transcended the laws of science, and when he moved outside a law, his action became a new law.[34] People like Lahiri rewrite the laws of nature as we know them. Sounds appropriate for a participatory universe.

The highly practical mathematician John von Neumann reluctantly arrived at the same conclusion: Consciousness creates the reality we know. Von Neumann wanted to determine the exact timing for the "collapse of the wave function," which is the moment when a potentiality becomes physically real. But everything in the world is physical, including scientists' measuring machines. Even our personal "tools of measurement," our eyes and our brains, are physical. *Everything* is made out of electrons and protons and quarks and quanta. All these *things*, von Neumann reasoned, can be represented mathematically, by what they call wave functions. So where does the "collapse of the wave function" occur? Being a down-to-earth left-brainer and after doing a bunch of mathematical equations, Von Neumann decided that the only *non-physical* step in the process that was the mind.[35]

We are the ones who *think* quantumstuff into chairs and blankets and picnic tables.[36] We influence events in our everyday lives. [37] For example, through the frigid hours of the Himalayan night, practitioners of Hatha yoga sit outdoors, naked and unafraid, using the psychic heat generated by their focused intention to melt and dry out icy sheets draped around their bodies. They use attention, intention, belief, focus, and passion, all of which are within our own grasp.

We determine the nature of what we will experience through . . .

- Attention: What we think about most often
- Intention: How we feel about the people and events in our life and how we plan to act
- Beliefs and imagination: Ideas of what is possible and what is not possible
- Focus: Determination
- Passion: Emotional content

Riding Waves of Magic with the Maker of Dreams

Well, let's see; I was divorced after nearly 30 years of marriage, starving, saddled with a house payment that totaled more than my monthly income, crying over a man I thought would marry me and didn't, and had lost my full-time job. Was I ever ready to rewrite my life!

How was I to start? By taking responsibility for what "happened" to me. The prerequisite to conscientious creating is to assume responsibility for our lives, without feeling constricted by or blaming any external agency—neither spouse, child, friend, stranger, nature, or God. I stayed in the marriage too long, went without a job for too long, should have moved and rented a cheap little house, should have picked a different man to fall in love with, and should have taken *any* job just to pay rent. As *A Course in Miracles* says, *I did this to myself.* And knowing that, the text says, is *the secret to salvation.*

Why does self-accountability matter? Because of the Law of Materialization. More than just transmitter/receivers, we are transformers. We are flesh-and-blood power plants that convert mental-psychic energy into the events that form our lives. $^E/c \times c = m$. This is another way of saying that the stuff we can touch is materialized (or matter-ized) thought.[38]

The creative force is like the gasoline that makes a car run; the car can be driven by a drunkard or by someone sober—but if an accident occurs, no one blames the gas or the car. It was the responsibility of the person behind the steering wheel to drive well, and it is our responsibility to steer ourselves through life.[39] Quantum physics holds us personally accountable. And awareness of quantum laws liberates us from self-imposed limitations. I was all for sloughing off unnecessary limitations! I wanted to learn how this system works.

The science is this: At the heart of quantum physics lie probability waves. A probability wave is what it sounds like, a wavy representation of all the things that are most probable, plucked from an infinite number of things that are possible.

Now, an ordinary wave is a surge of energy that carries information and spreads its influence, like a crime wave or a rumor that sweeps through a crowd. Abraham Lincoln began a wave of emancipation that Martin Luther King, Jr. added energy to with Freedom Marches a hundred years later. Elvis Presley made waves tuned to the beat of rock and roll and changed the tenor of our music. Quantum principles crashed through the arena of science like massive waves rolling through a previously placid pool. Quantum ideas carry waves that influence those of us who are crowded into time and space.

Outside time and space—we could even say "somewhere over the rainbow"—there exists a para-physical Force that allows our dreams and our fears to come true. One of the quantum laws *proves* that this non-physical realm exists beyond our universe. (Wheeler's "delayed-choice" experiment, which proves faster-than-light communications, discussed in Chapter Seventeen.) Aristotle and Werner Heisenberg called this Force *potentia*. Physicist David Bohm called it the implicate order, with the superimplicate order directing *potentia*, and the whole thing contained within the holomovement. And Deepak Chopra calls it the Field of Possibilities.

In *potentia*, every possibility exists. Let's listen to that statement again, for it affects every particle of our lives: Within *potentia*, EVERY possibility exists. The choices we make call into physical reality various possibilities.

> The Tao is like a well:
> used but never used up.
> It is like the eternal void:
> filled with infinite possibilities.
>
> *Tao Te Ching #4*
> Stephen Mitchell, translator

The superimplicate order is like a magical clearinghouse located beyond the warehouse of *potentia*. So how do our "abracadabras" get from here to there and back again? A telepathic wave carries the information, taking its direction from us and the energetic patterns we create in a dizzying system of give-and-take relationships. Our free will directs the orders and routing: We can make wise choices that contribute immediately to our fulfillment, or we can construct brick walls to beat our heads against. God may point us in certain directions, but God never sabotages our ability to choose.

I once dreamed of walking into a store where I found God smiling at me from behind the counter. Overhead stretched a colorful banner that read, "Dreams Are Always Free."

"Is it true?" I asked. "I can have anything?"

"Anything your heart desires."

"Oh, God," I exclaimed, "whatever You say, that's what I'll take."

God replied gently, "I am sorry, dear heart, but that I cannot do. I provide the means to make your dreams come true, but you must supply the vision."

Me? But I'd given up on my dreams. I was going to have to dust off my imagination, I realized, when I read what the great swami, Vivekananda, had said: "Whatever you dream and think of, you create."[40]

I read further, and learned that Einstein valued imagination above education. In fact, the seed for Einstein's theory of relativity came from young Albert imagining that he was riding a beam of light. It is imagination that designs what becomes real.

> If we didn't get so lost in our heads, whole new worlds would open up to us.
>
> Jon Kabat-Zinn
> Unity Temple on the Plaza, January 30, 2005

Why not dream big? Give potentia, give Goodness, the chance to work. God keeps the flow going, round about, if only we believe and accept and share.

Thinking about Thinking

Our inner world is creating our outer world, so we've only to look at the outer world to see if what we're thinking and feeling has been productive. Is life a nightmare? Congratulations to us! We've done a *good* job of *mis*creating!

Now that we understand this process, on to the business of internal housecleaning. We have to pay attention to what our minds do, that is, to *think about* what we are thinking about.[41] We must commit ourselves to becoming aware of—waking up to—what we think about all day long. Some of our most effective visions are fear-filled scenes we habitually imagine in vivid detail.

Yes, that's how it works for me. When I'm up the proverbial creek, what have I done in the past? Imagine what terrible event *might* occur. If I, as a creator with the divine ability to transmute my thoughts into matter, keep dreaming up vivid "worst-case" scenarios, what else could I possibly expect to materialize in my life? Yes, fear has been a potent fuel for real-izing thoughts.

For example, I spent years trying to avoid getting pregnant, and now I'm the mother of three children! (I think fear of pregnancy is the best fertility drug we have.) I'm beginning to learn!

One of the best tests for identifying a non-constructive thought is, I learned, does it make me feel good about myself?[42] Another telltale sign of destructive thinking is a shudder. I didn't understand that the shudder is my body consciousness trying to shake off the idea I just thought. Now when I notice my body using this language, I immediately cut off that thought pattern, pantomime erasing it, and replace the negative image with a positive one. The Sufis, who are the mystics of Islam, call such visualization "creative prayer."

All right, I'm committed to changing my nightmare, I'm watching what I think about, and I'm trying not to be afraid. I'm ready . . . but can my dreams *really* come true?

Four

Anything goes.

> The real problem is that even the most objective
> researchers have to *focus* before they can see, which
> means they have to decide where to look. This limits
> their options . . . Like the rest of us, scientists tend to see
> what they expect to see.
>
> K. C. Cole
> *Mind Over Matter*

Hitting the Bull's-eye and Other Weird Stuff

There's a riddle about a father and son involved in a car crash. The father is killed out-right and an ambulance rushes the son to the hospital. In critical condition, the youngster requires immediate surgery and is hastily prepped, cross-matched for blood type, and wheeled into the operating room. However, upon seeing the patient's face, the surgeon exclaims, "I can't operate on this patient—he's my son!" The boy is not a stepson, not adopted, not illegitimate. Nor is the surgeon a priest. The only possible answer can be that the surgeon is the young boy's *mother*. How obvious! Yet the male model for surgeons is so culturally ingrained that I never thought of the answer.

Although he grew up in a culture strictly ruled by religion, Jesus himself believed that "anything goes." Jesus said, "With men this is impossible, but with God all things are possible." In a similar vein, the *Tao Te Ching* states that nothing is impossible for someone who's not addicted to his or her own ideas.[43] Why? Because our ideas make a distinction between what is possible and what isn't.

Quantum physics has changed our ideas of what is impossible. In the Double Slit experiment, it was proven an electron passes through two slits *simultaneously* when it isn't being watched. That is, subatomic particles (like the photons that make light) behave like a wave *and* a distinct particle at the same time. This means that if I'm blindfolded and throw a baseball of quantumstuff, I might break my bedroom window and the neighbors' picture window, too . . . or the ball might end up in China.

In the One-Hole experiment, a gun shoots one particle through a small hole in a barrier placed in front of a phosphor screen. Now, if I shoot one bullet at a time out of a regular gun, the bullet would zoom straight ahead, following the straight-line trajectory of the gun barrel. But the particles in this experiment behave very strangely; after a number of them have been loosed off, a pattern forms on the phosphor screen that looks like a bull's eye of concentric circles fading out at the edges—yet *neither the gun's position nor its aim has been changed.* Between the gun and the screen, each particle spreads out like a wave flowing over a large area.[44]

Because of light's both-wave-and-particle behavior, physicist Werner Heisenberg formulated his Uncertainty Principle, which states that we can either know where a particle is or trace its path through space, but we can't know both at the same time. A simple way of picturing this is to imagine taking a photograph of Superman while he's flying faster than a speeding bullet. If we use a very high shutter speed we can capture Superman in flight, a look of determination frozen on his handsome face, but the background's nothing more than a blur; we've lost sight of the path Superman is taking. If we use a slow shutter speed, our photograph shows an indistinct Superman as a blurred trail across the snapshot; we capture Superman's path but not his position.[45] Every time I lose my train of thought (the wave) by being distracted by a detail (the particle), I've been governed by the Uncertainty Principle. Or when I hear the phrase, "You can't have it both ways," when someone flips a coin and calls "Heads," or when I miss something that's right before my eyes. Quantum mechanics rule our ordinary macro-life.

Quantumstuff is weird (subatomic particles called quarks come in flavors—I'll take chocolate!) and gets weirder.

- A subatomic particle moving from one point to another takes *all possible paths.*[46]

- When an electron prepares to change its orbit, it tries *every possible new orbit* at the same time.

- Until the electron has been observed, it is *everywhere, simultaneously,* a kind of electron-cloud.[47]

- In addition, subatomic particles have a "spin," yet what is doing the spinning is *nothing.*[48]

- In September, 2011, neutrinos traveled *faster than light.* They arrived in Gran Sasso, Italy *before* they had left the CERN facility outside Geneva.[49] These neutrinos knocked out the Theory of Relativity and made way for a whole new type of physics—and showed us that *our ideas about how life works are completely wrong.* This event is like my firing a gun again, but the bullet hits the target *before* my finger pulls the trigger. (The real miracle would be my hitting the target at all, but that doesn't mean the speedy neutrino and its implications don't still deserve a *Wow!*)

• The behavior of elementary particles *varies* according to who is paying attention to them and *what the people expect* or believe will happen.[50]

Fantastic, yes? There's more. An electron must turn around *twice* before it presents the facet to us that we saw before it started spinning.[51] Now, that eccentricity is *literally out of this world!* If a tiny bit of matter can do so much and humans are *made* of this stuff (or strings, which are just as odd), what could we do if we really "put our minds to it" and dreamed *big*?

We are made of quanta. We can do the strange and wondrous things that quanta do. Jesus performed what we call miracles. Yogananda's predecessor, Lahiri, did too. And mothers who rescue their children pinned beneath cars. Cats who survive twenty-story falls.

> What's true for the tiny electron is true for all of the objects within the material universe, since all things are made up of electronlike things.
>
> Fred Alan Wolf
> *Parallel Universes*

If we can believe, all things are possible. People living 2,000 years ago didn't even regard miracles as miraculous; the Jews didn't have a word for "miracle" because they *expected* miracles to happen.[52] So, if we can believe, then all things *are* possible . . . Like moving enormous stones to build the pyramids. Effecting world peace. Walking through walls. (Which happens every time we erase files off a flash drive—by "quantum tunneling," the particles pass through barriers.)[53] Diverting natural catastrophes, like tsunamis. Yes, really. There's a real-life example of this in Chapter 14. But how?

Maybe it's the Tao at work. Lao-Tzu's *Tao Te Ching* tells about the Tao, or "The Way." Lao-Tzu said the Tao is "like the eternal void: filled with possibilities." Anything and everything is possible because of the Tao, God's design, Heisenberg's *potentia*, George Lucas' Force. No matter what we call it, the non-physical realm is filled with possibilities just waiting to be drawn into physical reality.

> The electron does anything it likes. It just goes in any direction, at any speed, forward or backward in time, however it likes, and then you add up the amplitudes and it gives you the wave function.
>
> Richard Feynman
> quoted by Nick Herbert in *Quantum Reality*

To scientists, the non-physical is the realm of the probability wave, the "sum of possibilities."[54] The wave function describes everything that's possible, including things we might not expect. For example, we need to make a decision, so we flip a coin to help us decide: Heads, yes; tails, no. The coin, however, falls on its edge . . . or a blackbird flies by overhead and plucks the coin out of mid-air . . . or the wind blows the coin out into the street and a passing SUV smashes it beyond recognition. The probability wave of our quantum lives always contains an almost infinite number of possibilities. It's our *focus* that hampers our ability to see the options.

We know the element that makes the probability wave collapse is consciousness. As von Neumann discovered, the collapse can't be caused by a machine, because machinery is made of atoms and atoms are physical, and one part of any system cannot make a judgment about that system, according to Kurt Godel's famous Incompleteness Theorem. The observer can't be a physical part of the system that is being seen and continue to be the observer of it. It's like trying to act in a movie and watch it at the same time. The mathematical equations of quantum theory that represent the physical world *prove* the existence of observers who lie *outside* those mathematical descriptions.[55] In other words, part of us—and other living creatures, right down to those tiny electrons—exists outside this universe. We are divine, and we create life on Earth, what we see and feel and touch and taste, is a huge cooperative venture, drawing resources from *potentia*.

The Changing Truth of "Truth"

Potentia makes anything and everything possible. No, I'm not likely to sprout wings overnight or suddenly leap tall buildings in a single bound, but too many of our beliefs masquerade as truth when they are only mistaken ideas. Like first impressions. First impressions may turn out to be quite the opposite of what's really true.

In 1973 I was taking a Self-defense course, and my boyfriend volunteered to play the role of attacker so I could practice.

"Let's go into the hall," Neil said, "where we have more room." Since my apartment (which my mother referred to as The Fire Trap) was a tiny efficiency, we stepped into the hallway lit by a single hanging bulb and sunlight filtering through a dirty window in the front entry. Neil raised his hand holding an imaginary knife and moved in to strike.

Uh-oh. We learned that, if attacked, I would be stabbed, slashed, and easily spindled.

"Wow," Neil said, "you need a lot of practice. Let's try again."

This time his hands circled my throat and bumped my head against the staircase.

"Wait," I tried to squeak, "I'm not ready." The *Wait, wait* in my head kept time with my head rapping against the woodwork. I realized I'd no chance of surviving a strangler—especially if the slasher got me first.

"Wait," I croaked, but Neil stayed in character.

Then the entry door opened, and framed against the daylight stood a tall man wearing a battered cowboy hat and a great coat that hung to his shins. He paused, then ambled down the hall toward us and stopped right in front of Neil, who was still using my head like a maraca.

With a slow, crazy grin on his gaunt face, the stranger looked straight into Neil's eyes and said, "Can I help you, man?"

"Oh, God," I thought, "I'm going to get raped right in front of my boyfriend."

After explanations all around, I learned the identity of the stranger, John Price, and that he was, in truth, a gentle man prepared to defend a woman—a total stranger—being attacked. His *Can I help you, man?* was male-speak for *Back off!* My first impression was the polar opposite of the true situation. (Thank you, John.)

Our concepts of right and wrong fluctuate across the years and from one culture to another. As Robert Frost wrote, "Most of the change we think we see in life/ Is due to truths being in and out of favor." Today's American mother who drowns her newborn baby girl will go to jail, but an Oriental mother who killed a female infant during the mid-twentieth century was conforming to the ethnic practice of maintaining pure bloodlines.

Some definitions of truth are as fuzzy as an electron cloud: Glass, for example, is defined as a "solid liquid."[56] That sure sounds funny to me. And space—why do we think of space as being empty? Space is actually teeming with tiny bits of matter that continually pop in and out of existence.

To illustrate the changing nature of "truth," here's a joke about a manager interviewing three people for the position of accountant. The first applicant comes in and sits down, and the manager asks, "What does 4 + 1 equal?"

"Five," replies the applicant, who is quickly dismissed.

The second applicant enters the office and even before he's seated, the manager fires off, "What's 4 + 1 make?"

This applicant had witnessed the brevity of the previous man's interview, so he takes his time in answering. Deciding it's a trick question, he finally responds, "Forty-one?"

Out he goes. The last applicant enters and the manager says curtly, "What's 4 + 1?"

Quick as a wink, the applicant replies, "What would you like it to be?"

Guess who landed the job.

It's true, the truth is malleable. Four plus one doesn't always equal five. If we stir one cup of sugar into four cups of water to fill the hummingbird feeder in the backyard, we still end up with only four cups of liquid.

"Facts" that Cause Damage

What we believe we generally accept as fact, whose truth we thereafter never think to question, because what we see in the external world seems to support what we believe.[57] Indeed, whatever we believe does become *real*, even if it's not *true*. In 1946, it looked as if there was going to be a bumper harvest in South America. Then someone started the rumor of famine. Twenty thousand farmers left their farms to seek refuge in the cities, the abandoned crops withered, and famine struck.[58]

Gravity is another "truth" that has its exceptions. "I think we've underestimated the life on this planet," said Dick Solomon in the pilot of the comedy series, *3rd Rock from the Sun*. "The people have so much courage; here they are, hurtling through space on a molten rock at 67,000 miles an hour, and the only thing that keeps them from flying out of their shoes is their misplaced faith in gravity." John Lithgow's alien was going for a laugh, but Einstein's general theory of relativity discovered that gravity is an illusion. Curved spacetime is generally thought to be what holds us to earth and the earth orbiting around the sun.[59]

The force of gravity seems all-powerful and yet I learned that atoms, small spiders and plants are virtually unaffected by gravity.[60] And, as mentioned, there are yogis who defy gravity's pull. We need not be swamis, though, to experience levitation. Most of us have scooped up a balloon at a children's birthday party, rubbed a few electrons off its surface, stuck the balloon on the wall, and cried, "Hey, kids, look at this!" The levitating yogis merely carry the action a step further, allowing themselves to be en*lighten*ed, rather than to abide by the decree that caused Newton's apples to fall to the ground and remain there. The yogis refuse to accept that limitation.

Physicist Fred Alan Wolf says that any time we try to make an objective observation using anything physical (including our eyes), we're looking through filters, as if we were wearing a pair of rose-colored glasses or, of course, blinders. It's like my believing that there are good and kind people everywhere, so what do I find? Good and kind people everywhere I go. Why? Because we find what we expect to find; our expectations *affect* the probability wave.

Specialized sight like this is called "inattentional blindness." Dan Simons at the Harvard Visual Cognition Lab conducted experiments where the participators watched a video of students passing a ball back and forth, and he asked the viewers to count the number of completed passes. It was only when they watched the same video a second time, without trying to keep track of the ball, that they noticed a man dressed in a gorilla suit cross the screen.

IT ALL DEPENDS ON YOUR OUTLOOK

In another experiment, people watched a rapid sequence of pictures, and most viewers failed to see the missing object, even something as large and as essential as the engine that was missing from a jet airplane. They believed the airplane would be complete, so they didn't notice what was *not* there.

What we see, then, is determined to a great degree by what we expect to see. Our preconceptions act as barriers to sight.

Looks Can Be Deceiving

Familiarity may breed more than contempt; it can, like with the jet engine, cause things to vanish or appear through selective vision, which is manipulated by the brain in two ways. The first is a vanishing act, where the brain erases things like the sight of our nose in our own vision. Why? Because it's always there and we get used to our nose always being there, in the middle of our visual circle, so the brain filters out this information. The brain also performs a magic act of invention, filling in the blanks. Where the optic nerve connects to the eye, a blind spot forms. At this spot no information is recorded, yet we don't go around seeing "black holes" in front of us. The brain fills in the void in our vision with what the brain thinks we *should* be seeing.

Sight is not the only physical sense subject to manipulation. Think about people who lose limbs but keep feeling "phantom pain."[61] Here again is the power of the mind; it can create pain for something that no longer exists or forget about something as ever-present as a nose.

Our point of view does make a difference, and proves that reality itself is relative: If we hold a box of aluminum foil as if to tear a sheet of foil off, we see the full length of the box. If we hold it up so we're looking only at the end cap, it appears to have no length at all. These two points of view make truth seem a complicated matter. Or like magic.

We can experience an amazing "sleight of mind" for ourselves by reading the following passage:

The Paomnehal Pweor of the Hmuan Mnid: Aoccdrnig to a rseearch at Cmabrigde Uinervtisy, it deosn't mttaer in waht oredr the ltteers in a wrod are, the olny iprmoatnt tihng is that the frist and lsat ltteer be in the rghit pclae. The rset can be a taotl mses and you can sitll raed it wouthit a porbelm. Tihs is bcuseae the huamn mnid deos not raed ervey lteter by istlef, but the wrod as a wlohe.

The above jumbled but readable passage is incredible, huh? (This ability may explain why marketers cannot get the spelling right for every word in advertisements. They take a Quik Trek through English, depending on the quantum weirdness of our brains to translate.)

Or try this one:

7H15 M3554G3 53RV35 7O PR0V3 H0W 0UR M1ND5 C4N D0 4M4Z1NG 7H1NG5! 1MPR3551V3 7H1NG5! 1N 7H3 B3G1NN1NG 17 WA5 H4RD BU7 N0W, 0N 7H15 LIN3 Y0UR M1ND 1S R34D1NG 17 4U70M471C4LLY W17H 0U7 3V3N 7H1NK1NG 4B0U7 17. B3 PROUD! 0NLY C3R741N P30PL3 C4N R3AD 7H15.

I began to ask myself, *How valid can any of my perceptions be?* How can we discern what's real from what we made up? Our bodies, our world—both spirituality and quantum physics tells us that we make them up as we go along, filling in the pieces of the larger picture we cannot "see."

> *You made this up.* It is a picture of what you think you are; of how you see yourself.
>
> *A Course in Miracles*

This means that if we change our thoughts, if we are open to the possibility that our assumptions may need revising, we *can* change our reality. This is good news. If I've been conjuring up lots of things that aren't really there, I've been creating hells on earth. Get me the hell out of my nightmare!

Maybe I'd better go back to basics. Back to the foundation and rebuild, without false limitations. But how? By looking for simple truths that are all but hidden by man-made add-ons, dogmas, and just plain over-thinking. Like the rabbi, priest, Buddhist monk, and Muslim who were strolling through the park.

"What is the greatest teaching in the world?" asked Rabbi Tov.

"The Scriptures as interpreted by the Roman Catholic Church," replied Father Dennehy.

"The wisdom of Buddha and the patriarchs," replied Lama Das.

"No, no," said Mohammad, "it's the teachings of the Prophet, blessed be his name."

A young man sitting on a nearby bench disentangled himself from his girlfriend's arms and grinned at the group. "Naw, it's love, man," he said. "Love's all you need."

The Brick Wall School of Hard Knocks

Limiting ideas keep us trapped in smallness. They may have come from childhood or may have developed over time, but the list goes on and on. I know I've spent decades attending the Brick Wall School of Hard Knocks, where I failed to learn anything until after I'd beaten my head against those unyielding walls. This school wasn't a mandatory part of my earth-bound training. I built it myself, on cornerstones of feeling trapped and beliefs like . . .

> "Life is a struggle."
> "This is the way it's always been, and it'll never get any better."
> "If something can go wrong, it will."
> "Hope for the best; expect the worst."

Of course, some of the lessons I eventually learned are valuable, like it's easier to stay out of trouble than to clean up the mess afterward, or that kindness comes when I least expect it. But who of us would willingly pay tuition to learn lessons in the Brick Wall School of Hard Knocks? My tuition didn't come cheap, either; I paid in heartbreak, suffering, resentment, anxiety, bitterness, and depression—all of which can translate into broken relationships, high blood pressure, heart attacks, cancer, and suicide.

Avoiding the Brick Wall School requires a different curriculum: a shift toward optimism, a willingness to focus on whatever possibilities we can imagine, and the discipline for practicing peace, no matter *what* happens. First we work at tearing down the old structure, letting go of the programming that locked us into the Brick Wall School in the first place. Then we begin pouring a new foundation.

Fifteen years ago I was diagnosed with Grave's Disease (hyperactive thyroid) and was left with double vision, even after the thyroid condition cleared up. One day I noticed that in the fraction of a second before I completely woke up in the morning, my eyesight was perfect . . . until I thought, "Oh, I need my glasses," and reached for them on the bedside table. But for the remainder of the day, my eyesight was so bad that I learned to drive down two streets at the same time.

One afternoon I noticed Dr. Joseph Liberman's book, *Take Off Your Glasses and See*, on the library shelf and, since it was a pleasant summer day, I carried it outside to read. Optometrist Liberman presented this analogy: Suppose you break your arm and go to the doctor. The doctor says, "There's your cast. I want you to come back in one year—and every year afterwards, until you die—and we'll fit a larger, heavier cast on your arm at each visit." Liberman suggested that eyeglass wearers give our eyes "practice" every day, without looking through our lenses.[62] So I took off my prescription glasses and, by God, it *was* possible—I was reading the next paragraph! Eventually, I was spending more time looking for my mislaid glasses than I did looking through them. And when I lost them "for good," I decided it was the Divine telling me to let go of the visual crutches completely.

This experience was a true eye-opener. I began telling my eyes they were capable of regaining perfect vision. I praised them when they read small print, and reminded them of the exceptional sight they used to have—and though I had tested nearly blind in one eye, my vision has improved! I've come to believe that each of us is a god to the cells in our body and that the cells respond to our inner messages (thoughts) and encouragement.

The Mind-Body Connection

Bohm supports the mind-body idea, along with Deepak Chopra, and Michael Talbot, author of *The Holographic Universe*. Talbot once told an energy psychic in Los Angeles about a medical problem he had. The psychic took one look at him and said, "Michael, you haven't been yelling at your spleen, have you?" With chagrin, he admitted he had been doing exactly that. She reminded him to send positive messages to the parts of his body.[63]

Blessing what goes *into* our bodies is important, too. Many Americans have tried many different diets, but nutritional studies show that:

1. The Japanese eat very little fat and suffer fewer heart attacks than Americans.
2. Eskimos eat a lot of fat and suffer fewer heart attacks than Americans.
3. The Chinese drink very little red wine and suffer fewer heart attacks than Americans.
4. Italians drink a lot of red wine and suffer fewer heart attacks than Americans.

5. The Germans drink a lot of beer and eat lots of sausages and fats and suffer fewer heart attacks than Americans.

So does it matter *what* we eat? A neighbor, Ernie Potter, ate bacon and eggs every day of his life and lived to be 103. Isn't it more important *how* we eat? It's a case again of how we do something affecting the outcome. If we breathe easy, revel in what we eat, and tell our body the food will bless it, our bodies will benefit and respond in kind. "Everything I eat benefits my body," is a phrase I suggested to my friend, Kay, who loves sweets. She mentioned that Christmas was coming and, oh, she was going to put on unwanted pounds. Kay discovered that the proof was in the pudding, literally; she used the phrase regularly and ate treats *moderately*, and did not gain one pound over the entire season!

Going Through a Different Door

So what can I really do, I wondered. I learned to set an intention before I fell asleep, before the day began, before a difficult situation. In general, my intentions (life lessons) are to bless with every thought, to live without fear, and to let go of toxic relationships and compulsions like smoking and automatically reacting with the comment, "But I can't _____." To let go of possessions, which seem to breed, filling all available space! To remember to get peaceful and, so, beneficial.

> So what can you do? Anything you want to . . . From any branch there is a pathway leading to any other branch . . . *keep making the impossible possible*. Keep choosing which branch you wish to sample life on . . . think of the branches as branches of a tree and of the sense of self you now feel as the sap or lifeblood of the tree. Feed the good branches.
>
> Fred Alan Wolf
> *Taking the Quantum Leap*

Still, I often forget. I forget to laugh. I forget to focus on "what's going right." I made a daily checklist of things to do, like grounding out and sending out blessings . . . and forget to consult it every morning and evening. I forget grace, so I don't have to feel afraid. I've pretty well learned to look for the blessing or lesson in most situations, but tend to forget that *anything is possible*. But it is my responsibility and privilege on earth to aim for the (im)possible— dreams and joys—to set my intention and walk through a different door, because *anything goes*.

Anything goes, although, like the motto of the Army Corps of Engineers, "The difficult can be done immediately; the impossible takes a little longer."

What we used to believe was impossible may indeed be possible when we apply quantum mechanics to our lives instead of banging against closed doors.

There are so many closed doors at the Brick Wall School, but we've all heard the adage, "When one door closes, another door opens."

King Solomon once gathered the wisest men in his kingdom and ushered them all into one room. "On this door," said the king, standing beside the only exit, "are ten of the finest locks in the realm. The first man who can open the locks and walk through the door will be my prime minister." With that comment, King Solomon left the room, closing the door behind him.

What consternation arose in the wake of his announcement! Some of the sages paced frantically back and forth, while others sat silently, deep in thought. Some studied the locks; others tapped on the stone walls, looking for a secret passageway. While the rest of the group was so busily employed, one man walked over, pushed the unlocked door open, and walked through.[64]

That parable reminds me of the Sufi, Rabi'a, who asked, "Was the door ever closed?"

With no doors closed before us, anything goes.

Five

Goodness is a given.

Matter is spirit moving slowly enough to be seen.
                              Pierre Teilhard de Chardin

Like the butter hidden in cream is the Life Source that
permeates all.
                              Svetasvatara Upanishad[65]

Dandelions and the Divine

So many people fight the dandelions that pop up in their yard. My children used to bring me bouquets of dandelions, and I thought the little gifts of gold were beautiful. Sometimes our fortune depends on our outlook, on what we think is good, bad, or ugly.

Alternative healers use universal or divine energy, which takes its direction from their intention. The Source of the energy, however, is not neutral. Our Quantum God upholds life and promotes creativity.

"The earth," I read in Psalm 33:5, "is full of the goodness of the Lord." Even so, I worried that I'd have a lot of trouble proving the existence of goodness. I had to switch from the concept of good-that's-the-opposite-of-evil to the goodness that breeds and nurtures life. It's a goodness inherent in all, providing the drive for individual, global, and cosmic development. This goodness supports life, and there are diverse examples of the force in our physical universe.

People generally want God to be the God of the good. They don't realize that the same . . . Source of what we call the beautiful is the same Source of the ugly. In fact, it is the Source of Allness.

Rabbi Schachter-Shalomi
quoted by William Eliot in *Tying Rocks to Clouds:
Meetings and Conversations with Wise and Spiritual People*

Ten Thousand Things . . . and the Science of Goodness

In the macro-world, the good, the bad, and the ugly are all part of the Allness, the unity, the diversity that Lao-Tsu called "ten thousand things."

In the micro-world, quarks and electrons, gravity and electricity are the same energy. In the macro-world that we see, the particles and energy forces have slowed down.[66] What happens in this frozen place, after energy has slowed down? Broken tree limbs fall to the ground, water turns to snow, sleet, or ice, and teens sleep in messy rooms. We get caught up in broken relationships, in messy lives. We forget what is behind it all. We worry about dying and forget to live.

Once a group of students asked their teacher, "Master, what will happen when we die?"

The teacher replied, "We will look behind a veil and exclaim, 'So! It was You all along!'"[67]

The whole is made of its parts, both the sacred and the profane, the beautiful and the ugly. A Zen master once said that if we love the sacred and despise the ordinary, we're still living in delusion. Maybe we would feel better if we recognized the sacred *within* the ordinary.

> Life is this simple: We are living in a world that is absolutely transparent and the Divine is shining through it all the time.
>
> Christian mystic Thomas Merton

Goodness supports and nurtures life within our universe. Science has discovered manifold ways by which Quantum God does this:

- the improbable *im*-balance of matter and antimatter in a symmetrical universe;
- less than a huge number of energy-gobbling black holes;
- the delicate balance between cosmic expansion and gravitational crunching;
- the presence of the Moon and its gravitational effect on the Earth;
- the exact proportion of carbon dioxide to oxygen in the air;
- the precise fixing of the nuclear ("strong") force;
- the order that arises from chaos;
- the self-organizing properties of *inanimate* matter;
- the precise temperature of the Earth;
- the fact that life emerged at all;
- the incredible variety of life in "impossible" situations;
- the natural inclination toward cooperation;
- the astronomically high odds against the accidental emergence of our universe.

Let's look at the ways the universe supports life.

- *The improbable im-balance of matter and antimatter in a basically symmetrical universe*: Because quarks and anti-quarks are always created in pairs that annihilate each other, it is a miracle that matter formed in the first place. After "Let there be light," there certainly would have been light radiating outward—but nothing else. In one-millionth of the first second after the Big Bang, however, quarks outnumbered anti-quarks by 3,000,000,000 to 299,999,999. A few stray particles of our kind of matter blossomed into everything we now see.[68] Matter and antimatter should have wiped each other out, but because matter and antimatter decay at slightly different rates, the universe triumphed on the side of life.[69] For those of us who continually shoot for perfection, this fact may give us a new sense of freedom, because we owe our lives to *imperfection*.[70]

- *Less than a huge number of energy-gobbling black holes*: Scientists say the early universe should have been populated with a huge number of black holes, rather than star-forming gases. *The odds of a black-hole universe outnumber the accidental birth of a universe like ours at the estimated figure of 10 to the 10th to the 30th power.* That's a one with 300 zeroes after it!

- *The delicate balance between cosmic expansion and gravitational crunching*: If the explosive force of the Big Bang had been any weaker, the universe would have disappeared in a Big Crunch, and had it been any stronger, the initial gases would have spread too quickly for stars to form. The maximum give-or-take allowance of the explosive force of the Big Bang would be as small as if we fired a bullet at a one-inch target twenty billion light years away and hit the target.[71]

- *The presence of the Moon and its gravitational effect on the Earth*: Because the Moon exists in space where it is, in orbit around the Earth, it stabilizes our planet, so that the Earth's tilt wobbles only by half a degree of 23 degrees over hundreds of thousands of years. This relatively stable axis may cause ice ages, but it also allows for life on Earth.[72] Not too shabby for a temperamental man made of green cheese.

- *The exact proportion of carbon dioxide to oxygen in the air*: Were there any greater amount of carbon dioxide, oxygen-breathing beings never would have come into existence.

- *The precise fixing of the nuclear ("strong") force*, which promotes the creation of the most basic elemental building block, hydrogen. The "strong" force holds the nuclei of atoms together, and had it been any stronger, there would have been no hydrogen after the Big Bang. No hydrogen, no stars. No hydrogen, no liquid water. In short, no life.[73]

▪ *The order that arises from chaotic systems*: It may not seem like it, but the universe is becoming *more* ordered as it ages. The second law of thermodynamics says that the entropy (or disintegration) of a closed system never decreases; Humpty Dumpty never gets put back together again. But Bohm, for one, does not believe in closed systems; he viewed order as part of an infinite spectrum. As we travel farther along the spectrum, expanding our view to the "larger picture," *randomness gives way to orderliness.*[74]

Try It Yourself

To demonstrate the inclination of chaos to move into an ordered state, hold up a string tied to a pendant. If you shift the top of the string slightly, in a horizontal motion, the pendant rolls back and forth in a fairly uniform circle. But disturb the top of the string with a small but erratic movement and the pendulum swings wildly, unpredictably, in all directions.

When, however, you once again hold the string still and stable, the pendant will eventually abandon its random behavior and settle down into a back-and-forth motion, coursing through the same arc until it comes to a standstill. This return to order is called syntropy. It may seem as if everywhere we look, what we see is disorder, but the universe has actually become more orderly over the course of its history.

The early universe was a chaotic boiling soup of steamy particles and radiation. It has cooled down considerably—and it's only in cooler temperatures that stable atoms can form.[75] Today, we see in our universe stars made of numerous elements and galaxies made of billions of stars. Living organisms have evolved over the course of the Earth's history into more and more complex forms, and the level of order has risen.

In fact, Ilya Prigogine, the 1977 Nobel Prize winner in chemistry, insists that order emerges *because* of the myriad possibilities within entropy, not in spite of it.[76] Considering my life, I call that great news. (With typical wry humor, Wolf says, ". . . quantum mechanics indicates that there is an order to the universe. It simply isn't the order we expected.")[77]

In the computer game, "Bookworm," glowing red tiles occasionally drop down from the top; when they get to the bottom of the columns, the game ends. These red tiles alarm novice players, yet the "fatal" tiles sometimes align themselves so that bonus words can be made if the player remains calm and patient. This game reminds me of the ancient Chinese character for *crisis*; a compound word, it is composed of two terms: *danger* and *opportunity*. Chaos, in other words, leads to progress. Physicists say that the more chaotic a system, the greater is its inclination to re-establish itself into a higher order.[78] This is why the Hindus' Shiva, god of destruction, is also "the transformer." Thank God—I'm ready to be transformed!

■ *The self-organizing properties of INANIMATE matter*: There are many examples of increasing order in inanimate systems, like the growth of crystals,[79] or the bewildering behavior of granular materials. If we fill a jar two-thirds full with different-sized sand and give it several good shakes, the largest grains of sand will always rise to the top—just as Brazil nuts do in a can mixed with cashews and peanuts. I used to find the same thing when I opened a can of spaghetti rings; the meatballs had risen to the top. Why? Order, establishing itself out of chaos. Cool.

> Mother Nature wears geometry on her sleeve. She spins the stars around in spirals, molds planets into nearly perfect spheres, sends water undulating downstream in sine waves, pulls projectiles into neat parabolas, and holds together the hydrogen and oxygen atoms in water molecules at an angle of precisely 105 degrees.
>
> K.C. Cole
> *Mind Over Matter*

■ *The precise temperature of the Earth*: This is another case in which the universe promotes life. Had the Earth been any hotter, the life-giving rains and oceans would have vaporized, and any colder, the waters would have frozen solid. Liquid water means life. Even human beings are about 70% water.

■ *The fact that, as Bohm marveled, life emerged at all*: The first liquid to form on earth was so poisonous it killed all incipient life. Eons passed before a molecule arose in cells that caused the cells to develop an outer membrane that acted as a protective shield against the poisonous waters—and those cells lived and multiplied. And those protected cells still live inside us.[80] Bohm believed nature has the *intention* to create life, that it is "creative and purposeful." The universe, in other words, is predisposed toward life.

■ *The incredible variety of life in "impossible" situations*: Near the hydrothermal vents along the ocean floor at depths of up to nearly 12,000 feet, where the pressure is enormous and sunlight non-existent, poisonous waters roil in a scalding 750° F over the vent and drop to just 34° F an inch away—and yet, the sea teems with life: tube worms, clams and crabs, little lobsters, anemones, tiny eyeless shrimp, and bacteria. And then there are penguins living in the harshest climate on Antarctica.

As if these testaments to life were not enough, there is also the exquisiteness of the electromagnetic force, which holds a grain's worth of matter scattered through five or six feet of space, keeping "body and soul" together. Were the space between nuclei any less, we would collapse into an unrecognizable speck.[81] This fact makes me recall the Jewish proverb that says, "Each blade of grass has an angel over it, saying, 'Grow, grow.'" Gives you a warm, fuzzy feeling, doesn't it?

- *The natural inclination toward cooperation:* I've heard about dolphins saving people who were drowning; pets warning their masters before disaster strikes; pigs waking their owners during house fires. On May 9, 2005, Netscape News carried the story, "Stray Dog in Kenya Saves Abandoned Baby." The stray dog had found an infant abandoned in the Ngong forest and carried the newborn across a busy road to join her litter of pups.[82] Heartwarming stories like this have existed since before the beginning of human language and are cherished precisely because they demonstrate the intimate, compassionate cooperation shared among the living beings on Earth.

- *The astronomically high odds against the accidental emergence of our universe:* This is really cool. If our universe was nothing more than an accident, the odds against it containing any appreciable order are incredibly small. The odds of an ordered universe of stars and galaxies emerging out of unplanned and undirected chaos are:

100,000,000,000,000,000,000,000,000,000,000,000,000,000,
000,000,000,000,000,000,000,000,000,000,000,000,000,000,
000,000,000,000,000,000,000,000,000,000,000,000,000,000,
000,000,000,000,000,000,000,000,000,000,000,000,000,000,
000,000,000,000,000,000,000,000,000,000,000,000,000,000,
000,000,000,000,000,000,000,000,000,000,000,000,000,000,
000,000,000,000,000,000,000,000,000,000,000,000,000,000,
000,000,000,000,000,000,000,000,000,000,000,000,000,000,
000,000,000,000,000,000,000,000,000,000,000,000,000,000,
000,000,000,000,000,000,000,000,000,000,000,000,000,000,
000,000,000,000,000,000,000,000,000,000,000,000,000,000,
000,000,000,000,000,000,000,000,000,000,000,000,000,000,
000,000,000,000,000,000,000,000,000,000,000,000,000,000,
000,000,000,000,000,000,000,000,000,000,000,000,000,000,
000,000,000,000,000,000,000,000,000,000,000,000,000,000,
000,000,000,000,000,000,000,000,000,000,000,000,000,000,
000,000,000,000,000,000,000,000,000,000,000,000,000,000,
000,000,000,000,000,000,000,000,000,000,000 to 1. [83]

> We live in a universe that is far more benevolent than we realize.
>
> Michael Talbot
> *The Holographic Universe*

So there's a lot of scientific support that goodness exists. Goodness with a capital *G*, a force that designed and supports life in our universe. Scientifically, Goodness *is* a given.

For Goodness' Sakes!

> *Potentia* "provides us instantly with any knowledge we need. It computes probabilities in a flash. All That Is—the Absolute, the holomovement—is a constant presence that surrounds us. It is a well-intentioned, gentle, powerful, and all-knowing atmosphere, and each individual is a manifestation of this presence. It has a loving intent; it has everyone's best interest in mind."
>
> Norman Friedman
> *Bridging Science and Spirit*

Science now echoes what ancient wisdom from many cultures has told us for centuries. A simple Christian children's grace begins with "God is great, God is good." How great? In the Koran, God says, "I require no provision from them, nor do I need them to feed Me."[84] In other words, God needs nothing, not even our worship, which creates a feeling of separation inside us. The most persistent theme in the Kabbalah, the foundation of mystical Judaism, maintains that God is all-inclusive and lacks nothing. God is, therefore, "good, since all aspects of evil stem from a feeling of lack."[85] And what God creates is good.

The *Tao Te Ching* also speaks on this topic:

> The great Tao flows everywhere,
> to the left and to the right.
> All things depend upon it to exist
> and it does not abandon them.
> It loves and nourishes all things
> but does not lord it over them.[86]

Guiding without interfering, in other words. God allows us to be ourselves.

One from Column A, One from Column B

In the physical universe our lives are shaped by the decisions we make, and so we contribute to the process of Creation. One way the Hindus picture God is as a mother who provides delicious foods and lays them out in a cosmic buffet. When one dish is taken, two more platters appear in its place, each more exquisite than the last.

The Hindus' image of a banquet table represents *potentia*, but all too often we view life like a Chinese menu: "Pick one Appetizer from Column A and one Entrée from Column B." We limit the fund from which we may draw—and we skip the free fortune cookie, to boot. As we grow to believe in the bounty of life's

Source, we may choose, as Wolf put it, to "dance on the edge of chaos," living lives full of plenty and adventure and wonder.[87] In the wake of ongoing losses, changes, and indefinite income, I was forced to accept that *uncertainty contains all possibilities*. It was either find the good in my situation or kill myself with worry. A Brick Wall School lesson, but I learned.

Going It Alone

Living *is* an uncertain and often lonely process. I used to have dinner waiting for my kids when they got home from school, and I never knew whether we'd be feeding six or twice that many, but everyone was welcome. Now, with no one to cook for, I forget to eat at all. And, at times, the loneliness crushed me. I've learned to get out of that mindset (for the most part) and make my "alone time" count. I've also learned that the sooner I *stop*, breathe, and turn my thoughts to God, peace, and blessing, the sooner I'll feel better.

While we create our lives just as candy makers plan, pour, mold, and consume their works, or as producers weave together the elements of a play or movie, we don't have to do it alone. A para-physical Power (God, Allah, Tao, the Great Spirit,[88] the Prime Mover, or simply "the Force") exists that is inclined toward creating goodness and supporting life.[89] This is the Force that established both the chaos necessary for creativity and change and the impetus for order. This is the Force that manifests miracles and coordinates synchronicities, occasions such as an unexpected side-job that pays this month's mortgage, or like the day my friend, Roger, waited in line to pay for his coffee and recognized ahead of him the woman he'd loved 23 years before. By what long series of maneuvers had *potentia* arranged for Roger and Kathy both to be standing in line at the same Quik Trip at 8:05 on a Monday morning? (They are now married.)

I experienced a "miracle of coordination" at a time when I most needed help. My spirit had been shattered, and I was living like the walking dead—walking only because my children and friends had taken great pains to keep holding me up. The synchronicity occurred in a cafeteria. After looking around the crowded room, I finally sat at a table where a lone woman was eating her dinner. She introduced herself as Deb Holt and graciously asked how I was, and with heartache heavy on my mind, that's what I talked about. She began weaving with her fingers in my direction, pulling them back to the edge of the table, and brushing energy off her fingertips and toward the ground. As a healer, I knew what she was doing. As a woman, I felt the weight on my heart shift, lift, and ease to the point where I was more capable of functioning under my own steam. An unlooked-for blessing and a miracle of coordination that this Quantum Coach (UniverSelf.com) and I were both in that spot at the same time; this was a gift of the Force for good at its best.

The Goodness of the Creator extends throughout Creation. For nearly two millennia, organized religion has disempowered its adherents through the concept of "original sin." But "sin," translated literally, means nothing more than a frustrated hope or something that misses the mark.[90] We can be mistaken, and we can deceive ourselves and turn the power of our minds against us, but we cannot sin nor change what is our true identity—our divine nature.

> If sin is real, God must be at war with Himself. He must be split, and torn between good and evil . . . For He must have created what wills to destroy Him, and has the power to do so. Is it not easier to believe that you have been mistaken than to believe in this? . . . For the wages of sin *is* death, and how can the immortal die?
>
> *A Course in Miracles*

Significantly, as recounted in Luke 10:10-13, Jesus refrained from labeling the stooped teenager (perhaps from juvenile arthritis) a sinner. Unconditional love may note that a mistake has been made, but it does not judge and supplies no condemnation that requires forgiveness. We have learned that we are born sinful, but what if that isn't true at all? What if the serpent used in Genesis to trick Eve into disobedience was not a devil? The inclusion of a snake in the Adam and Eve story was actually an attempt to malign the snakes the ancient pagans used, so the reference to sin would reflect badly on the prevailing pagan worship.[91] And the "good and evil" that we now recognize demonstrates the polarity of *maya*.[92]

In contrast to the concept of original sin, the Kabbalah translates the Hebrew word for original sin, *hishiani*, as "He elevated" or "He lifted [me] up."[93] With the Kabbalah's interpretation of this single word, we are relieved of being sinners and are raised out of shame and blame, merely by being open to the idea that we have been *born to goodness*. That's enough to make me feel better about life on Earth. I was created good and holy, just like our Creator. And when I believe that of myself, that's how I live! (Well, try to.)

Saying Grace and Finding Treasure

When we "seek first the kingdom," we realize that no matter what happens, the kingdom of heaven is where we always reside—except when we forget it. The father in "The Prodigal Son" parable, Jesus implied, is like God. God's love is continual, even for those who reject it, and God's mercy falls on all without distinction. When the elder son, who had stood by his father and worked hard for him, resents the royal treatment for his dolt of a brother, their father says, "Son, you are always with me, and all that I have is yours." This means that we live in grace always, and all we must do is to *remember* that we live in grace; the elder brother had been enjoying everything his father had to share with him all along. This kingdom, or state of grace, is our natural state. When we pray for grace, it's as if we were standing neck-deep in a pool, crying out for a sip of water. [94]

> You need not God's blessing, because you have that forever, but you do need your own.
>
> *A Course in Miracles*

Kansas City jazz musician, Tim Whitmer, tells about visiting a nursing home during the Christmas holidays. During the deacon's short message, the group of elderly residents sat still and mute. Then Tim began playing "Silent Night" on his flute, and halfway through the first stanza, he heard a buzzing noise. He realized the hum was coming from his audience—off-key, to be sure, and wordless, but a many-voiced melody nonetheless. When Tim finished playing the refrain for the third time, the elderly group continued to hum another stanza. Tim attributed this reawakening to the grace that upholds all life.[95]

We may fail to notice the grace or order that is inherent within a system. The number *pi* (3.14159) which is non-repeating and so infinitely chaotic, is very useful, nonetheless. The chaotic characteristic of *pi* makes it perfect for its functions, and that perfection exists whether or not we are aware of it.

Often our sense of order relies on how we categorize things: Kansas City has a public rose garden, a botanical garden, community vegetable gardens, and beautifully landscaped homes. We notice only disorder if we focus on their different appearances. But we find order if we lump these places together as "gardens," seeing them as part of a larger set or spectrum.

The first verse of John says, "In the beginning was the Word [*Aum*], and the Word was with God," and—literally, reading from the Greek text—"the Word was God."[96] From the word *logos* comes our English word "logic." In the beginning our world and everything in it made sense.[97] What we call order—or the apparent lack of it—may be so far out on the scale that it becomes hard for us to appreciate its inclusion in an "invisible" part of the spectrum, like the radio waves and microwaves that are invisible to the naked eye.

Finding God in Good, and Good in Bad

Even if we expand our definition of goodness to a cosmic proportion, what about the truly tragic things that happen? How can they possibly fit into a Grand Plan? Why does God allow such things to occur? Rabbi Harold Kushner of *Why Bad Things Happen to Good People* fame says:

What sort of world would it be if there were no God? Some people would say it would be a world very much like the one we now have, a world of war and threats of war, of crime and corruption and random cruelty. For me, the answer is even more dismaying. Without God, it would be a world where no one was outraged by crime or cruelty, and no one was inspired to put an end to them . . . we would have no reason to feel "this is not the way the world is supposed to work," nor would we have any reason to believe that, with enough time and effort, we could make it better.[98]

Here's personal accountability, again. But we don't have to go it alone.

Six

We have constant access to wisdom, support, love, and strength via our connection to God.

I am the taste and the water.

Bhagavad Gita

Phoning Home

In the wake of a flood, Marcel prayed to God for help. He had decided not to leave with the wave of trucked-out evacuees before the storm, and now he is hanging out of his second-story window, hollering at the man in a boat.

"Go away, I tell you. God's going to save me."

Two hours pass and the floodwaters rise. Marcel is now straddling his roof peak. He clings tightly to his TV antenna as a helicopter approaches. "Go away," he yells. "The slipstream's going to throw me off the roof. Go away!"

"We're here to help you, mister," says a man through a bullhorn.

"God will save me," Marcel replies.

But Marcel is soon disappointed; he drowns, and when he gets to heaven, he angrily confronts God. "I had faith in You. Why didn't You help me?"

God tells him, "I tried three times, Marcel. I sent a truck, a boat, and a helicopter. Didn't you hear Me speaking in the drivers' voices?"

We have continuous access to the Divine Mind. Like E.T., we can phone home via the "Ethernet," which some refer to as the Akashic records, or cosmic library. (Akasha is Sanskrit for "ether.") Comparable to the Internet, the Ethernet is a treasure-house of information and a means for communicating internally.

> We don't have to go to gurus, mediums, or fortunetellers. If we really want to know, ask; it will be given—not easily, and perhaps not when we want it, but when the time is right.
>
> Dr. Elisabeth Kubler-Ross
> quoted by William Elliot in *Tying Rocks to Clouds*

Exchange of information is an integral part of Bohm's projection from the implicate order (*potentia*) into the explicate order (the world we know), and cyclically back again to *potentia.* He explained it like this: A wave rises (is projected) out of the ocean (the whole). Then it falls (is injected) back into the ocean. The first wave affects (influences) the next wave.[99]

This means that ever-updated information about the physical world is amassed in the non-physical realm and is available to everyone and everything at any time. Not only does God keep track of us, but at some level we know a lot more—a world more—than we ever dreamed we knew. One proof of this exchange is a series of tests done at Stanford, where "ordinary" people had the ability to do remote viewing. We all have access to cosmic information.[100]

I remember one Saturday evening when I "looked in" on my sleeping friend, Kay, to send her blessings, and saw lights in the shape of a Christmas tree at the head of her bed. In response to my email telling her about the vision, she replied that she had been looking at Christmas decorations the previous afternoon.

The Scientific Proof for Quantum God

We now know that consciousness is the agent of creation, and humans and other creatures—plants and elements and even subatomic particles—are the agents creating our life on Earth. But who is large enough to observe *all* of our universe? If the wave function isn't "real" until a mind collapses the myriad possibilities into a single actuality, *who collapses the wave function of the entire universe?*"[101] Who stands outside the universe? Quantum God.

The scientist Max Planck, "Father of Quantum Mechanics," believed in an intelligent Creator. In his acceptance speech for the 1919 Nobel Prize, Planck said, "We must assume behind [atomic] force the existence of a conscious and intelligent mind." This God Mind, he said, "is the matrix of all matter."[102] What I called the Science of Goodness—the exact "ingredients" of the universe's life-supporting qualities—has convinced many modern scientists to hold a deep belief in a "creative Designer."[103]

One Big Choreography

It doesn't matter what term we use: God Mind or Akashic Record or Christ Consciousness or Buddha Mind, or non-local mind. We can even eliminate the word "Divine" and call this a connection with our Higher Self. Within the Life Force resides the universe with all its physical components. The taste and the water. The dance and the dancer. The fragrance and the flower. Together. Nothing is separated from anything else, despite appearances. Why? Because the entire universe was initially correlated.[104] Or more simply, as mystics of every creed and philosophy have tried to tell us, we are one.

When my mother contracted mouth cancer, my tongue and palate and gums on the right side of my mouth turned mushy and very painful; a phone call to my sister confirmed that Mom's cancer lodged on the right side of her mouth. This was an undeniable, "in-my-face" demonstration of sympathetic resonance.

We are one in the Mind of God. One in the mass medium of quantumstuff. One in a system of relationships. The theory of Six Degrees of Separation theorizes that every two people on Earth are connected by a chain of six acquaintances, max.[105] As far as relationships go, it's a small world after all, a world the Romans called Terra, giving our mother planet a formal name because it, too, is a living organism.

Aristotle named the universe Gaia and thought of it as a single living organism working toward a cosmic goal. The fact that our sun exhibits pulses in regular five-minute intervals, like a heartbeat, lends scientific credence to those who, like Aristotle, believe the universe functions as a whole.

The wholeness of Gaia might be compared to a child who is part Jew, part Arab, with Cherokee and Indonesian mixed in. We can't divide the child, saying "This part is Indonesian," or pointing out which part is Arab. The whole universe is a single quantum system.[106]

> The mathematical proof of wholeness lies in John Stewart Bell's theorem of Interconnectedness, which some physicists believe is the most important single work in the history of physics.
>
> Gary Zukav
> *The Dancing Wu Li Masters: An Overview of the New Physics*
>
> Bell's theorem demonstrates that once-connected things that are separated—even by a transuniversal distance—influence each other *instantaneously*, through a non-local, quantum bond.
>
> Norman Friedman
> *The Hidden Domain:*
> *Home of the Quantum Wave Function, Nature's Creative Source*

Proof for interconnectedness was posited by Bell's Theorem, which states that "Reality is non-local." Bell's Theorem was proven at the University of Geneva in 1997, when twin photons sent seven miles apart showed an immediate connection, although information would have had to travel between them at a speed *faster* than the speed of light. That message was literally *out of this world*. Once again, ancient wisdom preceded modern science; the *Isa Upanishad* long ago wrote of non-locality in the passage, "The Spirit, without moving, is swifter than the mind."[107]

The Vedas of India compare the cosmos to "a spider's web that evolved out of Being."[108] On the other side of the world, the Hopi Indians say that before Creation, Grandmother Spider spun a web so that everything that came into being later was connected. Scientists figure that interconnectedness occurs through physical means, such as basic quantum foam, physical fields of all sorts—morphogenetic, electromagnetic, gravitational, the quantum wave, the weak and strong forces—but also through mental and emotional fields, energetic fields, and relational patterns: in short, *non-local mind*.

> The universe begins to look more like a great thought than like a great machine.
>
> Sir James Jeans in the 1930s
> quoted by Ian G. Barbour
> *When Science Meets Religion: Enemies, Strangers, or Partners?*

The non-local mind (or Akashic realm) is evident in the realm of discoveries, when more than one person independently latches onto the same invention or solution to a problem. An example from the scientific community is Heisenberg, who formulated his system of quantum mechanics at the same time that Schrödinger designed his wave equation; these were different names for the same basic idea. Where did the ideas come from? They are "quantum jumps" from that "virtual domain," where everything is potential.

Inspiration and revelations are examples of quantum leaps: Now you don't see it... now you do!

A QUANTUM JUMP: NOW YOU DON'T SEE, NOW YOU DO

The Sixth Sense and the Ethernet

Communication via the non-local mind is a form of telepathy or sixth sense employed by all living creatures. This kind of telepathic communication happens every day: A brother suddenly knows when his twin is injured. A mother immediately senses that her child has been in an accident. A widower smells his late wife's perfume as he gets ready for bed. A dog heads for the front door, knowing when his master leaves the workplace, even if the work schedule varies.[109]

> When one tree becomes infested with insects, it sends a warning to other trees of its species, probably through the interconnected energy fields, and the other trees become immune to the insect infestation by changing their chemical composition.
>
> Dr. Valerie Hunt
> *Infinite Mind: Science of the Human Vibrations of Consciousness*

Animals communicate with and through the non-local mind. So do plants.[110] It's all non-local communication at work on the physical plane, with the connecting wires stretching across the (non-)expanse of the para-physical dimension. Non-local mind might also be termed higher consciousness; Jung called it the collective unconscious. Biologists call it an altered state, and psychologists super-sentience. The spiritual call it Christ Consciousness, Buddha Mind, or God Mind. But how does it work?

Are we talking about an energetic resonance, about being "on the same wavelength?" In Matthew 18:20, Jesus said, "For when two or more are gathered in my name, I am in the midst of them." It may have been a vibrational level to which Jesus referred when he mentioned praying "in my name." Jesus spoke Aramaic and in the Aramaic language, the word *shema*—usually translated into English as "name"—can also mean light, sound, atmosphere, or vibration. Everything vibrates at its own unique *shema*, its own signature frequency. [111] From what we know of vibration attracting like vibrations, it seems probable that Jesus was referring to "tuning into" a high-pitched cosmic or divine frequency.

In the broadest sense, the non-local mind gives us access to any concept, any bit of knowledge formulated in all of timeless reality, for whoever quiets the ego-chatter in his own mind; for whoever raises her frequency high enough to tune in the station on the divine level. Non-local mind is supported by four contemporary scientists:

- David Bohm: He believes in a holographic cosmic memory.

- Neurophysicist Karl Pribam: He believes the brain is a hologram of an all-inclusive memory of the human race.

- Experimental physicist Bob Beck: He measured the brain waves of persons "tuned into" past and future events at 7.8 cycles per second, which is the level at which energetic healers operate and at which the Earth vibrated as of 2005.[112] (When we feel "spacey," worried, or mentally unstable, we are *literally* ungrounded. Walking barefoot on the ground, gardening, or simply "thinking green"—imagining ourselves in an outdoor setting—helps us reconnect with Earth and be grounded again. We can also seek out mountain air, running water, crashing waves, or devices that produce negative ions, like indoor fountains, potted plants, and salt lamps. Crashing ocean waves deliver energy 15 times greater than the energy that comes from the sun.)

- Dr. Valerie Hunt: People going about the business of ordinary living generally emit energy around the frequency of 250 Hertz (cycles per second). Mystics, on the other hand, emit energy up to the remarkable "cosmic" frequency rate of 20,000 kilohertz, as high as her instruments were capable of recording![113]

We tune into this wisdom merely by switching the radio dial of our consciousness to a higher frequency. Usually we tune into the physical realm but, like clairvoyants, we all have the capability to receive all stations. No matter how noisy our surroundings, turning the radio on is as simple as quieting our own mind. Meditation is one method to achieve this connection. (*Aum* is the breath that vibrates throughout the universe.)[114]

> The Voice for God is always quiet, because it speaks of peace, and it is as loud as your willingness to listen. It cannot be louder without violating your freedom of choice . . .
>
> *A Course in Miracles*

When in danger, a rabbit will run and a bird will fly away; their inner nature helps to preserve them. Human beings are the only creatures on Earth who doubt the inner wisdom available to them. We say, "Wait a minute. Should I run away?" or "I don't know . . ."

During one moonless night, a man was walking across a field when he heard footsteps. His village had heard tales of a man-eating tiger in the territory, and he was afraid. The man turned and ran blindly across the field, until he ran right off a cliff. With flailing hands, he managed to grab a sapling growing in a crevice of the cliff wall, and he hung on for dear life. The minutes crept by; his muscles began to ache.

"Let go," advised a soft voice from above.

The man thought for a moment and then asked, "Is there anybody else I can talk to?"

How do we know when we're tuned into the right channel? To distinguish divine aid from our own inner chatter, the test is whether the messages are based on fear or on love, and whether they plague us or speak only at our invitation.[115] Any insight we receive from the Ethernet will *always* make us feel good about ourselves, make us feel loved and supported. A thought that batters our self-esteem is our *own* ego-based voice, sometimes called the Inner Critic. Occasionally the truth is the last thing we want to hear, but even with a conviction—a revelation to which we'd like to respond, "No, I'd rather not do that"—we feel encouraged to break out of the status quo and follow the suggestion; we just "know" it'd be good for us. Divine messages generally concern *self*-improvement and making connections with others; they aren't a green light to "save the world" by castigating someone who believes differently, suborning the free will of others, or causing harm of any sort.

Intuition is another divine-to-human (or Higher Self-to-ego) channel. I know I'm out of alignment when I switch from my slow-moving check-out line to go stand in a faster moving line and the original, abandoned line picks up its pace while the newly adopted line grinds to a sudden halt. On the other hand, when I hit green light after green light along my route (whether while driving, writing, etc.), I know I'm tapped in and moving in a good direction. I had a hunch . . .

Some people are more attuned to feelings in receiving para-physical communications. The *Tao Te Ching* refers to masters as people who are guided by what they feel rather than by what they see. A "feeling in your gut." A chill down the spine. (In fact, I've learned that any time I shudder, my body is trying to shake off the thought I just had. Immediately, I "erase" it and replace it with a more positive idea.) It may be an impulse we don't recognize consciously but do obey, like the people who had seats booked on the tragic 9/11 flights but, "for some reason," they had an inspiration to cancel and make other arrangements. Intention, imagination, insight, intuition, inspiration—all these are qualities of the non-local domain.[116]

"Inspiration" is based on a Latin phrase that means "to breathe into." The Bible contains many accounts of divine inspiration coming in the form of dreams, including Joseph of the many-colored coat, and the three wise men. About 1855, Isaac Singer found inspiration in a dream for the way to thread his sewing machine. Fifty years later, an unknown clerk named Albert Einstein published three papers in a fit of divine inspiration.[117] One revolutionary paper might have been a fluke, but Einstein had connected with his scientific muse; he'd tapped into the Inspiration Channel, and his three papers boosted science to a higher plateau.

Once we are committed to self-evolution, we are guided to the right books, helpful people, and appropriate situations—but we must be open-minded and quiet in order to hear or feel the promptings, willing to follow the advice, and confident that we *are* "connected," even if it doesn't feel like it. In order to invite possibilities into our life, we have to be willing to let go of what's comfortable and familiar, regret for the (seemingly unchangeable) past, and fears concerning our future. As the Maker of Dreams confided to Pierrette, "I'm used to opening doors. And yours opens much more easily than some I come across. Would you believe it, some people positively nail their doors up, and it's no good knocking."[118]

Revelations knock at our hearts. Song lyrics echo through iPods. A variety of messages continually seek us out.

> Every event contains mysterious messages. Every encounter with another being is a point of contact upon which the universe pivots. When we enter into this frame of mind, reality as we see it becomes a vast opportunity to experience the interconnectedness of all creation, to see that every piece is integral to the unfolding of creation.
>
> Rabbi David Cooper
> *God is a Verb*

Because time is a by-product of our three-dimensional existence, time only exists for God as an eternal *now*, and God always acts in the present. What happened to Lot's wife when she turned and looked backward? She was paralyzed. If we're brooding about the past or fretting about our future, God has no way to help us, for our focus is removed from Divine Presence in the present moment, and we've shut down our direct, one-on-One wireless cable to God. We have disconnected from the blessings that God has for us right now.

Remember the man hanging from the cliff?

"Help me!" he cried again.

"Let go," advised the soft voice.

"Oh no," cried the man, "I'd fall to my death!"

An hour passed and the man's muscles began to cramp.

"Trust Me," said the voice. "Let go."

"No, I won't," cried the man, and somehow he managed to hang onto the sapling until dawn. Exhausted, he looked around him in the pale light and discovered that his feet were only six inches above solid ground!

When we are ready to take the next step—and there is always a "next" step—Quantum God will create the conditions to make it happen and will supply any support we need. God is not an external agent with a sadistic, ironic, or even whimsical sense of humor looking down upon us, tying us in knots. Although the tapestry of our lives sometimes reminds us of a tangle of twine, the string theorists see order and beauty in the warp and weft of creation.

String Theory postulates that quarks are actually vibrating strands of energy.[119] That tiny string or quanta represents a divine core in the subatomic shell around which the building block of matter meshes, like a brilliant, full-blown idea that "comes out of nowhere." God is the growing medium of everything that lives. God is All, outside and inside, looking out of our eyes at the world.[120]

"We are One" is supported by many philosophies:

- Judaism believes that everything is linked with everything else, and nothing exists outside God.

- The Koran agrees: "Wheresoe'er ye turn, there is the Face of God." (2:115)

- In Jesus' time and culture, the word for God ("I Am" or *Alaha*) meant Unity, the individual who could not be ultimately separated from the divine. [121]

- For monotheists like Christians and Jews, there is only one God. For Sufis and other mystics there is *only* God.

- According to South American Kagaba tribal tradition, "The mother of our songs, the mother of all our seed, bore us in the beginning of things and so she is the mother of all types of men, the mother of all nations. She is the mother of the thunder, the mother of the streams, the mother of the trees and all things . . ."

- The Hopis believe the Creator, Taiowa, constructed everything first in his mind, forming Mother Earth and the human body alike.[122]

Invisibility gives birth to the visible. Scientists and mathematicians brush against the invisible, the infinite, and the divine every day. When scientists include time in their equations, they use "imaginary numbers" like the square root of -16. Because -4 times -4 equals positive 16, the solution for the square root of -16 demands an imaginary number (i), and the answer is $4i$. Theoretical physicists use i and its "complex conjugate" to bring these extraordinary numbers down to earth, so to speak.

Infinity also crops up when gravity and quantum mechanics attempt to merge, approaching zero in infinitely small portions.[123] Although an imaginary number may sound too insubstantial to have any relevance to the "real" world, many of us are carrying minus dollars in our pockets: the dollars we owe for our car or house or children's education. These are "minus" numbers and ones that, unfortunately, are all too real![124]

Infinity. Imaginary numbers. Different dimensions. String theory. Inspiration. Places only traveled via the non-local network. Like the electromagnetism that pervades the physical universe, so does the non-local mind.

"The Force is with you," Obi-Wan Kenobi said to Luke Skywalker.

Seven

What we focus our attention on is what we come to experience.

Quantum physics suggests that by redirecting our focus, we bring a new course of events into focus while at the same time releasing an existing course of events that may no longer serve us. Buddha, Gandhi, Jesus, and those who participated in the mass prayer of November 1998 each experienced the effect of such change.

Gregg Braden
The Isaiah Effect

The Road to Stardom

W hen I was a little girl, I became familiar with the historic struggles of the Jews, thanks to Cecil B. DeMille. Long before Han Solo's *Millennium Falcon* zoomed across the silver screen, this Hollywood director gave us epics like *The Ten Commandments.* Swayed by passion and purpose, DeMille's characters never included people like Reuben and Esther in the following scene.

Setting: *The Red Sea, which has parted to make way for the exodus of the Israelites.*

REUBEN

Oy! Have you ever seen such a thing, mud all over the place!

ESTHER

How dirty my feet are, and the hem of my frock—I'll never get it clean again!

REUBEN

How much farther do you think we'll have to wade through this muck and mire?

ESTHER

I've no idea. It'll be a miracle if I don't have a heart attack
before the hour's out.

REUBEN

I should be so lucky. When I think of the hearth and home
we left behind![125]

Even as extras, DeMille wouldn't have ordered close-ups of Reuben and
Esther as they trudged along, eyes fixed on the muddy ground. Why should an
audience care about characters who gripe along their road to freedom and never
once notice the miracle taking place?

The Kabbalah likens awareness to a magnet.[126] Quantum physics backs up
the Kabbalah; it says we participate in the creation of our reality through what
we're aware of. Had Reuben and Esther raised their eyes, their focus would have
changed their dialogue and actions, and they might have been the next Burton and
Taylor or Brad and Jolie, starring in their own epic movie.

In my own movie-life, my basement was shipping water: In my own movie-
life, my basement was shipping water every time it rained, and the foundation
was leaking. It wasn't until the master bathroom pipes broke and flooded the
house with a torrent of water that I finally noticed the correlation between the
overflowing water and all the weeping I'd been doing because I'd lost someone
I loved. I set out to create a new belief, founded on the quantum ground of
endless possibilities—as simple as believing that help would come to me—and
concentrated on attracting new situations into my reality, knowing they might take
some time to materialize.[127] A whole string of aids came from friends who cheered
me on to the spiritual healer who energetically removed a great portion of the
sorrow; from a friend who repaired the foundation to my father, who simply and
practically suggested lengthening the drains at the end of the downspouts. I also
decided that if I felt like crying, I'd better do it outside, away from the house!

We don't need silence or solitude to focus. The absence of sound is less
important than the absence of self. I learned to concentrate at a crowded swimming
pool, where country music blared from loud speakers and three hundred children
crashed, splashed, and yelled, "Watch this, Mom!" In fact, in Burmese monasteries
monks noisily recite whatever material they're trying to memorize, having learned
to block out the voices of their fellow monks.[128]

Detours and Delays

Sometimes navigating through our noisy, do-it-yourself life seems just too
much. "Live and learn," we say with a sigh after taking a wrong turn.

Determined to meet a man who was said to be the wisest man on Earth, a
group of tourists climbed up a steep mountainside, stumbling across the rocky

screes. Finally they stood before a stooped old man and asked, "How can we become as wise as you?"

The wise man looked up and said succinctly, "Wise choices."

One of the youths then asked, "But how do we know what choices are wise?"

"Experience," he answered.

The youth said, "But how do we get experience?"

The wise man smiled. "Bad choices."

When I was a baby my grandma, Zelma, and my mom went shopping and returned to the parking lot, only to find that Grama had locked the keys in the car. Fortunately, a rear window was rolled down. Mom volunteered to climb through it. "No, Sandi," Grama said. Although she was forty pounds heavier and a bit taller than Mom, she insisted that since she'd forgotten the keys, she'd be the one to retrieve them. Grama leaned into the car, hitched up her hips . . . and got stuck. No going forward, no backing out. Stuck, stuck, stuck. The ladies finally made it home after Mom pushed and Grama pulled, laughing all the while. And Grama learned to keep track of her keys.

Of course, some are wise enough to learn from others' mistakes, like my little sister, Nancy, who watched me as she grew into a beautiful young woman and sidestepped the same problems I had landed myself in. But for most of us, doing dumb things is the way we learn . . . at the Brick Wall School. I ought to be quite wise by this time in my life! However, my father is quick to list all the bad choices I've made—thank goodness he doesn't know my whole history, or I'd never hear the end of it. But belaboring mistakes is no way to rise above them; blame and shame only weigh us down. The thing to do is to learn. Turn and face another direction. Refocus.

How can we do that? We make an effort to become aware of what we're thinking and change our thoughts, for repeated thoughts are what we're projecting outward. And it doesn't have to be hard; this can be as simple as throwing away an old VCR tape.[129] Indeed, Cambridge biochemist Rupert Sheldrake tells us that our eyes not only receive images, they actually project images *out* into the world.[130] *We are creating everything we see.*

We can, remember, choose whether we want the quantumstuff to materialize as a wave or a particle. So we can *choose* the possibility of prosperity, *choose* to make connections with others, *choose* health. As we envision what we desire, the intensity of our desire calls from *potentia* possibilities that are out-pictured into reality. Daydreamers, your time is not wasted!

Because of quantum mechanics, we have learned that the future is composed of ever-crystallizing possibilities. What we most often think about, the scenes we most often imagine, the messages we give ourselves eventually manifest in the physical world. (There are, however, two cautions to this principle: First, if we ignore "hidden" beliefs like "Life is a struggle," they will also manifest, because the fear underlying them provides the muscle to power them into physicality. Secondly, there's an exception: What we *long* for, feel we can't be happy without, or desperately need, we in fact *push away* because of the repulsive energy attached to the desire.)

What, then, are we to do? We imagine ourselves in the situation we choose to be in without brooding about what we don't want. Like toddlers who love the sparkles in cut-glass crystal but are easily distracted by a plastic Scooby-Doo cup, the trick is to develop something—an image, a setting, an affirmation—the equivalent of a Scooby-Doo cup with which we distract ourselves, latching onto the new image or affirmation so that we quickly change mental direction.

If this "mindfulness" sounds a little strange, think about it this way: Most of us must work with budgets, so why shouldn't we consider spending our thoughts as wisely as we do our money?

When I was a youngster—way before PCs, iPads, and Game Boys—we kids spent a lot of time outdoors. The streetlights coming on was the sign for bath and bed. But the kid who lived across the street often played truant. In desperation, Bobby's mom told him that ghosts came out when darkness fell. As he grew up, so did his fear, and he refused to take a paper route or run to the store down the block after sunset. So his mom gave him a medal for protection.[131] I always wondered about that. Wouldn't it make more sense to have faith in ourselves, rather than needing something external to put our faith in?

And yet, on autopilot, I dreamed up a nightmare that I could have avoided. When I was a teenager, Smokey Robinson and the Miracles sang "The Tears of a Clown." I understood that song. Because our mother taught us that we are each "a light unto the world," I learned to be cheerful and smile a lot, but underneath a melancholy always lurked (a drawback of being a Water-ruled INFJ). And once you've lived in despair, it seems as if despair is as close as someone tapping you on the shoulder. Eventually, I discovered tricks to elevate my mood when I finally got a good start on my Path, tools to use. Yogic breathing. Certain foods to eat (like dark chocolate, in moderation). Concentrating on what I'm grateful for or a joyful memory. Calling a friend, and making contact with the Divine.

But really, the first step was not to turn around when I felt that tap on my shoulder, but to keep going forward, to keep shooting for balance. For peace. For *some better feeling*. It takes self-discipline to turn from despair and depression but, with practice, it gets easier. I had to remember to take a deep breath, get up off my butt, listen to upbeat "moving" music, and get out into the green of the good earth. Little by little I increased the distance between that tapping finger and better times. But I had to take that first step.

I developed the practice of *thinking* about what I was thinking about—was I focused on what fear showed me, the worst possible outcome? It helped to recall the simple little electron, that sub-atomic particle that tries all possible orbits before changing course, like a baseball that's hit and while it's in flight, it smears itself over the outfield in the shape of a waffle cone, until it connects with a mitt, a wall, or the ground. The ice cream cone-shape includes a lot of possible outcomes a lot different from the "oh, no!" scene I'd been focused on. Whew! I learned to stop, laugh at myself, and refocus. Redirecting my attention keeps my mood lighter, my outlook brighter, my vibrational frequency higher, and the events that I attract more desirable. When I exercise some control over what I'm thinking, I can regulate how I feel. (Moods can be modified through specific techniques listed in Part Two.)

Keeping Your Mind on Mindfulness

One dark and lonely night back in the 'Seventies, Merrilee was hitchhiking. A car stopped; the driver motioned her in. They had been on the road for twenty minutes or so when the driver suddenly reached across the seat and shoved a screwdriver into Merrilee's ribs. Without panicking, without the paralyzed immobility fear induces, Merrilee acted; she wrapped her fingers around the shaft of the tool and thrust it away from her, speaking firmly and calmly. "Hey, man," she said, "you don't really want to do this." Mastering her fear defused the dangerous situation, and she arrived safely at her destination.

Waking up requires becoming aware of what goes on inside us and what we are doing, moment by moment. After the death of a particularly revered rabbi, one of his disciples was asked what had been most important to the great man. "Whatever he was doing at the time," replied the student.

What a great definition of mindfulness!

Every night, rain or shine, I take office trash out to the dumpster. It's a simple job and one I can do on autopilot. One night I lugged the bag outside, crossed the hot blacktop parking lot, wrestled with the latch, yanked open the big wooden door, and manhandled the garbage bag over the high dumpster rim—along with a full set of building keys. My trash-stowing had become so automatic an action that out of habit I tossed away everything in my hands. Guess what mindless employee had to go dumpster diving.

> Mindfulness is about being right here where you are anyway.
>
> Jon Kabat-Zinn
> Unity Temple on the Plaza, Kansas City, Missouri,
> 30 January 2005

Mindfulness, which the Sufis call remembrance of the soul, comes from disciplined focus, and focus from practice.[132]

Eight

Most people go about their daily routines in a highly suggestible state of mind.

A man with advanced cancer was no longer responding to radiation treatment. He was given a single injection of an experimental drug, Krebiozen, considered by some at the time to be a "miracle cure."

. . . The results were shocking to the patient's physician, who stated that his tumors "melted like snowballs on a hot stove." Later the man read studies suggesting the drug was ineffective, and his cancer began to spread once more . . . his doctor administered a placebo . . . The man was told the plain water was a "new, improved" form of Krebiozen. Again, his cancer shrank away dramatically. Then he read [that] Krebiozen was a worthless medication. The man's faith vanished, and he was dead within days.

Rupert Sheldrake
Seven Experiments That Could Change the World

There's One Born Every Minute

One day a high-priced psychiatrist overhears his new receptionist talking on the telephone.

"Recurrent mild headaches? Your problem is a simple neurosis. I'm sure the doctor can help you."

Before the doctor can speak, the phone rings again, and again the receptionist listens briefly and tells the caller, "Trouble sleeping? Your problem is a simple neurosis. I'm sure the doctor can help you."

When the receptionist hangs up, the psychiatrist looks at her sternly and says, "Please, Ms. Dannon, you must not make diagnoses."

"But, doctor," the receptionist replies, "I'm just drumming up new business for you."

In our high-tech world, we're bombarded with suggestions every day, but even in a state of sensory deprivation, most of us still have one companion we react to, much of the time without the awareness that we *are* responding to suggestion. My most constant companion is myself. In my head or out loud I talk to myself a lot of the time. "Intelligent people talk to themselves," I'll say with a smirk when someone overhears me. "I'm good company, too," I add. But how good am I, really?

We like to be with people who make us feel good. People who make us laugh. People who love, or admire, or at least like us. We all talk to ourselves, and we can gauge what sort of company we're providing ourselves by stopping to take note of what we're saying.

"Idiot!" I used to exclaim when I made a mistake. "I'm tired," I used to say when I felt worn out. "I can't!" I still groan when faced with a challenge. *These are all messages that our inner self takes very seriously.* These are not the remarks of anyone we would seek out to spend time with; these messages do not make us feel good about ourselves, our abilities, or our bodies.

The Power of Words

The Japanese scientist, Dr. Masaru Emoto, has spent years exploring the power of words. Emoto performed three types of experiments: First, he typed out phrases like "Love and Gratitude," or "You make me sick," and attached the strips of paper to glass containers of both spring water and tap water. He also set a series of containers on pictures of scenic spots and, finally, exposed another group of containers to different types of music. Then he froze the water samples and took pictures of crystals that had formed in the water. The photographs in his book are amazing proof that our words deeply influence whatever they touch.[133]

What makes Emoto's findings relevant to us is that we are approximately 70% water (newborn infants are 50% water). What we think and what we say affects us biologically and psychologically, along with the words or names we wear on our clothing, the things we see, and the music we listen to and shows we watch all have a physical effect on us. So now I use discretion when choosing what to read, watch, listen to, and wear, including clothing, "singing the blues," negative thinking, and toxic people. I even had the small Chinese character for "Joy" tattooed on one shoulder, "Trust God" on the other, and the master healing symbol at the back of the throat chakra.

Emoto's findings are good news or bad news, depending on what sort of company we're supplying ourselves, but the situation becomes even more important when we realize that most people go about their daily lives in a highly suggestible state of mind.

The Babemba tribe lives in southern Africa. These people have no rules, and they have no crime. On the rare occasion that someone does something unkind or immoral, the people hold their own sort of intervention.

In the middle of the village sits the offender, with the tribe circling around him. For hours or for days the meeting goes on, with the offender listening as each member, one at a time, speaks about the best qualities, stories, and kindnesses of the offender. When the "intervention" is finished and all the members have said every last good thing they can think of about the person in their midst, the offender is then welcomed back into the tribe with a celebration. The offense is rarely repeated. How affirming!

Grama Zelma had pneumonia, which landed her in the hospital. At the end of a week, an ambulance took Grama to a nursing home, for she was ninety-two years old, and the illness had left her weak and spiritless. My father flew in from the coast, and for three days he kindly tended his mother. He plumped pillows, brought her favorite chicken nuggets for lunch, and time and again with the best of intentions said, "No, Mom, don't. Let me do that for you, you're too sick." By the time he headed for the coast again, Grama had become more an invalid than when she was suffering from the initial bout of pneumonia. In a mindless manner, Grama was focusing on illness rather than health.

The night my father left town, I entered Grama's room with four-year-old Kate and three-year-old Cecilia. We kissed her hello and then I spoke in a firm tone of voice. "Come on, Grama, get up now, or you'll never get out of this place. We're going to practice walking. I know you can do it." With the little girls and me at her side praising her efforts, Grama paced up and down the hall outside her room. Every night we practiced together, walked a little further, felt a bit better. At the end of a week, healthy, cheerful Zelma signed her discharge papers and proudly walked out of the nursing home.

Mindlessness, or operating on autopilot, is like being in a trance. This "mechanical" behavior is the reason most auto accidents happen within a few blocks of home; we talk, walk, drive, and work in an unfocused condition. And when we lose focus, lose awareness, slip out of mindfulness, we easily react to external or internal promptings, just like someone who has been hypnotized. In fact, quantum psychologist Dr. Stephen Wolinsky wrote that the job of the hypnotherapist was "no longer to *induce* a trance but rather to *de-hypnotize* the individual out of the trance she was already experiencing."[134]

When we walk around in a trance, we are highly sensitive to suggestion. What does a child grow to believe about himself if he often hears, "You're so dumb!" What shall an employee believe if she is told, "You can't do anything right!" The subconscious even reacts to "He's such a drunk," or "I'm so stupid!" when we've made a mistake. (A valuable affirmation is "I respond only to suggestions that benefit my well-being.")

> Frequently things turn out just as expected or prophecied . . . because people's behavior tends to make the prophecy come true. For example, a teacher who predicts that a student will fail may treat the student in ways that make failure more likely, thus fulfilling the original prophecy.
>
> Rupert Sheldrake
> *Seven Experiments That Could Change the World*

What messages are we bombarding ourselves with, day after day? If our life is not satisfying and our minds not at peace, we need to become aware of the inner dialogue that is undermining our sense of well-being, and we can refuse to participate when people are discussing dire predictions, say, for the national economy.

The unnecessary South American famine in 1946 demonstrates the power of suggestion. This is one of the reasons why both advertisements and affirmations work. Advertising is perhaps the most ubiquitous form of suggestion in our society. Television and radio spots, billboards, the Yellow Pages, flashing Internet ads. Medical and pharmaceutical advertisers create business by hinting at all the ways our bodies can go *wrong*, and the seeds they cast out take root needlessly. Advertising everywhere suggests that we need this product, that service, these connections, toothpaste and deodorizer. Sometimes less is more.

Less is certainly more than enough when the inner voice of our most constant companion tears us down. We talk to ourselves all the time; our thoughts are a continuously flowing stream of messages. Many of these suggestions pertain to our physical appearance and health, and *when it comes to our bodies, our own words and thoughts are taken as literal commands.* [135] Mark Twain knew what he was talking about when he warned us about reading health books. "You may die of a misprint," he said.

> **Try It Yourself**
>
> See how the following short message affects you. Supposedly, Hemingway once won a bet for writing a complete story in only six words:
>
> "For sale. Baby shoes. Never used."
>
> K. C. Cole
> *Mind Over Matter*

Words carry a lot of weight. If my internal dialogue revolves around a theme such as, "I've always been sickly," or "I am prone to strep throat," is it little wonder that sickness is what I experience? I've commanded my body to operate at less than optimum level.

"I am . . ." may be the most potent creative statement we can utter. When I changed the directive to "I am always healthy," good health was my reward, especially when I stopped giving germs—*external* agents—the power to

affect me. No bouts of influenza. No thyroid imbalance. No kidney disease. (I'm now working on not giving my power away to poison ivy: Name it; claim it! "I am immune to poison ivy.")

I discovered a wonder drug—a new thought—by accident. In 1972, I was diagnosed with a chronic bleeding kidney. In the late 1990s, when my HMO went through restructuring and lost *all* of my records, I had the revelation that, with the record of my condition being lost, the kidney problem had also vanished. My idea was that the kidney dysfunction had been *wiped out* along with the charted diagnosis, and this actually effected a physical cure; in that instant of mind/body cooperation, I was totally cured. I agree with both quantum physics and the Kabbalah, which says each moment we live is a new beginning in the cycle of ongoing Creation. If we conceive it, if we believe it, that is what we manifest.

Because internal suggestions work, many oncologists now recommend visualization and affirmation as techniques in fighting cancer. Louise Hay goes one step further and maintains that *every* word we speak is an affirmation. She suggests that an affirmation is like a visit to the cosmic kitchen; you place your order and assume it will be out when it's ready, without your going back to the stove to hover over the chef.[136]

Our words' influence does flow outward into the environment. (Check out "The Power of Words" posted by Andrea Gardner on youtube.) The famous horticulturist, Luther Burbank, used words to develop a spineless cactus. He would tell the plant, "You have nothing to fear. You don't need your defensive thorns. I will protect you." Both his intention and his speech worked; he developed an ouchless cactus. How? Thoughts amplified by emotion or intent affect matter; "will directs energy." *Energy follows intention.*[137]

Emoto's studies and ouchless cacti prove that those of our mothers who were forever telling us "If you can't say something nice, don't say anything at all" were wiser than we children gave them credit for.

> In the Gospel of Thomas, verse 15, Jesus says, "If you enter into any land and walk through the countryside, and if they receive you, eat what they put before you. Those who are sick among them, heal them. For what goes into your mouth will not defile you, rather what comes out of your mouth is what will defile you."

Since abracadabras come out of our mouths, we now know to

- Conceive it
- Believe it
- Name it
- Claim it . . .

and act mindfully, as if each thought *will* manifest.

Nine

Judgment separates us from what we are judging and destroys our peace of mind.

It is you who put your hands
before your eyes and say it is dark.
Take your hands away and see the light.

Vivekananda
Living at the Source

Sweeping Out the Old

When we needed our chimney cleaned, we called a chimney sweep. On the doorstep appeared a tall, dark, handsome man, lean and strong and, I thought, intimidating. He looked a bit like my stepfather, he seemed to carry within him an explosive element like my husband, and immediately I formed mental associations and reacted emotionally: I was scared. It was not until the man had been working for a while that I moved beyond my fear and talked with him, and I discovered Michael was a soft-spoken, not-scary gentleman.

My ego had separated me from the sweep and made him frightening, but when I let Spirit direct me, acceptance became possible. The ego judges and then our judgments control us, in a manner of speaking, for quantum physics has discovered that *what we think should happen is virtually always what we think we find.*

Our thought processes mostly involve liking or not liking, accepting or rejecting. And sometimes we become slaves to our thoughts, our associations, and our judgments.[138] When we say, "It shouldn't be like this," or "This is bad," we are resisting the situation as it undoubtedly exists, which thrusts us outside the realm of action, where we cannot make positive changes. We may strive for tolerance, but tolerance implies, at the least, an irritation to be set aside rather than unconditional acceptance. If we moved beyond our polar differences, beyond should and shouldn't, there'd be nothing left to find fault with.

> Humans take their wishes, wants, and likes (almost all of which are fairly legitimate), and they foolishly change them into Jehovistic commands, demands, shoulds, oughts, and wants, which do not really exist in the universe—because man invented them. So they upset themselves needlessly and make themselves depressed, angry, horrified, and anxious . . .
>
> They hate and pity themselves, which interferes with their going after what they want and avoiding what they don't want in this life. Try to change whatever is against your interest . . . but don't *demand* that the things you like exist or that because you dislike something that it *must not* exist. These Jehovistic commands and demands constitute the core of human neuroses.
>
> Psychologist Albert Ellis, founder of Rational Emotive Behavior Therapy quoted by William Elliot in *Tying Rocks to Clouds*

Buddhists maintain that our ideas of polarity—hot/cold, good/bad, body/soul—are the binding factors that keep us stuck in the physical, but the polarities themselves are necessary composites of one whole. Polar opposites are the yin and yang of our existence. Niels Bohr so believed in quantum wholeness that he had his coat of arms made with the yin/yang emblem on it, symbolizing the interconnectedness of the universe.[139]

> **Try It Yourself**
>
>
>
> A "Möbius" strip demonstrates the "Many are One" concept, or "the not twoness" of *advaya* Buddhism. To make a Möbius strip, cut a length of paper, give one end a half twist, and tape the two ends together. Then, starting anywhere on the strip, draw a line down the middle of the paper . . . until you find you've covered *both* sides of the paper and ended up at the starting point. The strip has only one side, although—to your eyes—it is positive proof of being a two-sided object!

In 2004 to 2005, the United Church of Christ ran a thought-provoking television advertisement, in which two hefty bouncers stood before the doors of a church. It was the bouncers' job to turn away "undesirables." Among the faces they rejected were those of a black woman and a gay couple. The tag line at the end of the spot stated: "Jesus didn't turn people away. Neither do we." Good point. Who are we to exclude from *We are One*?

A Different Kind of Perfect

The matter of exclusion becomes all the more liable to error when we consider Jesus exhorting his listeners to love their enemies: "Be ye therefore perfect, even as your Father which is in heaven is perfect." The Aramaic word traditionally translated as "perfect" can also mean "all-embracing."[140] What a tremendous change in attitude this alternate interpretation produces: God is *all-embracing*; Divine perfection comes from not leaving out any part or particle. Makes sense if God is all there really is.

Furthermore, how can we make wise decisions when one person's sense of goodness is not recognized by another? G. K. Chesterton said good has many meanings: "If a man were to shoot his grandmother at a range of five hundred yards, I should call him a good shot, but not necessarily a good man." Baruch Spinoza wrote that good is whatever is useful, which renders the standard of goodness dependent upon our changing outlooks and varying needs. Echoing Taoist philosophy, the Baal Shem Tov, the founder of mystical Judaism, believed that good is closer to God and bad is farther from God; in any case, bad is part of the spectrum.

> How is it possible to believe in God, who is eternal love and mercy, and at the same time to believe that this good God could create a being capable of evil to the point of eternal—eternal!—damnation? If one posits unrestrained personalized evil in a being or beings, then anything can happen and God's hands seem to be tied . . .
>
> All creation is subject to infinite, unconquerable goodness. We either believe in the mystery of the eternal love of God or we believe in a creator who, at least once, miscalculated badly and could do nothing to correct it.
>
> Donald Spoto
> *The Hidden Jesus*

When we deny that the opposite of good exists at all, we come nearer to recognizing that opposites really don't exist.[141] The figure of Satan represents the opposite of goodness and the epitome of evil, and yet the great swami Yogananda wrote that the "Satan" to which Biblical prophets and scripture writers refer is *maya*, which diverts people from the spiritual to the material.[142]

A Course in Miracles proposes that the Devil is the *ego's sense of isolation*.[143] Anytime and every time I've been mired in despair and depression, I certainly felt isolated from the world and from God. In exploring the question of evil, I learned that Satan in the parable of Job is actually *Ha-satan*, an "employee" of God's, a sort of loyalty assessor or prosecuting attorney. I also learned that early Christian writers of the New Testament who mention "devils" were actually referring to pagan cults.[144]

Bad. Good. Falsity. Truth. As Einstein would say, it's all relative.

Buddhists and Sufis (among others) avoid the problem of judgment and exclusion by revering all life, but reverence for life is not limited to "spiritual" people. Despite his background as a scientist, Bohm felt that whatever lies behind nature is holy.[145]

[Sheikh] Sunbul Efendi, in looking for a successor, sent his disciples out to get flowers to adorn the lodge. All of them returned with large bunches of lovely flowers; only one came back with a small, withered plant.

When asked why he did not bring anything worthy of his master, he answered, "I found all the beautiful flowers were still recollecting the Lord—how could I interrupt this constant prayer of theirs? I looked, and one flower had finished its recollection." It was he who became the next sheikh.

James Fadiman and Robert Frager
Essential Sufism

Lao-Tsu wrote, "When people see some things as good, other things become bad."[146] The fact that we make distinctions in itself creates undesirables.

Many wise people maintain that evil is only ignorance. I know that when my grandma Da took me out to find leaves for a 7th grade science assignment and I thoughtlessly stripped all the leaves off a forsythia limb in passing, she informed me that the leaves were the method by which the bush breathed. I was horrified that I had done damage in my ignorance. In fact, motivational speaker Jean Houston believes that if the young Adolph Hitler had been awarded an art scholarship, all of the horrors of his political career might never had occurred. If, however, evil *does* exist, we only resonate with negative energies when we think like thoughts and react to negativity at its frequency.[147]

Fanning the Sparks

Jewish mystics of the Kabbalah believe there lives a divine spark of holiness, however well-hidden, in everyone; that it is our purpose on Earth to fan this spark into flame, and that evil is only that which is not aware of its own spark.[148] In fact, the root of *shem* (*kevod* in Hebrew) implies a vibrating force at the core of every being.[149] *Shem*-light includes all frequencies, which in turn include darkness—and it is darkness, or dark matter, that makes up most of the universe.

> Sparks . . . Left over from the creation event. Caught now inside everything and everyone. A light-like consciousness. Echoing the beginning. Hovering just above 3 degrees Kelvin. Somewhere between spirit and matter. Hidden away in galaxies and trees and you and me. Shimmering. Like sunlight on water that will not be still.
>
> Rabbi Lawrence Kushner
> *River of Light*

In our culture, a "light in the darkness" has great significance. But the flip side is, darkness defines the value of light. Something as common and useful as duct tape has a light and a dark side, and yet it certainly holds the stuff in our lives together!

After we accept the role that darkness plays in our universe and our lives, we can then consider how to interact with darkness. Jesus urged his disciples to be as "harmless as doves" while they made their way through the world. And Paul said, "Be not overcome of evil, but overcome evil with good." In like manner, the *Tao Te Ching* proposes we give evil nothing to oppose and it will disappear by itself (#60). This concept is the basis for the martial art of aikido. The martial art of aikido teaches us that when we come into contact with "evil," we sidestep it and allow its momentum to cause its own downfall, which is better than resisting the attack with the same energy it comes at us with.[150]

This reminds me of the man who was held up by a teenager. Julio couldn't help but notice that the young man was shivering in the cold. He willingly handed over his wallet and insisted that the teen also take his winter coat, then invited him to a nearby diner for a hot meal. When it came time to pay the bill, Julio grinned and said, "I'm sorry, son, but you have all the money." In gratitude for the man's generosity, the boy handed Julio the wallet, along with his knife, saying, "I won't need this anymore." This was a real turning point in the young man's life.

> Have compassion for everyone you meet, even if they don't want it. What appears bad manners, an ill temper or cynicism is always a sign of things no ears have heard, no eyes have seen. You do not know what wars are going on down there where the spirit meets the bone.
>
> Miller Williams

The Aramaic word usually translated as "good," *taba*, involves something that maintains its integrity and health and also means whatever is in harmony with "Sacred Unity," or God. The Aramaic word traditionally translated as "evil," *bisha*, is nothing more than that which has fallen out of rhythm with God. [151]

The Greek word usually translated as "evil," *paneros*, comes from a root that means "to toil." So evil is a labored effort. The Chinese have a philosophy of "effortlessness," or *"Wu-Wei,"* also translated as "not forcing." We're not talking doormat here, but flexibility and an open mind, like the nonviolence advocated by Gandhi and Martin Luther King, Jr. Victory, says the *Tao Te Ching*, goes to one who knows how to yield (#69).

One of my favorite stories is *To Kill a Mockingbird*. In both book and movie, Atticus Finch tells his daughter that you never really know a man until you "stand in his shoes and walk around in them." Like the chimney sweep who came to our house, when I make a hasty judgment against someone, maybe it's only a case of my not having learned enough about that person.[152] This is a lesson Barney and Violet learned during a trip to Las Vegas.

The Color of Kindness

Each year, an elderly couple my mom knew took time off from volunteering at Trinity Lutheran Hospital in Kansas City and treated themselves to a week of good food and light gambling. One year, after they'd arrived in Las Vegas and checked into their hotel room, Violet said, "I believe I'll go downstairs and gamble a little bit."

"Well, I'm too tired," Barney replied. "I'm going to bed. Will you be all right alone?"

"Oh, yes, don't worry about me. I'll be up in an hour or so."

She stepped into the elevator. After descending a couple of floors, the car stopped and in walked a big black man with four of his friends. As Violet was moving back to make room for them, one of the black men said, "Hit the floor!" Frightened out of her wits, Violet fell down on all fours.

The men were horrified. They helped Violet up and she returned to her room.

The week passed, and at the check-out counter, Barney asked the desk clerk for their bill.

The clerk replied, "There's no charge."

"But we made long-distance calls to our children. We ordered room service," Barney said.

The clerk told him that the hotel bill had been paid in full.

"Who paid our bill?" asked Violet.

The clerk smiled. "Eddie Murphy."

We were *truly* all the same (brothers)—because their belief in one God had removed the "white" from their *minds*, the "white" from their *behavior*, and the "white" from their *attitude*.

Malcolm X, *Letter from Mecca*
quoted by Philip Novak in
The World's Wisdom: Sacred Texts of the World's Religions

Regarding everyone as part of our family runs through many traditions. The Dakota Indians include everyone with the phrase *mitakuye oyasin*, "all my relations." In like manner, the Sioux Indians pray, "Teach us to walk the soft Earth as relatives to all that live." Shintoism teaches its followers to regard heaven as their father, earth as their mother, and all things as their brothers and sisters. Finally, with delightful humor, Confucius made the wry comment that "All the people are your relatives; expect, therefore, troubles from them." [153] Sounds like Thanksgiving dinner at a lot of American homes.

> We are one with God. God is everywhere and everything. All being derives its reality from God. According to this paradigm, if God is within all creation, then what *appears* as evil can only be a distant, albeit distorted, expression of the divine. This doesn't make it "good." But nothing can be entirely separate . . . from God. Everything, therefore, is the way it is 'supposed' to be.
>
> Rabbi Lawrence Kushner
> *Invisible Lines of Connection: Sacred Stories of the Ordinary*

Evil seems destructive, but an ancient parable illustrates how everything in the universe is an expression of the Tao. Three vinegar tasters sipped the brew of life in the Land of the Morning Calm. Buddha found his sip bitter, and Confucius decided his tasted sour. But Lao-Tsu pronounced the vinegar sweet, for its acidity was indeed what made the vinegar truly vinegary.[154] The vinegar was perfect because, in accordance with its own nature, it tasted the way it was *natural* for it to taste.

I've experienced a lot of sour and bitter things in my life, from starving for months on end while an unemployed college graduate to being raped. Lack of food taught me compassion, and rape taught me to use my voice, to stand up for myself, and to stop feeling like a victim.

Compassion helps me understand difficult times and difficult people (including myself). Compassion helps me accept without "judging against." I've found that I can often avoid "judging against" when I remember that everyone and everything is evolving at different rates, and then I can allow people to act according to their own natures. (Then it's my choice, of course, to pick the people I want to associate with.)[155]

> Practically nothing makes me angry anymore . . . Once in a while I get angry . . . Then I immediately say to myself that being angry at [people] is foolish, because I'm telling myself they *shouldn't* be the way they undoubtedly are.
>
> Albert Ellis
> quoted by William Elliot in *Tying Rocks to Clouds:*
> *Meetings and Conversations with Wise and Spiritual People*

According to One's Own Ideal

Allowing people to behave according to their own nature sets the stage for peaceful relations; it's acceptable when children shriek with delight, though the high pitch may strike a live wire inside their parent's head. It's all right when a teenager does what teenagers are supposed to do—rebel against conformity—especially when that passion is directed down a constructive road, like my friend, Chelsea, who stood up for a mentally challenged student being teased by their high school classmates.

Most of the creation verses in Genesis end with "and God saw that it was good." In our world of polarities, we tend to assign the label of "good" and "bad" to people, things, and events, but those distinctions involve judgment for and judgment against parts of God.[156]

In the *Silmarillion*, the prequel to *Lord of the Rings*, J.R.R. Tolkien wrote his own version of the Creation story, in which the gods were singing a great anthem that would ultimately lay the groundwork for the world. Like Sauron after him, Melkor desired more power and glory, but his music disrupted the entire composition.

> Then the discord of Melkor spread ever wider, and the melodies which had been heard before foundered in a sea of turbulent sound . . . And it seemed at last that there were two musics progressing at one time before the seat of Iluvatar, and they were utterly at variance. The one was deep and wide and beautiful, but slow and blended with an immeasurable sorrow, from which its beauty chiefly came. The other had now achieved a unity of its own; but it was loud, and vain, and endlessly repeated; and it had little harmony, but rather a clamorous unison as of many trumpets braying upon a few notes. And it essayed to drown the other music by the violence of its voice, but it seemed that its most triumphant notes were taken by the other and woven into its own solemn pattern . . .

> Then Iluvatar spoke, and he said: "Behold your Music! . . . And thou, Melkor, shalt see that no theme may be played that hath not its uttermost source in me, nor can any alter the music in my despite. For he that attempteth this shall prove but mine instrument in the devising of things more wonderful, which he himself hath not imagined . . . And thou, Melkor, will discover all the secret thoughts of thy mind, and wilt perceive that they are but a part of the whole and tributary to its glory.[157]

> All things work together for good. There are no exceptions except in the ego's judgment.
>
> *A Course in Miracles*
>
> In harmony with the Tao . . . all creatures flourish together, content with the way they are, endlessly repeating themselves, endlessly renewed.
>
> *Tao Te Ching #39*
> Stephen Mitchell, translator

All We Want is a Good Hug

As an alternative healer, I know that non-judgment is an essential component of energy healing; in non-traditional energy work, one of the first things we learn is that our idea of healing may not bring the "cure" we would like to see. A general intention for whatever outcome is best is appropriate, especially when working with someone who is dying. We might think the "cure" is to keep the person with us, when what he or she really needs is to find peace and acceptance within, and courage to let go of this life. Thus, healing facilitates the adoption of peace and acceptance; the disease or disability may remain but the condition no longer matters, for it has been literally transgressed, or "gone beyond." So, too, may a condition remain because the lesson it symbolizes has not been learned; the underlying mental (a false belief) or emotional (an old anger or hurt) problem has not been addressed, so that resulting blockage of energy continues to recreate the physical malady. Indeed, images of physical dysfunctions appear in the human energy field before manifesting in the physical body, but if we replace old programming—"The flu is going around; I'm sure to catch it"—with sustained, healthy visions of ourselves, we can *program* our bodies for good health. We become what we *think* we are.[158]

All things contribute to the progression of an unfolding Creation, even the things that seem bad. Unconditional love helps, accepting the less-than-ideal without condemning it. Unconditional love does not say, "I'll love you, but first you have to act like this."

A Hindu swami once told about spending a day alone with his nephew: "It was a hard day for the swami and the three-year-old. We messed up the house. He threw a tantrum. Finally I took him in my arms and just held him . . . I realized that's all the world wants, to be held in spite of it all."[159]

One of my most favorite quotes from *A Course in Miracles* asks, why be angry at a world that "merely awaits your blessing to be free?"[160]

Speak kindly. Touch softly. Give hugs. Bless indiscriminately. Each of us is a bright light that shines into our world and makes it better.

Everyone must be judged according to his own ideal, and not by that of anyone else. If you are a strong man, very good! But do not curse others who are not strong enough for you. People are doing all right to the best of their ability and means and knowledge. *Woe unto me that I cannot lift them to where I am!*

Vivekananda
Living at the Source

Ten

We can only hope to change ourselves and how we respond to any event.

The most excellent jihad is that for the conquest of self.

Islamic *Hadith* [161]

Dealing with the Good, the Bad, and the Ugly

Our marriage was deeply troubled. My husband and I acted like enemies, and I was resigned to getting through each day of the decades stretching ahead of me until I could die. My only option was to embark upon a self-improvement campaign. One of the first books I read was Dr. Louis Tartaglia's *Flawless: The Ten Most Common Character Flaws.* (See Part Two, Principle #1.) Over the course of the first chapter, I found myself saying, "Oh, yes, that's him," referring to my husband, "and that flaw, too!"

The book stopped me in my tracks as my comments changed to "No, now, that one's me," and "Honestly, *I* do that." It was a moment of sublime revelation when the practice of blame loosened its claws on my side of the relationship. How silly I'd been, thinking in such a one-sided manner. I began to notice my *own* habitual behaviors and to hold myself accountable for my own actions and feelings. My husband became one of my greatest teachers.

We tend to see the other person as the "bad guy." Assigning blame makes us feel better about ourselves, but if everyone is behaving at their own particular level of development and no one *else* is responsible for how *we* feel, then blame evaporates.

When my friend, Steve Schieszer, wrote a screenplay about the time he served in Vietnam, he gave the finished script to a lawyer. She arranged for the sale in Hollywood, and had his money transferred into her bank account. Although her agent's fee amounted to more than $200,000, she eventually embezzled the entire amount, and Steve never saw a penny of his payment. I can't imagine how I would have reacted, but Steve knows that anger and resentment can only hurt him and those he loves, and he has coped with the loss without letting it make him bitter.

At any given moment, we may face a traffic jam, unpleasant person, or difficult situation. The good news is, we can choose how to respond. When I remember that I have all sorts of possibilities from which to choose (the quirky "impossibilities" of quanta and the limitless *potentia*), I depend less on people outside myself for approval and am less often hurt by their actions or criticism. I've learned that whenever I feel sad or anxious or frightened, I'm operating at base-ego level—and I don't have to! Now I rarely worry about merging with highway traffic or about my personal safety. I am on my way to learning fearlessness.

Living Free

No one outside ourselves can rule us inwardly. As soon as we understand this, we become free. By governing our own thoughts, emotions, and behavior, and maintaining our self-esteem, we can decide the course of our lives, rather than allowing fear or automatic reactions to make our decisions for us.

> The main theme remains constant: man owes it to himself to reject despair; better to rely on miracles than opt for resignation. By changing himself, man can change the world.
>
> Elie Wiesel
> *Souls on Fire: Legends of Hasidic Masters*

We are like animated characters in a virtual game. Although our souls have chosen us as their avatars, they have granted us autonomy; we are the ones who make up the play-action as we go along. We decide to hunt for treasure, fight the dragon, rescue the oppressed, or blow away other characters we have denoted as "the enemy" within the bounds of the animation. One reason we chose to participate in this game is because we wanted hands-on experience at discovering the rules of reality from scratch. We are learning the process of god-ing, which is constructive creating. We're learning the fundamentals of processing power on the physical level and, as ever, this process is governed by what we hold to be true within the virtual arena.

A Polish newspaper once reported the terrifying voyage of the freighter, *Phenian.* The freighter was heaving through heavy seas in the Atlantic Ocean when the crew heard mysterious voices calling from the cargo hold below deck. Believing the hold was inhabited by demons, some of the crew wanted to abandon ship, but the captain wanted answers. He used an ax to break open the crate from which the sounds were coming. Hundreds of dolls came tumbling out. "Mama, Mama!" they cried as the ship rocked on the high seas. Fear of the unknown had unnerved the *Phenian's* hardened sailors, but their fear turned out to be unfounded.[162]

A Course in Miracles maintains that God did not create fear so fear, therefore, must be an illusion.[163] What God did not create has no ultimate power over us—unless we give our power away. One of the highest levels of evolution for a Sufi comes when a person neither fears nor asks for anything.

Fear basically comes from a lack of trust in God, in the Life Force, in ourselves.[164] Although fear itself has a simple source, the fears we allow ourselves to feel are myriad, with various, unnecessary results:

- Fear of taking responsibility leads to blame.

- Fear that no one will love us leads to hatred and aggression.

- Fear of not being accepted leads to shyness and feelings of rejection— which then cause separation and loneliness.

- Fear for the future causes worry.

- Fear that life will never get any better engenders despair.

- Fear of looking foolish leads to boastfulness.

- Fear located in the past for something done or left undone causes regret.

- Anger has diverse causes, among which are the fear of "what is" and that things will get worse because they are not going the way we think they should.

- Fear of dying or leaving loved ones in the lurch contributes to prolonged comas.[165]

- Fear of not being good enough and perfectionism contribute to migraines.

- Fear of new ideas can lead to structural mutations, including cancer. (Frequency generators are being used now in cancer at 7.83 cycles per second, the vibratory field at which both the sacred spots of the Earth—Stonehenge, Delphi, the pyramids—and healers themselves radiate.)[166]

Co-workers and Angels in Disguise

Many of our fears can be eased by building up a healthy self-esteem, and our challenges dissipate when we learn whatever lesson we need. Until then, we keep attracting the same situations. Here's the old Brick Wall School, again. If we feel clueless about what we're supposed to be learning, we can look at the friends and acquaintances who have come into our life and ask ourselves what problems they are facing, for we attract both people who are involved in the same curriculum, and people who can help us work our way through those lessons.

The first group occurs because we make acquaintances with people who are working on life issues similar to ours; like vibrations attracting each other. My stressed-out spouse used to vent his anger on me; then I met Kyle, who was in a similar situation. A year later, I met Rachel, whose husband frequently berated her in front of their children. (This situation presented an ongoing spiritual dilemma for me: Did I try to find an even bigger bully to threaten my friend's husband into being nicer, or did I instead surround him with loving light every night in my blessings? I chose the latter course, and it took 15 years, but her husband is finally responding to life situations with more consideration and patience.) Along with my new friends came the idea that their similar circumstances held a lesson for me, and I began to consider changing my living arrangements—not just *wishing* for a change.

As for the second group, they may be what the Jews call *lamed-vav tzaddiks*, or angels in disguise.[167] People addicted to anger, for example, will meet persons or creatures that precipitate their anger—until they learn that "the other guy" is not the one responsible for creating their internal emotion.

A parable tells about a guerilla fighting in the Middle East and a wise man sitting beside the road. Laying his rifle aside, the soldier asked, "Heaven and hell, old man. Do they really exist?"

The wise man frowned and with a sneer replied, "Dolt! You're too dense to discuss such deep matters!"

For a moment the soldier was stunned; he was a big man with a big gun, and the locals would have done anything not to offend him. How dare the old coot talk to him like that!

"Leave me," commanded the wise man.

Irate, the soldier leveled his rifle at the old man. As his finger moved behind the trigger guard, the old man said softly, "This is the way to hell."

The soldier stood stock-still. He realized the wise man had risked his life to show him that his anger had landed him in hell. Slowly the soldier lowered his gun and then he fell on his knees before the old man.

"Rise," said the old man, as he himself rose to his feet. He offered his hand to the soldier and helped him up. "And this," he added, "is the way to heaven."

A few years ago, I learned about heaven and hell in my dreams. I was having recurrent nightmares about a huge bull that chased me through the house. I finally consulted a psychologist. The therapist agreed to treat me, saying that our visits would probably last a year or two or three, but together we'd discover the origin of my monster.

Three years of therapy? No way. "Never mind," I said. "I'll just make friends with it."

That's a joke, actually. What really happened was that I again dreamed of the angry bull, and again he chased me through the house. At the end of the hallway, a locked door barred my forward flight. Frantically I jiggled the knob and the door swung open—with my ex-husband standing squarely in the doorframe, barring my escape. I turned to face the bull, who raced down the hallway, only to come to a shuddering stop inches in front of me. He lowered his horns, but at that moment what struck me was the sight of the bull's deep brown *friendly* eyes. I reached out a quivering hand to pat his head and in the dream wept with relief. Why, I wondered as I woke up, had I been so afraid?

A Handful of Nuts

> Be not forgetful to entertain strangers: for thereby some have entertained angels unawares.
>
> Hebrews 13:2

Why are we so afraid of the unknown, the "not-me," the "ten thousand?" The ancient Hebrew word for God, *Elohim*, has a plural ending, which can be interpreted as "the One that is Many" or "Unity in Diversity."[168] We tend to think of God-Out-There as being sacred and "good," forgetting that if God is Everything, then God is also the mundane: the soil, the hops, the drunkard relieving himself. Even the idiot driver, the cashier who shortchanges us, the petty tyrant. Those people serve to teach us patience, understanding, ingenuity, and compassion. The Sufis (Buddhists, Taoists, etc.) say that everything in our world can remind us of God. I know, at any rate, that I can't make Waldorf salad with apples alone—I have to throw in a handful of nuts, too.

Although we often wish our lives were not so bumpy, science reminds us that without friction we couldn't dance, play golf, or walk over an icy patch of sidewalk.[169] In the "Mind and the Matter" episode of the *Twilight Zone*, Serling's misanthropic Archibald Beechcroft, played by morose comedian Shelley Berman, makes everyone in the world disappear. When he finds life without people too lonely, however, he repopulates the world with people just like him—dour, miserable, and whining—who quickly teach him tolerance and appreciation for diversity.[170]

When we come up against a brick wall of a person, our instinct is often attempting to persuade the other to accept our own ideas. On such an occasion, the Buddhists would say that it is easier to don a winter coat than to persuade the bitter wind to stop blowing. Christianity reminds us that "A soft answer turneth away wrath: but grievous words stir up anger." The *Tao Te Ching* says, "The soft overcomes the hard; the gentle overcomes the rigid" (#43). Quite true; what do we get if we hit a body of water with a sledgehammer? A rusty tool!

> You cannot be hurt, and do not want to show your brother anything except your wholeness. Show him that he cannot hurt you and hold nothing against him, or you hold it against yourself. This is the meaning of "turning the other cheek."
>
> Every loving thought is true. Everything else is an appeal for healing and help, regardless of the form it takes.
>
> *A Course in Miracles*

Peppery personalities serve as red flags that we are "judging against." I understood that my husband's anger came from disappointment, depression, and blame. Arguing (I found) didn't help. But I learned that people who have high self-esteem can step away from an argument, choosing to maintain peace of mind over demonstrating that they're right.[171] *A Course in Miracle*'s phrase, "I can choose peace instead," has served me well.

The obnoxious, the critical, the arrogant, and the hateful also want to be loved; they just have a lousy way of inviting it. Kindness is what they need.[172] Sufis, who believe that service is a form of worship, agree: Be kind, they say, to people whether they deserve your kindness or not.[173] The jerk who cuts us off in traffic may be a man rushing his pregnant wife to the emergency room, or a single mother hurrying to her second job; the man who snubs us in the elevator could be a veterinarian who had to put down a beloved pet, or a widower who just lost his wife; the sullen child may be a victim of abuse.

Spotting the Rainbow

A Course in Miracles proposes that when we fight or argue or defend our viewpoint, we're actually making a falsehood more concrete, more "real," or an existing condition worse. Talking about the sorry state of the economy adds energy to "what is." And if we name a physical condition, we are making the idea of sickness acceptable instead of focusing on wholeness, health, and life as a part of the Whole. There is no need to make a falsehood real and then attack it by attesting to the reality of what is untrue and trying to argue it into non-being.[174]

Anyway, most things are not worth the time and energy it takes to argue about. On one occasion religious scholars were having a field day discussing the question of which side they should stand on when carrying a coffin. Finally their rabbi settled their argument. "What does it matter," he asked, "as long as you're not in the coffin?"[175]

> God grant me serenity to accept the things I cannot change,
> courage to change the things I can,
> and wisdom to know the difference.
>
> Reinhold Niebuhr
> "Serenity Prayer"

While this is a participatory universe and we do affect everyone and everything around us, our greatest accomplishment is that of changing ourselves. Many situations can be defused by one person who remains calm and peaceful. Other times, the best course of action could be to avoid difficult people, or to allow trials to come into our lives like a thunderstorm that makes a lot of noise and then passes on. We may get wet, but how much better shall we see the rainbow?

Eleven

A deliberately directed intention of good will is a more powerful force that we can imagine.

Actions, words, or thoughts set up reverberations in the universe. The universe unfolds from moment to moment as a function of all the variables leading up to that moment . . . even a seemingly insignificant gesture could have weighty consequences . . . Where we place our feet, the people we see, the traffic we encounter, the impressions we make all should be envisioned as intersecting lines in the great tapestry of life.

Rabbi David Cooper
God Is a Verb

When the Warning Lights Don't Work

On a three-lane interstate approaching the point where another two-lane highway would feed into my road and with vehicles moving at 65 mph, my van—in the middle lane—began to lose power. I didn't know it was the fuel pump going out; I only knew, as an energy healer, to pour energy into the car. I punched on the emergency flashers, gripped the steering wheel firmly, and tried to sidle through three lanes of unyielding cars, heading for the far right side of the highway. Like a water-logged piece of debris stuck in the middle of fast-moving tree trunks flowing downriver, the van moved ever more sluggishly but it *did* keep going, while traffic around me paid no attention to the emergency taking place in its midst. Energy flowed from universe through me to my disabled vehicle, and finally we came to rest on the shoulder, more than two miles from the initial collapse of the fuel system. When my son, Tad, arrived, he discovered a malfunction in the emergency lights; they had *not* been flashing a warning to other drivers at all! It was only the intentional direction of energy (and divine providence) that helped the dogs and me reach safety.

Does this act of aiding my failing vehicle sound incredible? Think about people who spontaneously combust. We humans produce nuclear energy, and intention gives energy its direction. Studies show that seeds thrive when provided with water that has been blessed by healers, bacteria is stimulated by compassion, plants respond to loving conversation, and persons suffering from grievous illness recover because of their own optimism and the blessings of friends and family members.

Whatever we eat and drink, whatever we think or imagine, every emotion we feel—they all have a physical affect within us, and those changes cause chemical, electromagnetic, and para-physical waves to ripple outward, ultimately influencing everything that exists. This is how prayers and blessings work.

An elderly woman once went to see her doctor, who shook his head over her faint, irregular heartbeat. He knew her life would end in a matter of days, if not hours. "Terminal old age" he noted in her chart.

The woman hobbled out of the office and was waiting for the bus to arrive when a carload of college coeds parked nearby. "Mrs. Lottridge," cried one of the young women. "Mrs. Lottridge, do you remember me?"

"Of course," she said, smiling. "I remember all my students. Hello, Laura. Hello, Matt. Oh, and Mark and Cari—hello, hello!"

Around their old Algebra teacher the former students gathered. They told her they were going into the bar and grille across the street from the medical building and persuaded her to come along.

When the group was seated at a table, Mrs. Lottridge asked what her "children" would like to drink. They decided on red wine, and the retired teacher ordered two bottles of the best wine in the house. The coeds began to empty their pockets to cover the bar bill.

"No, this is my treat," Mrs. Lottridge said, whereupon the kids rejoiced at their good fortune. Every time they refilled their glasses, the room rang with their toasts. "To your good health!" they said in one clear voice. "To your good health, Mrs. Lottridge."

When the wine was finished and merry goodbyes said, the elderly woman rose and made her way toward the front door. In the foyer she met her doctor, who was coming in for dinner.

"Why, Mrs. Lottridge," he said, "you look like a different woman." He shook her hand then measured her pulse; her heart was beating in strong, regular beats. "I must be doing something right," he murmured to himself.

Smiling wisely, the old woman whispered, "It was the power of blessings."

A century ago the poet Francis Thompson wrote about the interconnectedness of our lives being such that "thou canst not stir a flower/ Without troubling a star." In speaking of quantum wholeness—the "We are One" concept—Bohm says it is

". . . a true mingling of distant beings that reaches across the galaxy as forcefully as it reaches across the garden." Everything is a seamless whole.[176] Because of Bell's Theorem of Interconnectedness, we know that once two things have been connected, an instantaneous line of communication continues to exist between them, and if everything in existence came out of the Big Bang, then everything was initially related.[177] In short, everything we do has some effect upon the Whole.

> Force, not substance, is the true being of the world, and it . . . reaches from one end of the universe to the other.
>
> Arthur Zajonc, Amherst physicist
> quoted by K. C. Cole in *Hole in the Universe*

Waves of Connection

We are only separated from other living things by the illusion the ego fosters.[178] At one point in the history of human consciousness, a man might have said of a river, "My water self flows over the rocks and through the valley." Or a mother could transfer part of her consciousness outside to the tree her children were climbing to keep track of them at a distance.[179]

> **Try It Yourself**
>
> Go outside on a clear night and look at a star. Any star. The light coming from the star and touching your eyes has created a physical bridge between you and that distant being. You *are* connected to the star so far away.

Age-old religious and spiritual doctrines of "We are One, we are all connected," are precursors to the scientific proving of Bell's Theorem. Like a sandy shoreline that looks solid from way out at sea, our universe is connected by a system of quanta, which close up look like minute grains of sand.[180]

One summer I flew out to see my friend, Jody, in San Diego. I was walking along a cliff, stopping frequently for a last, longing look at the sea, when a woman came up to me. She said, "I saw you, and I was just drawn to you. Isn't that strange?"

It didn't sound at all strange to me. I asked her name.

"I'm Mona. I just can't understand why I was drawn to you," she said again. "Doesn't that sound strange?"

"No, it doesn't, Mona," I said, placing my hand on her forehead to bless her.

With the waves of high tide crashing against the cliffs, I was "Connected." I was reveling in the symphony of the sea and "flying high and rising," radiating vibrations of joy, empowerment, appreciation, and wonder. It's little wonder that Mona sensed our connection and felt an attraction to the aura of goodness I was feeling and more than happy to share.

MAKE ME ONE WITH EVERYTHING
Riddle: What did the monk say to the short order cook?
Punch line: "Make me One with everything."

Biologists say we are interdependent upon all the life forms on Earth and that our fate rises or falls with theirs. Physicists have discovered that the atoms of our bodies and all other physical matter form one continuous, faster-than-light fabric,[181] "divine" energy of a denser, slower frequency.[182] Poets, too, have felt this union. John Donne wrote his famous "Meditation XVII: For Whom the Bell Tolls" in the 1600s.

> No man is an island, entire of itself; every man is a piece of the continent, a part of the main; if a clod be washed away by the sea, Europe is the less, as well as if a promontory were, as well as if a manor of thy friends or of thine own were; any man's death diminishes me, because I am involved in mankind. . . .

Like Donne but three hundred years later, Einstein felt strongly about the illusion we experience as separateness:

A human being is part of the whole, called by us "Universe," a part limited in time and space. He experiences himself, his thoughts and feelings as something separated from the rest—a kind of optical illusion of his consciousness. This delusion is a kind of prison for us, restricting us to our personal desires and to affection for a few persons nearest us. Our task must be to free ourselves from this prison by widening our circle of compassion to embrace all living creatures and the whole of nature in its beauty."[183]

Cardiologist Randolph Byrd included almost 400 patients in a coronary care unit and prayer groups across the country in a double-blind study: No patient, physician, or nurse knew which of the patients was being prayed for, but Byrd discovered that the prayed-for heart patients recovered better than the control group. Moreover, *distance was not a factor.*[184] Experiments like REG and studies like Byrd's show that no matter how great a distance, nothing can stop a blessing. The only amazing conclusion may be that someone feels any need at all to prove that prayer (or good will) is effective.

All this [instant transmission of information], of course, places us firmly in the territory of the metaphysical, the spiritual. Think about prayer, or meditation. If you were to pray to God, and God was hanging out on the far side of the galaxy, and your prayer traveled at the speed of light, your bones would long-since be dust before God responded. But if God, however you define God, is everywhere, the prayer doesn't have to travel.

Cleve Baxter
quoted by Derrick Jensen, "The Plants Respond"

A Butterfly in Texas

Based on the holographic nature of our universe, the Butterfly Effect proposes that what happens in one part of the hologram affects every other part. For example, a butterfly flapping its wings in Texas could generate a typhoon in Indochina. So intricately are we all connected that one small action initiates a long, complex chain of effects.

The event needn't be enormous to have an effect; like the meteor that wiped out the dinosaurs and made way for the proliferation of mammals, one person's explosion of temper or act of kindness also sends out ripples that affects the psychological climate of the immediate population. The Kabbalah agrees, but warns that good intentions must be accompanied by great awareness, so that they don't have an adverse affect.[185]

Dr. Larry Dossey, an advocate of the mind/health connection, illustrates the danger of good intentions with the case of a well-intentioned aunt who prayed fervently for her niece's conversion to the aunt's own brand of religion, but her prayers gave the niece blinding headaches at the same time that they were being said every day. After the niece realized what was happening, whenever she felt the onset of the next headache, she sent a flood of love along the negative current, backwards to her aunt, and that action ended her headaches for good.[186]

Just as a single small disturbance can alter a chaotic system, so can an extremely small adjustment stabilize situations.[187] If a little butterfly can disrupt the weather system half a world away, one person emitting a strong wave of intentional peacefulness can defuse a volatile situation, as when my family was hunting for a new house. We can call it prayer or we can call it active meditation, but a peaceful intention for general good will reach the farthest limits of everything that exists through Quantum God, for all thought vibrates forever in the cosmos.[188]

Raindrops of Blessings

We might think about our potential either to help or to hinder the next time an inconsiderate driver crosses our path—who needs a blessing more? Indeed, who needs a blessing more than a bully or fanatic? Jesus said we are to love our enemies and bless them, because God makes the rain to fall "on the just and on the unjust." This reminds me of the Sufis' adage that encourages us to be like "the rain that waters all things, whether it loves them or not."[189]

Words are powerful. Blessings work.

> The Lord bless thee, and keep thee; the Lord make His face to shine upon thee, and be gracious unto thee; the Lord lift up His countenance and give thee peace.
>
> Numbers 6:24-25 (KJV)

Twelve

Positive effects are created only from a state of peace.

A Sufi master once said: "My life is complicated and still I suffer a lot, but it doesn't mean anything. It is ephemeral, just a part of living. I also feel the suffering of the world very deeply. I do what I can. Yet it is also very clear that things are as they are, and to have any helpful impact my actions must come from the heart of peace. This is my goal: to show the peace in the midst of it all."

Jack Kornfield, *After the Ecstasy, the Laundry: How the Heart Grows Wise on the Spiritual Path*

Things Which Make for Peace

I experienced a miracle of manifestation recently. I took a short teaching assignment for a Wednesday afternoon. That night I arrived home long after the school closed and discovered the assignment extended into the next day. Agh! Was Thursday's allotted time also from 1 to 3 p.m.? All-day? A mistake? I spent some time fretting over details, like the fact that I don't do all-day teaching jobs, the school was a good half hour distant in non-rush hour traffic, and when were teachers expected to show up in the morning, anyway?

I went to bed early so I could get up early, but wakefulness lent itself to worrying. However, I tried to remain peaceful and practiced visions of my exclaiming (all too soon), "Thank God!" The miracle came a scant four hours later when I called the secretary. She told me the regular teacher had emailed her the night before, saying he would be at school Thursday and needed no substitute. I got to say "Thank God" on my way back to bed.

In Hebrew, "jerusalem" means "vision of peace." In John's revelation, Jerusalem represents the ultimate heaven on earth and peace among the members of humankind. Positive effects arise out of a state of peace, which also creates feelings of compassion, joy, appreciation, and gratitude. If the vibrations of affirming words have positive effects on us and our world, whereas the vibrations from negative words have the power to destroy, we might seriously consider Paul's advice to the Romans to "follow after things, which make for peace."

Peacefulness, compassion, joy, appreciation, and gratitude cause higher frequency signals to go out from and *come back* to us, because the universe is like a gigantic copy machine that reproduces the images we show it. When we're stuck in the 'Poor me' mode, the universe keeps giving us 'poor me' scenarios that we've just ordered.[190] When we think, "This job is gonna give me a headache," or "It'd be just my luck for the car to break down in the middle of nowhere," or I'm afraid of _____," can we as creators hope to receive anything else?

Prosperity is a Shared Sandwich

If we're bound to get whatever we're putting out, then *giving away* whatever we choose to have more of is a good idea. On a bright September morning in 1912, my grandpa, Rusty Baum, waved good-bye to his mama and set off for his first day of school with a paper lunch bag in hand. Louisa had packed roast beef on homemade bread and, as any proud cook might, after school she asked her son if he had enjoyed his lunch.

"Didn't eat it," he replied.

"*Was ist das?* What did you do with it?"

"I traded with Jimmy," Rusty said. "Jimmy's mama makes *gut* sandwiches, *Mutti.* You will make some like his? *Bitte?*"

Louisa knew that Jimmy's family was struggling to keep a roof over their heads. What could they provide that was better than her own sauerbraten? She asked Rusty what kind of sandwich Jimmy had brought to school.

"Fat and white."

Fat and white. Cheese?

Rusty caught up his mother's arm and pulled until she rose from her rocking chair. Tugging on her hand, he led her into the kitchen. "There, *Mutti,* over the stove—what you make pies with."

"*Gott in Himmel,*" Louisa exclaimed. "Lard!" She sat on a straight-backed wooden chair and pulled the boy close. "Russell, from now on I will give you two sandwiches. One for you, one for your friend. We'll save the lard for pie crust, *ja?*"

"Yes, mama. Teacher says, say 'yes.'"

"*Ja, ja,* I will say yes." Louisa laughed and began to set the table for dinner.

Almost twenty years later, the stock market crashed. Soup lines snaked down sidewalks, fathers grew desperate, and children went to bed hungry—if they had a bed. Louisa greeted her husband when he returned from work and before him on the dining table she set his favorite dinner, scrambled eggs and brains. A thick slice of fresh-baked coconut cake completed the meal.

Louis finished the last bite of cake, then turned to his wife and said, "All right, Mother, what's going on?"

"Now, Lou," she said, "Everett and Roberta have fallen on hard times. They need to move in with us for a while."

Instead of chiding her young son or, later, railing about national economics, my great-grandma focused on finding a practical and compassionate solution to the problem at hand and shared her family's resources and, even during the Great Depression, they prospered.

Magnetic Fields and Manifestation

Positive images of what we choose to manifest are vitally important right now because the gap between the thinking of a thought and its materialization is decreasing. The magnetic fields of the Earth act as a buffer between our thoughts and their manifestation, and the fields are growing weaker—over the last 4,000 years, the geomagnetic field has declined by 90%—so that manifestation is happening more and more rapidly.[191]

The time gap between thinking a thought and its materialization is becoming shorter.

Try It Yourself

On a day when the winds are gusting, try walking against the wind. How long does it take to walk a block, and with how much effort? On a sunny day when the air is still, travel the same route. How much easier was the walk without the hindrance of strong winds? Make it a daily game of noting "What I Need Comes to Me" and how fast.

Our goal is to learn to *think as if each thought will be instantly made manifest*, and to *think ONLY the thoughts we wish to see come into our world.* What better way of beginning this process than by cultivating a relaxed and peaceful core?

If, for example, we want peace in our lives and in the world, we must *be* peace, becoming that which we desire. This process is illustrated by the story of a large, disheveled, middle-aged man, who disrupted the crowd at a subway platform with his ranting. A vendor called security, who approached with their nightsticks drawn. Before they had cinched their circle around the distraught man, an elderly lady approached him and appeared to falter when her cane toppled to the ground before his feet.

"Sir," she said gently, "I can see you're busy and I hate to bother you, but would you help me, please?"

The man looked at the old woman and his face softened. He gave her his elbow and guided her to a bench.

"Won't you join me?" she asked. As the man sat beside her, she added, "Thank you, sir. I'm not having too good a day. And you? What about you? Not too good a day for you, either?"

The man's face contorted with grief. "I just came from the morgue," he told her. "My wife and daughter were killed in a car crash this morning."

The old woman raised a frail arm to embrace the large man, who crumpled onto her shoulder and wept. "Thank you," he said when he was able to speak again. "Thank you for caring."

The old woman could have felt afraid or disgusted and have chosen not to become involved, but her compassion and wisdom brought good results. Instinctively she was following the advice of the *Tao Te Ching*: "There is no greater misfortune," wrote Lao-Tsu, "than underestimating your enemy. Underestimating your enemy means thinking that he is evil."[192] The old woman saw not an enemy but an isolated person in need of TLC. Her choice demonstrated the peace-promoting martial art of aikido when she refused to react to the situation with the same emotion as that of the ranting man. This, I think, is the physiological basis for *A Course in Miracles*' admonition that we not share a brother's belief in sickness, but rather to allow our light of wholeness and holiness to shine into his mind. (The text adds, "If you believe you can be sick, you have placed other gods before Him.")

Nightsight Around the World

A teacher once asked her students how to tell when night had ended and it was time for morning prayers. "When you can see if the animal in the distance is a cat or a dog?" asked one youngster. "When you can see well enough to tie your shoes?" asked another child.

"No," said the teacher. "It's when you can look at any person and see he is your brother, or she your sister. Until then, it is night for you."

Jack Kornfield
After the Ecstasy, the Laundry

In Islam's *Hadith*, God says, "Shall I not inform you of a better act than fasting, alms and prayers? Making peace between one another . . ."[193] But what can I do? Sure, I can make friends with my neighbors next door, but how will that help the volatile situation in the Middle East?

I did some research, and what I learned was really cool. An average-sized adult contains a minimum of 7×10^{18} joules of potential energy, a force equal to thirty large hydrogen bombs. Everything contains this kind of energy trapped within it.

The energy comes in part from the food we eat and the oxygen we breathe, which are combined in the cells into electricity, and partly from the Force that gives life to all matter.[194]

To use my energy with good effect requires deliberate intention and keeping myself centered in high-frequency emotions. An added bonus, I learned, is that whenever we do this, we also strengthen our immune system and actually *change the genetic coding of our DNA*. With this one bit of knowledge, I have freed myself from the family history of heart problems! Compassion raises the frequency at which the body's cells are vibrating to a level, so that it has less resonance with disease.[195]

How practical is that? Love and joy keep us healthy. For example, the resistance of HIV patients increased by 300,000 times when they were in the presence of people thinking kind and loving thoughts.[196] So acts of kindness do good things to the physical heart, brain, and genetic code. And, experimenters in electromagnetism say, *the higher the frequency, the greater the impact.*[197]

> Watching the evening news, I know it is my story. Breathing in calmly, I hold us all in compassion.
>
> Zen master Thich Nhat Hanh
> quoted by Jack Kornfield in *After the Ecstasy, the Laundry*

The phone rang. It was the call all mothers fear; my daughter needed to go to the emergency room. Worried, distraught, paralyzed—all natural reactions, but none that I chose. I took time to breath, to center in peace, and then got into the car to pick Merrie Kate up. Instead of being "reactive," I had to be "responsive" and deliberately choose how I was going to behave.

Blessed are the Meek, for They Shall Inherit the Earth

In the same way that a skinned knee activates the process of physical healing, we can learn to use emotional hurts and crises as prompts to climb out of old, destructive thought patterns that keep us apart from high-frequency emotions. This takes a new way of thinking.

In Aramaic, "meek" literally means people who have softened what was once rigid inside themselves—their ideas and their hearts.[198] They are willing to be guided by Spirit, not by ego. Lama Chogyam Trungpa approached what Jesus meant by "the meek shall inherit the earth" when he said, "It is the open and tender heart that has the capacity to transform the world."[199] The *Tao Te Ching* addresses this topic, too:

> Whoever is soft and yielding is a disciple of life. The hard
> and stiff will be broken. The soft and supple will prevail. [200]

In the Aramaic phrase "inherit the earth," "earth" includes all of nature, and "inherit" means to be given power and sustenance. The "meek," then, have made a passageway within themselves for the powerful and divine "I Am" to move through them.[201] It's a "can-do" attitude.

Why don't we *give ourselves permission* to expand, to grow, to live? I'm still working on an "I can do anything" mindset, rather than "I can do better," even though I never really felt at home on this Earth. But the Australian Aborigines, the American Indians, the tribal peoples of Africa—they all sense a sacred living universe of which humans are a part. The divine "can-do" power permeates the earth, the water, the air, and our own being. We all belong.

> Every part of the earth is sacred to my people. Every shining pine needle, every sandy shore, every mist in the dark woods, every meadow, every humming insect. All are holy in the memory and experience of my people . . .
>
> This we know: the earth does not belong to man; man belongs to the earth. All things are connected like the blood that unites us all. Man did not weave the web of life, he is merely a strand in it. Whatever he does to the web, he does to himself . . . We are all brothers after all.
>
> Chief Seattle, 1883

From peace, from compassion and joy, from knowing how powerful we really are comes goodness that blesses the entire universe.

Thirteen

The most effective prayer is a repeated and unvarying image . . . or just plain letting go.

> . . . a prayer just wants an answer
> And twists time in a knot until it gets it.
>
> There's the door. Will anybody get it?
> That's what he's wondering; the bath's still warm;
> And by the time he towels off and puts on
> His pajamas, robe, and slippers and goes down,
> They'll be gone, won't they? There's the door again;
> And nobody's here to answer it but him.
> Perhaps they'll go away. But it's not easy,
> Relaxing in the tub, reading the paper,
> With someone at the front door, ringing and pounding,
> And—that sounds like glass—breaking in.
> At least the bathroom door's securely bolted.
> Or is that any assurance in this case?
> He might as well go find out what's the matter.
> Whoever it is must really want . . . something.

Mark Jarman
Unholy Sonnets, "The Word, 'Answer'"
Sarabande Books

Practice Makes Perfect Patterns

Bullwinkle J. Moose knew that persistence paid. When he tried to pull a rabbit out of his hat, out came a rhinoceros. Or a tiger. Or Rocky the Flying Squirrel. Anything but a rabbit. "This time for sure," he'd say and then try again.

When our thought and intention are consistent and intense, we create power in the morphogenetic field (from *morphe*, form, and *genesis*, coming-into-being).[202] Bullwinkle knew this, without the fancy words: Practice makes perfect. The more often we repeat a behavior, the better skilled we become at it. Co-creative repetition is like scooping up handfuls of invisible divine matter and sculpting reality; the first hundred scoops form the foundation, the next hundred erect joists and walls. As time passes, the structure is "concretized." This is the Law of Materialization, and *the Law of Materialization works whether or not we realize what we're doing.*

Bullwinkle probably wasn't aware that repetition establishes an energy field that makes successive actions "take" more easily, but he kept trying anyway.[203] He was a man—well, a moose—with a mission. To me, morphogenetic energy fields mean that if anyone has ever completed a sewing project without being reduced to tears, swearing, and incoherent sobs, then I too can attempt projects using a sewing machine, but that particular theory has yet to be proven.

Everything begins as an idea; the most beautiful building began as an idea, a blueprint that was transferred to paper and then to wood and steel and concrete. Okay, I get it. First comes the idea, then the thing or event. But Bohm suggests we not even distinguish between "mind" and "matter."[204] So the mind and body—which is the mind's closest construction—are one cohesive functioning unit.

This means that manifesting what we desire is helped along by our *becoming* what we desire, like *being* peace in order to *create* peace in the world. While we're waiting, we may have to make-believe, acting "as if" the outcome were already real. For example, a man applying for an executive position would do better if he acted the part of a professional beforehand and showed up for his interview calm and confident, rather than tugging nervously at his tie and worrying about the mortgage payment that's due. $E = mc^2$ in real-life.

But just wishing—without energy to fuel the thought—won't work. Perhaps this is the answer to why our prayers sometimes appear to go unanswered . . . [And] more often than not, our perceived need for anything is based in fear. When we say we "need more," that there is "not enough," or that we are "running out of," fear is the emotion driving such statements.

The soup of creation exists as a state of possibilities . . . Into the possibilities of creation, we place a feeling picture, enough energy to allow for a new possibility. The picture tells the soup of creation where we have placed our attention. The emotion that we attach to our picture attracts the picture's possibility. When we don't want something, our fear actually fuels what we claim not to want. These laws invite us to empower our choices by focusing on the positive experiences that we choose, rather than by preparing for the negative things we don't want.

Gregg Braden
The Isaiah Effect

Missiles to Matter

Do we really have the energy to convert mental into material? Absolutely. Physically, each cell in the human body carries 1.17 volts of energy, and each human being possesses a quadrillion cells.[205] Imagine the power of 1,170,000,000,000,000 volts of energy at our disposal! That figure is a truer assessment of our power than our normal self-image. Each of us is a nuclear power plant harboring enough energy to send a missile to the moon, and it is our emotions that propel thoughts through the barrier between the non-physical and the physical realms.[206] *Et voila*, manifestation.

Our vision (idea) supplies the blueprint for what we choose and emotional energy that supplies the power necessary to scoop up Einstein's E and thrust it into his m, or matter. Repeated thoughts powered by emotion access the nuclear forces within us and flip the para-physical switch for creation. That, in essence, is superstring super symmetry theory. Or, in other words, prayer.

But if we cry out to a God who is "out there" somewhere, we have actually, *in our own minds*, separated ourselves from our Source; we've cut our supply lines. When we stop asking, begging, and placing the responsibility for our lacks on God, then we cease being a subordinate and begin acting like a true partner in creation.

> Perhaps you have noticed that even in the very lightest breeze you can hear the voice of the cottonwood tree; this we understand is its prayer to the Great Spirit, for not only men, but all things and all beings pray to Him continually in differing ways. For the Great Spirit is everywhere; He hears whatever is in our minds and hearts, and it is not necessary to speak to Him in a loud voice.
>
> Black Elk of the Oglala Sioux
> quoted by Philip Novak in *The World's Wisdom:*
> *Sacred Texts of the World's Religion*

Prayer is not only words but is a relationship and *our awareness* of that relationship. The way life works, works for the atheist as well as for theist or deist, for pagan or Hindu or Hopi, for Moslem or electron. Prayer is a pathway to awareness of the process that God uses in creating. Creation is an ongoing process, and occurs in every *now* (even if we feel our nows passing along in a series of moments). Prayer keeps us connected to the Power behind it all.

Neither can we call on God or take God's name in vain, for God always answers. God supports us in everything we do. Part of the Divine plan is making things concrete in the physical realm, and everything we could ever desire (as long as it causes no harm to another) already exists, waiting to be chosen from *potentia*.

God cannot help but answer every prayer, because that's the way the system works, which we call universal laws.

Already Given

We get what we expect. That's basic quantum mechanics. And if we get what we expect, that's God saying yes. If we expect life to be a struggle, God says, *Yes.*

> God always says yes; we say no.
>
> James van Praagh
> *Reaching to Heaven: A Spiritual Journey Through Life and Death*

Whoa, wait a minute . . . God says, *Yes, you need not live in poverty.* Our responsibility, however, is to believe we are an integral part of the abundant universe. God says, *Yes, you can be healthy*—but we can't sabotage the basic health of our bodies by believing that germs or genetics have ultimate power over us. God says, *Yes, you can have anything you can attract*—pleasant events in your life, if we are pleasant and kind and don't use brick walls to batter our thick heads against, and if we have a smattering of "smarts" that enable us to make wise choices: I am a warm-hearted person, but my husband wisely drew the line at my bringing a homeless Vietnam veteran home for dinner and bath and bed.

> Why did the ancient Masters esteem the Tao?
> Because, being one with the Tao,
> when you seek, you find . . .
>
> *Tao Te Ching #62*
> Stephen Mitchell, translator

In Matthew 7:7, Jesus says, "Ask, and it shall be given you; seek, and ye shall find; knock, and it shall be opened unto you: For every one that asketh receiveth; and he that seeketh findeth; and to him that knocketh it shall be opened." However, in the previous chapter of Matthew (6:8), Jesus was even more emphatic: ". . . *your Father knoweth what thing ye have need of before ye ask him.*"

I found personal proof for this "Already Given" principle recently. I'd met a man who was kind and sexy and smart; it was little wonder that I fell for him! Everything was going fine until one Thursday, when Valdi told me he needed to leave town. Oh? For how long? Five weeks. Or maybe five months. Maybe even twice that long. Whoa! To a woman in love, five *hours'* separation is too long!

On Thursday night we kissed goodbye, and I immediately missed Valdi. On Friday I felt wretched but put the time to good use, working on a surprise for him, but by Saturday I'd gone totally bonkers. Miserable as all get-out, I railed against circumstance and fretted over whether he was feeling the same way about me. I did write a poem about meditating and redirecting my thoughts but, ha, didn't get around to *actually* quieting down. At church service the next morning, here came Rev. Sandra Campbell to give the Sunday talk; she reminded us that . . .

1. worry never does anything to change our circumstances,
2. only a new attitude produces change,
3. and the Kingdom of Heaven never changes at all—
   it's always inside us; just be *still*.

She added that when we feel grateful, we don't have room to be sad. And I had to admit, I was truly grateful for having Valdi in my life to cause me this misery now!

Then this thought struck me that on Thursday my need arose, but it was two weeks *previously* that Sandra began composing the talk I would so welcome later, the talk that recalled me to my Self and the principles of conscious creating and well-being. The answer to my prayer was "already given" *before* the birth of my need!

God knows what we need. God knows what we desire. Indeed, I'd heard that God has given us everything, but I always felt like rearing up and saying, "Wait a minute. I don't have everything. My job's being phased out and the kids need new winter coats." This was my ego speaking, which defines existence by "having" and "getting."

Once, it is said, the mystical rabbi Baal Shem Tov turned to his companion in a tavern and asked for money to buy a drink. Although penniless, the friend obediently put a hand in his pocket anyway and wasn't surprised when he pulled coins out of his pocket.[207] This reminds me of the Maharishi in Fairfield, Iowa, who was asked where the money would come from for a new university building. "From wherever it is now," he replied.

Likewise, when I was despairing of ever seeing my dreams come true in *this* reality, Valdi said for me to imagine that I had a suitcase full of money, as large as I wanted, and *then* told me to dream. He said, "The money is where the dream is," and that I should start with my dream and work backwards. The vision would activate *potentia* and draw forth all the machinations necessary in the form of synchronicities.

Perhaps we should say that, rather than every *thing*, God has given us every *how*, every capability we need in order to fulfill our needs, along with spiritual guidance to help us create beneficially. We have not everything; we *are* everything. Through our godlike creative ability, we have power that comes from the Power.

> You may recite His name 1000 times for this, 7000 times for that, and 8000 times for the other, but even if you recite it 50,000 times you will not receive anything. Why? Because God has already given everything to you.
>
> M. R. Bawa Muhaiyaddeen
> *Ama'Ul-Husna: The 99 Beautiful Names of Allah*

Indeed, if we and everything physical are all made of the same quantumstuff, then *whatever we desire is already within reach.* This is in part to what Jesus was referring when he spoke of the Kingdom of Heaven being at hand; once we get into a heaven-frequency, we both "have it all" and need nothing more. We're being given everything we need at every moment.

Jewish tradition says the Red Sea didn't part until Moses stepped into the waters, with the faith of "deep knowing" that God would provide a way to facilitate the Israelites' flight from Egypt. Whether the waters then drew apart like a CGI special effect, or whether a drought dried up the waters for Moses and company, with seasonal rains flooding the area by the time the Egyptians arrived, the moral remains the same: We must yank our attention away from worrying about the problem to *knowing* an answer will come.

When Jesus fed the five thousand with five loaves and two fish, he first "looked up to heaven and gave thanks." He looked away from the appearance of lack, *knowing* the Divine would answer with abundance.

Wills in Probate

> "God" means love, and "will" means thought. God's will, then, is loving thought.
>
> Marianne Williamson
> *A Return to Love*

The literal meaning of "Muslim" is "surrendering one's will to God." All too often we believe God's Will involves something we'd rather not do. We figure if we comply with what God wants, it follows that we must sacrifice something we hold dear. We fear that the life we'd like to experience falls short of "Thy Will be done." God becomes a personage to fear rather than an idea to love; we have made God in our own frightful image. When God is quoted as saying "Vengeance is mine," it is because vengeance has no place in either this world or in God's realm; God would remove vengeance from our hands completely, in favor of God's all-accepting nature. And so Divine Will conforms to God's nature, that of unconditional love.

Saying "Your Will, not mine" does two paradoxical things:

1. It sets us as apart from God, and implies that what God wants is not what we want.
2. It gives God the green light to work in our lives, maybe because we give up desperately wanting what we desire, which had set up a barbed-wire energy around us that kept us apart from what we wanted.

In *A Course in Miracles,* there are 32 references to God's Will, including:

God's Will is not demanding, and is nothing more nor less than . . .

- We be happy, through a "deep knowing" that goes beyond faith and beyond trust in God (which places God outside what we recognize as "us").
- We maintain a relationship with God, united in Oneness, rather than worshipping Something separate and unattainable.
- We use our creative ability constructively, and behave in a loving manner.
- We never feel anxious, fearful, "small" and powerless, judgmental, or unpeaceful, feelings that are "fruits" of the ego.
- We realize that God does not condemn us, so there is nothing we need to be forgiven for.
- We realize that the only reason we have to ask for anything is because asking gives permission from ourselves to ourselves to receive what is ours, as well as an invitation to the Divine, without which God—who will not suborn free will—cannot proceed.
- We realize God has given us every power and resource we need.
- We participate in sharing, which brings love, which brings joy, which evokes truth.
- We seek knowledge.
- We experience complete peace and joy.
- We know that God doesn't want us to be alone because *God* doesn't want to be alone.
- We reside in Heaven, which nothing can keep from us; our nightmares will not prevail against the peace God wills for us.
- We know we are guiltless, without which we cannot know God.
- We realize it is impossible that we are bound or limited in any way.
- We receive because it is God's will to *give.*

- We perceive the body as completely healthy; what God created is what God wills, and we cannot destroy anything God made.
- We see evil nowhere and feel no injury that would require forgiveness; then we will have the power to heal and bless. *There is no appearance that can't be overlooked, and no mistakes that can undo what God has created.*
- We know that no one can suffer for God's Will to be fulfilled.
- We know every miracle is possible when we see that our wishes and God's Will are one.
- We realize that we generally ask not too much, but far too little.
- We not make idols or use false beliefs as means for "getting more."
- We know the ego makes it seem possible for God's Will and ours to conflict, but God, Who wants us to be happy, is not capable of this.

It isn't God-Out-There Who is saying *Yes* or *No* or *Wait*. More often, it is we ourselves who say "no." We feel unworthy, we feel that a solution isn't possible, or we miss the answer that comes while we're looking for something different. Finally, we must be utterly confident that an answer of some sort *is* coming. *Jesus never doubted that what he pronounced would be realized*; he was supremely confident that his command would materialize.

> This is the day that the Lord has made; We will rejoice and be glad in it.
>
> Psalm 118:24
>
> Be content with what you have; rejoice in the way things are. When you realize there is nothing lacking, the whole world belongs to you.
>
> *Tao Te Ching #44*

Feeling There Leads to Being There

When we begin to grasp the concept of how life works, we can breathe easier, feel more confident and carefree, and enjoy ourselves. Quantum physics assures us that what we want really *does* exist somewhere.[208] So can I levitate? Not if I *want* to; wanting separates me from achievement. But if I work on *imagining* myself levitating and *loving* the feeling of floating on air, someday the me-floating in *potentia* will link up with the me-doing the imagining.[209] (Douglas Adams gives a hilarious account about human flight in "Live in Göttingen—Learning to Fly" on youtube.)

> **Try It Yourself**
>
> After the danger of a hard frost, plant some seeds outside, say, morning glories. For the first week or so, there isn't any noticeable growth, much less flowers. But you *know* the morning glories are there; you can see them in your mind's eye.
>
> "We can hear the future call to the past in the same way that the sun, rain, and warmth of spring call to the seed sleeping in the earth and awaken it to bloom."
>
> Neil Douglas-Klotz
> *Hidden Gospel*

Potentia is more than some nebulous realm; here is a level of reality we've hardly dreamed of, a level containing "real" experiences that we can *will* to materialize on our physical level. This, in fact, is one of the tenets of shamanism. The North American shaman, or medicine man, acted as the agent who traveled between the spirit world and community while in a trance. Because of this ability, the shaman had the power to effect cures, foretell the future, and communicate directly with spirits.[210]

The Kabbalah, the Tao, the Bible all agree.[211] Ours may be a slower but just as sure route, and it can be fun, too, if we pretend *each thought will instantly be made manifest.* Pretend (Lat.: *prae tendere*) literally means "to stretch out before [you]." First we have to figure out what we *don't* want so we can latch onto what we *do* want. Then we imagine what the experience feels like (and of course do what we can—like applying for the job we want). Finally, we expect it to happen and *allow* it to happen.[212] When Jesus said to ask and you shall receive, the word usually translated as "receive" implies being surrounded by the outcome of our request. So we need to place ourselves in the picture and then become "lost" in how it *feels* to be there, thankful that everything is possible. This is the changing shape of prayer.[213]

The danger arises when we want something so bad we think we can't live without it. When we feel desperate, we're operating at the level of fear and lack, and all we get is more "not having." In this case, the best thing to do is avoid thinking about the issue altogether. For example, if our parents both died of heart disease and we can't help but think of dying in the same manner when we repeat the affirmation, "I am always healthy," it's better not to turn our thoughts to health at all.

Carrying an Umbrella

A woman is walking down a dusty country lane when she sees three farmers in a nearby field. The men are kneeling and, with clasped hands, imploring the Lord to send rain for their withering crops. The woman leans across the stile and asks, "Hey, there. Whatcha you up to?" One of the farmers cocks an eye at her and speaks slowly, as if he was addressing an idiot, "We're praying for rain." The woman shakes her head. "Well," she says, "if it was me wanting rain, I'd be carrying an umbrella."

Remember the record-setting drought of 2012? Imagine it again: triple-digit temperatures that wouldn't go away. Green lawns that turned brown, and pasturelands parched, so that cattle were slaughtered early and food prices shot up. Heat so bad that people died and overloaded energy plants failed.

Now open your imaginary umbrella, and *hear* thunder roll across the skies . . . *Listen* to the *splish-splash* of raindrops hitting the fabric of the umbrella. *Feel* the rain cool against your hot skin. *Smell* the grass as it greens up again, *see* roses blooming, and *taste* vine-ripened tomatoes. *Imagine yourself* wading through puddles or dancing in the rain.

Now *feel thankful* that the scene you just imagined is entirely possible. *Know it is possible.* And carry your umbrella with you. That is an "umbrella prayer," combining visualization with action and confidence.

When we "carry an umbrella," we generate positive energy that accompanies being confident of success. In Mark 11:24, Jesus said, "Therefore I say unto you, What things soever ye desire, when ye pray, believe that ye receive them, and ye shall have them." Notice how the statement is worded: "believe that ye receive" right now, not "*shall* receive." This is why *A Course in Miracles*, the Bible, and modern masters tell us to thank God in advance for what already exists (in *potentia*), because the *feeling* of fulfilled desires attracts the probability wave fulfilling those desires. Quantum physics says, whatever it is we want, *it already exists.*

As Meister Eckhart pointed out, the best and shortest prayer is "Thank You."[214] Jesus gave thanks for the loaves and fish that he did have, *knowing* he would have enough provisions to feed the crowd of listeners. We must cultivate the confidence that Jesus possessed in his ability to work the "miracles" of manifestation, and completely trust that God is happy to fulfill any desire that neither harms nor infringes upon another's free will.

We must remember, however, that we can't expect our "castle in the air" to come true if it involves someone whose head is stuck in a different cloud. Just as we learned to focus on our own self-improvement and not "shoulding" others in their evolution, we focus on experiences particular to ourselves when manifesting.

Confidence! We've gotten so good at worrying that it feels like a natural state of being—but it's not. An old Jewish story illustrates our tendency to worry, instead of "letting go." One day a young man sought out his Rabbi.

"What am I doing wrong?" he asked. "I don't understand. I plant and I plant, but the seeds in my garden never sprout."

"Calm down now," said the Rabbi, "and tell me how you're planting."

"I plant the seeds and then I water them. But after I go to sleep, every night I wake up, and I get so worried! Are seeds growing? I wonder. So I pull on my robe and traipse outside and dig up the seeds and I was right, they're not growing at all!"

"I think I know what's wrong," said the Rabbi, nodding his head. "Wash the dirt off your hands and go chop some wood."[215]

It may seem contrary, but if we need something, the way to get it is to *stop needing* it. Manifestation requires a light touch, a certain nonchalance. There is truth behind the adage, "Good things come when you least expect them." When we least expect them—like remembering a previously forgotten telephone number—is when we have let go and allow the Current to flow. One day while I was at my secretarial job, my pen ran out of ink. The pen wasn't anything special, but I liked Jim, who had given me the pen with his company's name on the cheerful, red-colored barrel. Nonetheless, I tossed it in the wastebasket and finished my task with a different pen. Twenty minutes later—right out of the blue—the *same* salesman came in and tossed another red pen on my desk.

I hadn't spent months on repeated envisionings of new writing utensils. The new pen was a spontaneous gift from the universe in answer to my unspoken, un-desperate need. This supremely unselfconscious way of being (letting go) brought nearly immediate results. Now I try to trust that I will always have whatever is necessary to get on with my life.

Singing the Blues and Other Tunes

Is this why some prayers seem to go unanswered? Remember *wu-wei*? Because we're trying to force a particular outcome, like swimming upstream. When we go against the flow (or the Tao) and try too hard, both prayers and achievement may get lost in our efforts. The athlete who is "in the flow" isn't *trying*; that athlete is just *being*.

Another reason may be that we actually work against what *is* trying to reach us: We can't hope to win the lottery if we unconsciously equate being wealthy with being unspiritual, for instance. We can't pray for friends to alleviate our loneliness if we don't get out and meet people. We can't be happy if the only song we sing is filled with the blues: "My baby done left me and I feel so all alone. My dog, he got run over and the rain, she's coming down. My joints, they be a-painin' me, and I ain't got no friend." What a litany of self-perpetuating defeat! Better to sing the blues, if need be, but allow hope to color them a different shade: "When the sun don't seem like it'll shine, come morn, that's when you gotta let hope be born, because you never know what's gonna come tomorrow."

Then again, some unanswered prayers are blessings in disguise. One autumn, my employer closed his doors. That winter I opened my home to a homeless family, fed and loved them for five weeks, and when they finally moved, they left with everything they could carry, relieving me of most of my valuables. Then I lost my house and had nowhere to go. But the low-paying job made way for a home-based business that allows me time to teach and write. The lost possessions reminded me to be grateful for steadfast friends. And my son, Thad, took me in and shared his apartment.

Many times I've been my own worst enemy, crying over things that didn't happen. Now I try to remember Midas, who wanted everything he touched to turn to gold, and he ended up freezing everyone he loved into hard, cold statues. Midas neglected to reflect on the consequences of what he thought he wanted. Some losses, I'm coming to realize (looking back on my life), are grace providing blessings in disguise.

In the fifth book of Douglas Adams' *Hitchhiker's Guide to the Galaxy*, an old man offers hilarious (but true) advice: "There's another prayer . . . It goes, 'Lord, lord, lord . . . Protect me from the consequences of the above prayer. Amen.' And that's it. Most of the trouble people get into in life comes from leaving out that last part."[216] Our predilection for getting ourselves into trouble is demonstrated by the adage, "Be careful what you wish for—you might get it."

How true it is, that we don't always know what's best for us, like the man came into a diner on Monday; with him was an ostrich, which sat at the opposite side of the table. The waitress hurried over to this unusual couple and took the man's order: hamburger, fries and coffee.

"And you, dear?" asked the man, turning to his companion.

"I'll have the same," said the ostrich.

At the end of the meal, the man glanced at the check, stuck his hand in his pocket, and pulled out the exact amount of money necessary to pay his bill (including a tip, we hope). Every day that week this scenario was repeated, with the man ordering a hamburger and fries and coffee, the ostrich ordering a hamburger and fries and coffee, and the waitress receiving the correct amount of cash, right down to the penny.

By the time Friday rolled around, the curious waitress had to ask, "What's going on?"

"Well," the man said as he held the chair for the ostrich, "I was granted two wishes; the first was that I'd always have enough money in my pocket to pay for what I needed, and the second wish was for a long-legged blonde who agrees with everything I say."

Sometimes we miss the answer because it fails to coincide with what we thought it would look like. We are so intent on what our future *should* bring that we fail to notice the wonder that has cropped up, right before our eyes. Like a treasure of cheerful, golden dandelions.

Other times we concentrate so hard on what we desire to manifest that we lose our foundation for making it happen—our internal core of peace. Nothing good can come unless we are functioning from a nucleus of peace.

One Sunday afternoon I patted my hip pocket. My wallet was gone. I remembered having it at church a couple of hours before. I hopped in the car, trying to drive sedately, since I wouldn't be able to supply my driver's license if a policeman stopped me. I imagined finding the wallet in the lost-and-found bin at church, but half my mind was frantically lining up an agenda: call the credit card company, take time off work to stand in line at Motor Vehicle for a replacement license . . .

Back at church, I found nothing of value (to me) in the lost-and-found tub. Methodically, I retraced my morning's steps, from back door to fellowship room to sanctuary. Still nothing. Absentmindedly, I put a hand to my breast pocket, looking for a pack of cigarettes, and there was my wallet.

I'd lost my center of peace and allowed conditioning to lead me astray: "I always put my wallet in *this* jacket pocket." My next mistake was to focus on externals: "If it's not here, it must be there." Then judgment kicked in: "It's *supposed* to be here. If it isn't here where it *should* be, it's gone." We may fail to recognize the answer to our prayer because it fails to match our idea of what it should be like. *"Should" is always a tip-off that we are making a judgment.*

Many of our judgments are inappropriate. God's answer is always immediate and loving. It is we who have confused perceptions of reality. Once there was a man who died and awoke in a walled garden so beautiful it might have been Eden. The groundskeeper gladly granted the man his wish for a mansion, a gorgeous wife, a Corvette. Finally the man felt bored, for he had nothing to look forward to if all his wishes would be granted. The next morning when the groundskeeper strolled into sight, the man said, "I wish I could see what Hell's like on the other side of that fence."

"Where do you think you are?" said the gardener, chuckling.[217]

The Law of Manifestation goes hand-in-hand with the Law of Giving and Receiving. We receive as we give as we receive. So our motto would become, "We reap what we sow what we feel we have in abundance and share." Giving away what we desire is the trigger to getting more of it in our lives. When I feel prosperous enough to share what I have, that feeling of prosperity attracts more prosperity into my life. Like my sharing my house with the homeless family, and my son later sharing his apartment with me.

The second part of the Law of Manifestation, ". . . give as we receive," means that we cannot be given what we think we can't have, what we're not quite sure we want, or what we feel unworthy of. I want to live in a Craftsman bungalow, but it won't happen as long as I'm thinking, "I'll never find a house I can afford."

On the way to answered prayers, we can ease the waiting period by trusting in the process God has set up—by having confidence in the constancy of quantum law. Confident (*cum fide*) literally means *with faith*, like the old man on a pilgrimage, who was preparing to cross the desert on foot. "Father," said a fellow traveler, "you are so frail. How can you make it to Mecca?"

"I see it now," replied the ancient. "My heart is already there. How difficult can it be for the rest of me to follow?"

Fourteen

Groups are dynamic.

> Now Jericho was straitly shut up . . . So the people
> shouted when the priests blew with the trumpets: and
> it came to pass, when the people heard the sound of the
> trumpet, and the people shouted with a great shouts,
> that the wall fell down flat . . .

> Joshua 6:1, 20 (KJV)

Two or more gathered . . .

When I watch football at home, alone, there's no chance of someone sloshing beer on me, standing up and blocking my view, or yelling obnoxious slurs. I don't have to pay for parking, walk a mile to the stadium, or wait endlessly in line to leave. But, while I get to yell at the television from my comfortable couch, I do miss the surging, vital energy of people gathered together with a common goal—that of rooting for their team. This kind of energy is the reason that, in all of the NFL, Arrowhead Stadium is one of the places visiting teams most hate to play. The home football games draw sell-out crowds, and the crowd is often loud enough to cause false-start penalties. The spirit of 80,000 people becomes a tangible factor that the Chiefs encourage and use to complement their performance.

Because he knew that groups are dynamic (football notwithstanding), Jesus said, "For where two or three are gathered together in my name, there am I in the midst of them." Jesus was not denying the power of the individual, but he likely knew that the ego maintains its existence by making us feel like selves apart. When two or more people come together with a common purpose, their union raises them above the separation that the ego fosters and exposes them to a higher truth: spirit unifies.[218]

Furthermore, the word usually translated as "name" in the verse above (*shem*) we know also means "sound." *Vibration*, in other words, and *resonance*. Super-sized sowing and reaping.[219] Princeton's REG machine experiments proved the greatest effectiveness came from "pairs of operators with shared intentions."[220] Anyone at a largely attended sports or musical event has felt the dynamics of "two or more" vibration.

The dynamics of group power is seen in flocks of Canada geese. The geese honk to encourage one another. They instinctively use *wu-wei*, or effortlessness, by flying in a V-formation to take advantage of the slipstream of the forerunner. The geese also cooperate by taking turns; one leads and when it grows weary, another takes the point position. Their cooperation extends to compassion: If one goose is too tired to go on, at least one other goose falls out of formation with the exhausted bird, and they remain together until they can fly again.

> The repetitive words and actions of a religious service may alter reality, the studies show, and the more people who observe and participate in these rites, the more powerful the waves of energy produced, confirming what the faithful say they've known all along.
>
> *Curiosity*: "10 Biggest Questions Raised by Quantum Physics" at discover.com (September 4, 2011)

I participated in a dynamic group intention at Kansas City's Loose Park. Led by Rev. Dr. Gary Langston (Red Bear Who Sees All Worlds), over a hundred people gathered to bless the pond. Masaru Emoto's laboratory in Japan analyzed "Before" and "After" water samples, and his photographs provide definitive evidence that our words and intention have a direct effect on bodies of water. Before the blessing, the photograph showed only a few bleary bright spots. The blessed water produced a well-defined snowflake-like crystal.

As this demonstration showed, the collective power of a group with a common intention, like sending out blessings, is potent. The most beneficial groups are composed of caring individuals. Martin Luther King, Jr. knew this.[221] King was familiar with the Jewish philosopher and theologian, Martin Buber, who wrote a treatise titled *I and Thou* (*Ich und Du*). Although English no longer distinguishes between familiar and formal "you," German does. "Du" is the person, the thing, the animal, or God in an intimate relationship. Someone who has an "I-it" relationship with the world relates to people and things as objects. Whoever says "I-thou" has no boundaries and allows that the other person or thing also has feelings. When we live with an I-thou attitude, we cut down on the separation we might otherwise feel; we *care*. Latin, too, has a phrase for this type of relationship: *Alter ipse amicus*, or "A friend is another self." King devoted his life to changing social mores to encompass an "I-thou" relationship.

God (It) does not create a person's cancer or a tidal wave or a drive-by shooting, but God (Thou) is present when we use ourselves and our resources to help improve another being's life. A modern parable tells about the forks in heaven being three feet long, but no one goes hungry because the people feed one another.

Shouldering the Burden

Once there was an inner city neighborhood in great disrepair. The preacher at the local church finally cried out, "Oh, God, why don't You do something to help us?"

God replied, "Why do you cry out to Me? What are *you* going to do?"

The preacher knew from experience what great results cooperation can bring, and he thought about the walls of Jericho tumbling down. Inspired, he gathered a few willing teenagers, and together they started at the church and worked their way down the street. Singing as they went, they picked up trash and painted fences. They fixed the hinges, raked leaves, and trimmed scraggly bushes growing in yards. At the first house, the residents looked out their windows with expressions of suspicion that slowly turned into smiles. At another house, the grateful residents offered the clean-up crew cookies. By the time the teens arrived at the last house on the block, their crew had doubled in size and the neighborhood gleamed with new hope and good fellowship.

In the movie *Matrix*, the ruling government of machines used people as its power source. These plugged-in humans functioned like batteries, supplying all the energy necessary to keep the civilization of artificial intelligence running. Although the story was fictional, the science was real: In correspondence with the Earth/atmosphere being a giant capacitor (battery), the human brain contains millions of magnetic particles.[222] These particles serve as physical links with the Earth, with which we continually seek a harmonic/magnetic balance.[223] With 1,170,000,000,000,000 volts of energy literally at hand for each of us, the thought that becomes incredible is that *anything* could be impossible for us to accomplish. Multiply one person's power by two or more to create an enormous mental and emotional vibrational field, and the world of *potentia* seems entirely accessible.

Dominion of the Earth and Critical Mass

Dr. Valerie Hunt proved the power humans can access when working in partnership and harmony with Earth. While visiting the island of Bora Bora with a friend, Hunt saw a violent storm out over the ocean rolling in so quickly that she knew they wouldn't have time to move their expensive electronic equipment to shelter. She and the technician sat on the beach and concentrated on the image of the sheet of rain splitting into a V-shape. They calmly used will and intention to manipulate the energy fields surrounding them, and the force of the storm passed by on either side, leaving them dry and safe.[224] Notice that Hunt didn't *wish*; she deliberately used her *will* to effect a change. Nor was Hunt's an isolated experience. My own energy teacher told us about coming home from holiday and hearing on the radio that a tornado was touching down in their neighborhood. After pulling the car over, he and his wife immediately surrounded their house with protective energy. They arrived home later to find their whole block safe, while the surrounding areas had been ravaged by the twister.[225]

> But it is arrogant to lay aside the power that He gave, and choose a little senseless wish instead of what He wills. The gift of God to you is limitless.
>
> *A Course in Miracles*

In Jerusalem in 1983, a scientifically monitored group of meditators proved the relationship between prayer and active meditation (which uses visualization) and the lowering of crime rates, accidents, fires, and suicides throughout the city. This study, now known as the "Maharishi Effect," has been repeated with the same success many times and in many countries. In fact, Braden believes that only the square root of 1% of any population, concentrating on emitting peaceful blessings at the same time, is necessary to benefit the entire population.[226] And if that small group of people were to sustain its blessing, a critical mass would be reached and all of humanity rise to a higher level of consciousness. This is the Butterfly Effect at its best, and something called the Hundredth Monkey.

On the island of Koshima in 1952, the native Macaque monkeys loved to eat raw sweet potatoes. One young monkey began washing the sand off her food, and others of her generation soon followed suit. When most of the monkeys in that island group washed their food, a critical mass was reached, and their food-washing behavior was transmitted *non-locally* to monkeys living on other islands. The critical mass caused other groups to resonate with the Koshima monkeys. It may be that critical mass is transmitted through resonance within morphogenetic fields. [227] Through fields, through consciousness, and through all space and time.[228]

Resonance is a pattern of waves that harmonize with one another, and resonance is the reason soldiers break step when crossing a bridge: If their marching in step matched the natural frequency of the bridge, the soldiers would cause the structure to collapse.[229] This did, in fact, happen when two suspended walkways collapsed at the Kansas City Hyatt Regency Hotel in 1981, because of inadequate structural supports and the vibrations caused by dancing people.

We can view resonance in a room full of grandfather clocks. After a while, the clocks will synchronize themselves so that every pendulum (oscillator) is moving in a rhythm uniform with all the others. All the clocks will align (or *entrain*) themselves to the *largest* clock with the *strongest* rhythm.

What does that mean to us? The heart is a living oscillator with an electrical field up to 100 times stronger than that of the brain.[230] Because of this, a group of hearts will entrain to the heart whose vibrations of compassion are radiating at the highest frequency. The practice of focusing attention on the heart area and concentrating on feelings of appreciation and love (which may be as short as a one-minute technique) instantly increases coherence in the meditator's own heart energy field and then pulls other meditators into entrainment.[231] Heart-entrainment occurs, for example, within a group engaged in a *metta* meditation. Metta, or "Loving Heart Meditation," is the Buddhist practice in which one repeats intentions of goodwill toward oneself, others, and the world at large. (For more on meditations, see Part Two: 7. *Make personal peace a priority*, and Meditations section.)

Our thoughts, our feelings, our despair and our hopes all affect everything that is. As long as we view the world from a perspective of "Me/Not Me," we leave ourselves open to strife and loneliness and unconscious mis-creating. When we know ourselves as part of a great Biohood, then we begin to use the power of compassionate resonance to work toward gluing our world back together. Just as we are drawn to happy people who then help us to feel happy, an unconditionally loving presence moves all people and things—"two or more"—toward entrainment with that love. And that is when a ripple effect can shift the energy for the whole human race.[232]

Fifteen

One person can make a difference.

We have found a strange footprint on the shores of the unknown. We have devised profound theories, one after another, to account for its origin. At last, we have succeeded in reconstructing the creature that made the footprint, and lo! it is our own.

Sir Arthur Eddington
Space, Time, and Gravitation

Each particle of consciousness is dependent upon every other. The strength of one adds to the strength of all. The weakness of one weakens the whole. The energy of one recreates the whole. The striving of one increases the potentiality of everything that is.

Jane Roberts
Unknown Reality

Forging a Chain

According to urban legend, a New York teacher once honored her students by presenting each of them with a blue ribbon with "Who I Am Makes a Difference" embossed in gold. She also handed out three extra ribbons to each student, which they were to share the ribbons with other people.

One young man went to a local company and used a blue ribbon to thank a junior executive for help in planning his career. He described the class project, gave the executive the two extra ribbons, and asked him to keep the chain going.

The junior executive decided to pass the honor on to his boss who, in spite of being a grouchy sort, was a creative genius in the younger man's eyes.

When the senior executive arrived at home that night, he sat down beside his teenage son. "The coolest thing happened today," he said. "I was at the office, and one of the junior execs came in and gave me a blue ribbon that says, "Who I Am Makes a Difference."

"Big deal," said the teen.

"It was a big deal to me," his father replied, "but that's not the end of it. See, the guy gave me another ribbon. He said I was supposed to give this to someone who's made a big difference in my life. Besides your mom, you're the most important person in my life."

For the second time that day, the man was astonished; as he pinned the ribbon on his son's T-shirt, the teen began to cry. "Aw, Dad," he said between sobs, "I thought you didn't care. I was going to commit suicide tonight after you and Mom went to sleep, and now this—" He fingered the blue satin and beamed at his father, who hugged him as he had not done in ten years. When he arrived at work the next day, his fellow employees benefited from his newfound consideration.

Elie Wiesel felt that God was guilty for the atrocities of the Holocaust. In *The Trial of God*, Wiesel staged a mock trial where two Russian Jews indict God for remaining silent when there is evil in the world. His play illustrates the Jews' attitude of treating God as an equal and, on occasion, calling God to account. Such an attitude is the fulcrum for a balanced and sane relationship. But it's time for humanity to shoulder the responsibility for the inhumane acts committed by human beings.

"Now wait," we might say, "what could I have done? I wasn't alive during World War II." Or "I was living in the United States." Many Europeans might say simply, "I was afraid." Certainly a viable reason. What about the ethnic cleansings in Bosnia, Rwanda, Tibet? What about the homeless on our streets right now? What about the animals used in testing for food, drugs, and cosmetics? Now I'm going into overload: too much to do and too little "me." Before a sense of utter helplessness sets in and paralyzes me, I have to ask: Can Quantum God help here?

The answer is *Yes!*

The Necessity of One

> In the universe great acts are made up of small deeds.
>
> *Tao Te Ching #63*

No matter how high we count, we can always add one to the previous number and come up with a larger number. By adding one . . . and one . . . and one, we travel toward infinity. One makes all the difference.

Remember how small an atom is? If, however, the nucleus of an atom were the size of a grain of salt, the diameter of its electron cloud would span three football fields! That image is a good illustration of how far the influence and power of one person extends. We need not be big or strong, charismatic or dynamic. The Dalai Lama has pointed out that zero seems like nothing, but without it we can't make ten or one hundred.[233] A person may feel insignificant, but he or she *can* make a difference.

Nikola Tesla, one of the greatest engineers of the early twentieth century, theorized that if a person stood in the topmost room of a skyscraper and, in time with the natural swaying of the structure, gave an exterior wall a nudge, rhythmically and repeatedly, the whole building would eventually topple down. The mechanical resonance involved might take months, but it *would* happen.[234] Tesla also believed in the power of resonance so deeply that he boasted he—one man—could use electrical resonance to split our planet in two (like Ella Fitgerald's high note breaking the wine glass). Tesla's claim brings to mind the Hebrew *Zohar*, which says, *A person should always imagine that the fate of the whole world depends on his or her actions.*[235]

Knowing that my thoughts may be giving birth to or destroying worlds helps me remember to "watch" what I'm thinking; sometimes I wonder if I'm creating rainbows or cataclysms in other dimensions. And at home, in this time and this world, I know that one smile can light a life in peril; one meal can help the homeless; one affirmation can rescue a lost soul. It might be something as simple as stepping into an elevator and making an off-hand comment that changes someone's life. Or shoveling snow from a neighbor's driveway. You never know the beneficial influence you had, but it exists just the same and grows as it's passed on from person to person.

> A man was walking along a beach littered with hundreds of starfish stranded there at low tide. He picked up a starfish and tossed it back into the ocean water, then walked another pace and did the same for the next stranded starfish. A jogger coming up behind him said, "You can't save them all."
>
> "Maybe not," said the man, flinging another starfish into the sea. "But I made a difference to *that* one."

When my son, Thad, was sixteen, *Chicken Soup for the Teenage Soul III* published his poem about a suicidal teen who was saved on her birthday by a phone call from her mother. (See endnote.)[236] His poem has had an impact that reaches around the world and across the years since its publication. One young woman wrote to him:

> "i've had some hard times where i felt like shooting myself in the head wasn't the worst idea . . . [your poem] will stick with me forever, and undoubtedly hold me together . . . at least one person will always love me. you're the reason i know this."

One small kindness can have a tremendous effect. Indeed, the Dalai Lama says that his religion is very simple, for it is nothing more nor less than kindness.[237] He knows that one is a powerful number. A geneticist has estimated that the difference between a mild virus and a killer disease can be as small as one atom in more than one and a half million atoms. And the difference between a human being and a plant amounts to a single atom![238]

Brandon Moore, a retired elementary school teacher, used to ask his fifth-graders whether they would rather receive a million dollars or the proceeds from any calendar month during which they are given one penny the first day and two cents on the second day, with each successive day doubling the previous date's amount until the end of the month. That exponential figure totals $5,375,109.12 for a thirty-day month! Moore's thought exercise gives new meaning to "Paying it forward," doesn't it?

The idea of paying it forward idea was expressed by the teacher who handed out the blue ribbons. Any chain reaction begins with just one spark. No matter how insignificant we feel, a single action is liable to have far-reaching effects. Fifty years ago, a woman refused to give up her seat on a Montgomery, Alabama bus and her creation of a new morphogenetic field made it less difficult for blacks later to claim full personhood. One woman: Rosa Parks.

In scientific terms, quantum field theory explains the scientific basis for a little yeast that leavens a lot of bread, or the idea that each of us stands at the center point of a cosmic web of probabilities that is affected by our thoughts and feelings.[239]

I'm the One I've Been Waiting For

"Gee," we might say, "that sounds like the Second Coming of Christ. You don't mean me. You can't mean *me*." Elie Wiesel, who survived internment at Auschwitz, firmly believes one prayer can change the course of events. And, he writes, the Baal Shem Tov, was a one-man spark that engendered hope in thousands of families living in the 18th century, a spark that "fanned itself into a huge flame that tore into the darkness."[240]

I've spent a lot of my life in the dark, waiting for a man to come and recognize the light shining inside me. I didn't feel "at home" in this world. And I thought a lot about not living. I used to have enough life insurance to leave everyone sitting pretty, if not gorgeous, after I died, but my life insurance policy bit the dust when my job dried up, so I didn't even have the consolation of an option I would never take.

Some people have dynamic personalities; they glow and show a zest for life. Some are stubborn, tenacious, or just plain too nasty (let's say "becoming") to die early on. Some people are driven by the momentum of their responsibilities; their ever-changing, never-ending To Do List carries them from day to day.

But I'm too laid-back to be zesty, too nice to be nasty, too responsible to die in an "accident." And I knew all the right things to do—to smile at my reflection every day ("Hi, beautiful!"). To appreciate the beauty of nature, the kindness of a stranger. To feel grateful and give something back, even something as small as a compliment. I knew to give myself nightly personal pampering (a bite of chocolate), and to get physical exercise (living in a two-story house helped), mental exercise (crossword puzzles) and spiritual exercise, as in affirming, "One person *can* change the world." So, heal thyself, right? Still, right felt more like "left." Oh, well, it was time I learned to be ambidextrous and light up my corner of the world—beginning with myself.

The Baal Shem Tov preached that the world would only be transformed when people realized the Messiah is not someone other than themselves.[241] This idea is the heart of the Kabbalah.

What happens when you ask yourself: "What if I were the Messiah? What if I were a Christ? What if I'm another Buddha?" Maybe your ego rears up and cries, "No way!" That's not surprising. We have learned to regard ourselves as small, weak, and helpless. We have let the ego do for us what it believes is a favor, keeping us safe by keeping us in a rut.[242] Even if the rut has led to a hell. Even though one step forward may be, if not heaven, at least not quite so dark and solitary. Where we are and who we (mistakenly) think we are seems safe because it feels familiar. It's our comfort zone. But this small self is not where we have to stay or who we must remain. One person can shine like a sun in the dark throes of a storm.

> Learn the Zen of a lone lamp shining in a death ward.
>
> Zen master Ying-an
> Thomas Cleary, *Zen Essence*

A century ago, one man had the persistence to create a thousand light bulbs, one after the other, until he happened upon an improved design that worked well. The man was Thomas Edison, who in his moment of triumph handed the precious light bulb to a junior assistant. The fumble-fingered young man dropped it and, of course, the glass shattered. Edison and his team worked for the next twenty-four hours straight to craft another perfect bulb—which Edison then handed to the *same* young assistant, lighting what might have become a very dark life.[243]

Physically, if all atoms were once star-stuff (and they were), then the power of the stars resides in every particle within each of us. I remember how good it was when I was a child and had skinned my knee; my mother bent over my hurt and kissed it and made it feel better. How does this work? Because everything in the universe is part of a single holographic unit, and because Einstein proved that energy and matter are different forms of the same substance ($E = mc^2$). This is why both love and alternative medicine works. Energy healing is a natural, innate human potential, especially potent in fairly healthy people who have a *strong intent* to help and heal.[244]

One Light Shining Everywhere

One year I wondered what I could do for a friend who was going to be alone during the holidays. "Coco, you want to go?" The dog chuffed and sprinted to the front door. I grinned and began packing.

We left Kansas City to drive twelve long hours away. The Saturn didn't look much like a sleigh going south on Interstate 35, but it did carry presents and chocolate macadamias. After our pre-Christmas delivery, Coco and I hit the road the next day, using the "shorter" Highway 7. However, along this two-lane route another small town always popped up as soon as we'd gotten up to speed after the *last* small town, with dreary fallow fields in between, and I learned I'm an *Interstate* sort of girl. At least my co-pilot had the chance to bark at cows all afternoon.

Six hours into the trip (after turning the wrong way and backtracking), we reached Interstate 540, but by now it was dark. The road snaked up and down mountains and spun out before us for a hundred miles. I was worried that I'd missed the connection for Highway 7 north. I wasn't even sure what *state* we were in. We came to a college town where lines of traffic stretched ahead and the oncoming glare of white lights hurt my tired eyes. The streamers of bright headlights and red taillights sparkled like lit Christmas trees, but I was so weary—and still no sight of Highway 7.

After eight hours on the road, we stopped for dollar burgers. Although I felt grateful when the clerk told me we were less than an hour south of Joplin, the thought came to mind, *Oh, now there's the whole length of Missouri to go!* Discouraged, I squatted in front of the counter. A little girl three or four years old was standing a couple of feet away.

"You have on a pretty shirt," I said with a weary smile. Then I noticed the characters printed on the sweatshirt. "Do you like *Cars*?"

"That's her favorite movie," her daddy said.

I searched my mind for modern Disney movies. "My favorite movie is *Monsters, Inc.*"

Suddenly, the little girl stepped across the space separating us and gave me a hug, holding, holding, holding onto me. When she finally let go, I caressed her cheek and said, "Thank you, sweetheart."

She didn't say a word. Her daddy collected their order and led her to a table.

Before leaving with my bag of hamburgers, I stopped to say goodbye.

The man turned to his wife and explained how their daughter had hugged me. Then he told me, "She never does that—especially with strangers."

"What's her name?" I asked.

"Grace," they replied.

Back in the car, I handed Coco her hamburger and marveled, "Grace embraced me, just when I needed it the most. Grace embraced me!" I laughed with joy and wonder. The light of one little girl carried us the rest of the way home—sunshine in the dark of night.

The sun is a good way to illustrate the nature of human beings. The sun is comprised of the core, radiative zone, convective zone, photosphere, chromosphere, and corona, along with sunspots and huge flares called prominences. So too can we imagine the human with . . .

- a divine core or soul,
- a physical body,
- and the "shining" bodies:
  energetic,
  emotional,
  mental,
  intentional
  and finally the most far-reaching, the spiritual body.

Anxiety might be represented by sunspots, and the individual effects of self-will (blessings and curses) act like the far-reaching flares. Such a flare, carried by solar winds, could knock out all the Earth's electronics in a huge electromagnetic pulse (EMP)—that's the potential power of light.

The following meditation is one that will help us feel enlightened, empowered, and expansive. First we begin with the image of a light within our heart. This light is our own which, in turn, is fueled by Life Force. Next, we let the light grow until it fills every part inside our skin. We allow this living, throbbing life force to radiate outward until it surrounds us. Now we imagine the light growing, expanding, until it has surrounded our home, our community, our country, our planet. Eventually, the light expands until it has grown as large as the cosmos; living inside it are the stars and the birth of stars. In this Tibetan practice of light-meditation, the meditator *intends* to project this light energy into the surrounding space, and wills it to radiate the energy of compassion to all corners of the cosmos.[245] As quantum physics has shown, there is no doubt that the grace of intentional-light touches someone, something, somewhere.

More power to the power of one!

Sixteen

Lessons will be repeated until they become disasters dire enough to claim our attention.

Through us, the universe questions itself and tries out various answers on itself in an effort—parallel to our own—to decipher its own being. This, as I reflect on it, is awesome. It assigns a role to man that was once reserved for the gods. [246]

David Bohm

We tend to think along the lines of the most *probable*, thereby failing to notice all sorts of other *possible* paths. Cruising along the major highways on autopilot, we may miss the small signposts that point to beneficial by-ways, lucrative turn-offs, even delightful detours—until an event crashes into our lives with the force of a freight train, and finally gets our attention, turning us to head off on a new direction. Default settings are shortcuts that allow us to go through life without a thought as to what we are thinking. They are insidious because the default—in our minds—becomes the *only possible* scenario.

K. C. Cole
Mind over Matter

Figuring Out What the Lesson Is

One morning I was driving to work. I'd left home early and I knew I'd get to work on time, but my habit was to drive a bit over the posted speed limit, and the nearby drivers were irritating me; I'd gotten stuck behind slow-moving cars. I looked at the Celica in front of me, the ancient Volvo in the left lane, and then glanced up the road. Ouch! I spotted a police car half-hidden in a driveway about a block away, and the officer had his radar gun pointed in my direction. Those slowpoke drivers had saved me the cost of an unnecessary speeding citation.

> Praying is not about asking . . . It is just opening your eyes to see what was there all along.
>
> Changdud Tulku Rinpoche
> *The Essence of Zen*, Maggie Pinkney, ed.

There's always something more to learn, and what we learn adds to our appreciation of the "larger picture." The threshold to learning stands at the beginning of an open mind. For years I'd pooh-poohed the kids' chigger bites—until three of those nasties bit *my* ankle. I discovered really fast that chigger bites cause pain more intense than childbirth. The itching drove me crazy! Those chiggers gave me insight into the larger picture, that of my children's lives; I learned what it's like to suffer from bug bites (and that calamine lotion's a lousy treatment). Learning is an important part of life if we wish to graduate from (or skip) the Brick Wall School because the best thing about lessons is, if we catch on right away, we avoid beating our heads against brick walls.

> If you don't change the way you think about yourself and the world around you, you'll be bound to repeat the same old patterns, and the fabric of your life will be the same tomorrow as it is today.
>
> Richard Dupuis
> *From the Mouth of God*

While we attract the events that "happen" to us, *potentia* will always provide the gentlest lessons first, the mildest tribulations. Our job, then, becomes twofold: to accept the situation, and to understand the spiritual lesson underlying the pain. Why does the air traffic controller come down with a headache at the end of his workweek, and why have the occasional headaches grown into weekly migraines? Because his job demands perfection, and perfection strains both body and soul? Because he carries the tension home with him? Because he'd really rather be stocking shelves or painting houses, but the job paid well, or his parents pushed him into it, or . . . (The profession could as well be law, or teaching, or dealing with a houseful of children, etc.) So his first task is to figure out what's really going on inside him emotionally, psychologically. At the same time, he must acknowledge the situation as it is—that for some reason he's hurting.

Of course, the grieving widow cannot shunt aside a heart full of pain; she must accept the fact that she misses her husband. But the process of loss and recovery is more easily borne if she remembers that the grief is an emotion, and the emotion will pass if she embraces the feeling and then allows it to pass through her. The word *emotion*, in fact, means "to move out of." *This, too, shall pass* became my motto, my mantra, when I was trying to overcome grief and depression, especially when the effort involved getting through the next two minutes, the next two hours . . . one day . . . one night at a time.

Angels that Look Like Devils

Our teachers are not only those people we love and esteem but also those who try our patience or test our strength, even those who commit crimes that cry out for our understanding and forgiveness. Like the Buddhists who believe that gods can look like demons but still be working toward our own good, the Kabbalah believes in earthly angels who are often mistaken for unpleasant people. And *A Course in Miracles* teaches that if we take no offense in the first place, there's no need for forgiveness.

> A *lamed-vav tzaddik* [miracle-worker] who holds the universe together may hide in many disguises. The person giving us the hardest time actually may be saving our lives. We can never tell from one moment to the next if an event is for our well-being, so it is wise to give everything and everyone the benefit of the doubt.
>
> Rabbi David Cooper
> *God is a Verb*

No matter what happens, no matter how stupidly we act or what harm a person causes, there is a lesson to be learned from every experience. The purpose of lessons is to nudge us out of our ruts, startle us out of complacency, lure us out of our comfort zones, and prod us on the journey of self-evolution. The people who "push our buttons" act as red flags, pointing out areas where we're putting conditions on the love we give.[247] Unconditional love doesn't say, "But first you have to clean your room . . . get a better job . . . do it my way."

Difficult people may be the last people we'd like to listen to, but they may bear the most important messages for us.[248] Messages like:

- A Special Ed student I was working with taught me patience and ingenuity. I finally gave the disruptive but good-natured kid the task of calling bingo numbers, and he latched onto sneaking peeks at the scrawniest kid's card to help him win. I gave him a discreet thumbs-up sign, and afterwards hugged him and told him he'd done a fine job. He lived up to the responsibility he was given.

- A difficult person is our savior if we discover our self-worth and decide to move toward freedom. The task of ending the marriage fell to me; I had to overcome my fears, to speak up and get both of us moving in different directions. It was a scary but necessary step.

- We learn to slow down and notice beauty when we walk with the elderly. Grama used to apologize for moving so slowly with her walker, but I enjoyed walking at a leisurely pace. I had time to smell my roses, literally!

- We learn to frolic when we find ourselves in the midst of rowdy youngsters.

According to the Gospel of Thomas (78), Jesus said, "Those in garments which are soft upon them cannot know the truth." Ideas that cloak us and hold us in complacency act like soft garments for us, but remaining in our comfort zone will not move us forward.

Coming Through Fire

> I will put Chaos into fourteen lines
> And keep him there . . .
>   He is nothing more nor less
> Than something simple not yet understood;
> I shall not even force him to confess
> Or answer. I will only make him good.
>
>   Edna St. Vincent Millay
>   *The Oxford Book of Sonnets*, John Fuller

Some of the best opportunities for learning may seem like chaos, or what scientists call entropy. Opportunity can disguise itself as a catastrophe, and it is our job to find the advantage in the debris. For example, the seeds of the giant redwoods germinate only *after* they've been exposed to the intense heat of a forest fire.

Scientifically, the system that disintegrates into disorder once sat at an unbalanced point, the "edge of chaos," which in itself *attracted* the element that pushed it into disorganization. This "strange attractor" shows why we attract through our vibrational energy fields the events that seem to "happen" to us. We are then faced with a crisis—a lesson—and when we've tumbled out of our comfort zone we can, with practice and awareness, *stop* and think differently.[249] And unless we do this, we're liable to experience avoidable pain.

Suffering is avoidable pain. On any occasion when we're suffering, we can be sure we're stuck in a rut and functioning out of the mindset of a victim: "This shouldn't be happening to me. It isn't fair," or "I'm afraid of what might happen *to me*." Suffering comes from wanting to change something that cannot be changed. Molly Schaffer, a Beagle, once gave birth to nine pups soundlessly and painlessly—she wasn't afraid. By not resisting the inevitable and not being afraid, Molly suffered no pain in pup-birth.

Pearls of Humanity

The simple question "What is the spiritual side of this situation?" can change our focus from "Poor me" to a "What can I learn?" attitude. Any tragedy, like Hurricane Katrina that hit the southern seaboard of the United States or the United flight that crashed in Sioux City, the meltdown at Chernoble, the World Trade Towers of 9/11, or the 2011 tornado that devastated Joplin, Missouri— such tragedies also become the setting for brotherhood and heroism: incidents of love for one's neighbor borne into actuality, the compassion of volunteers, and the strength of survivors and family members. (For example, in less than one week, $300,000 was donated for the Medley family's hospital bills after the July 20, 2012 *Batman* shooting in Aurora, Colorado.)

Tragedies provide a stage for great deeds. The hurts are grievous, but our heroic acts are the pearls of humanity. Even small kindnesses, like giving up our seat on a crowded bus or subway, emit a spiritual light that had not shone forth in the previous moment.

> The knowledge that whatsoever happens to you is for your good, raises you to the heights of living in Paradise.
>
> Hasidic hero, the Bratzlaver
> Louis I. Newman
> *Hasidic Anthology*

Redirecting our attention to the lesson suffering brings also teaches us to value laughter and gives us the chance to "practice joy." If we often experience suffering, surely at some point we will decide, "Enough! There must be more to life than this. There must be another way to live." It is then that we turn our backs on darkness and learn to shine. And when we brighten other lives, the shining grows stronger inside us and we no longer give free rein (reign) to the *Why me?* question that invited suffering in the first place.

Depression or difficulties in our lives are signals that our thought patterns are not serving us well. Perhaps the most easily deciphered signals are physical symptoms: For example, an aching upper back—you are not feeling supported; remember that Divine support is always available, and breathe in and out of the back of the heart chakra. Disorganization or "spaciness"—you are ungrounded; stop, calm down, "grow roots," and breathe. Constipation—you are holding onto something you would do better to let go of. Diarrhea—you are not processing something you need to think about. Or if the difficulties are financial, maybe we have been thinking, "I've always been poor," or "I'm so deep in debt, I'll never dig myself out," or "This is the way it's always been, and it's never going to get any better."

We need, as Einstein observed, to solve problems with a different sort of thinking than that which plunged us into hot water in the first place.

Every year, two sculptors hired a small plane and pilot and flew to a wooded lake to hunt for raw material. Rick and Dave had great luck on their latest trip, and when the pilot returned to the campsite, they produced six black walnut tree trunks to be transported back home.

"I can't take six," the pilot told them.

"But you must!" replied Dave. "Look at what beauties they are!"

"That's too much weight for the plane to carry."

"But it can't be," said Rick. "We found six last year, and the pilot helped us load every one of them."

"Same kind of plane as mine?" the pilot asked.

"Sure thing. Same plane, same number of trees."

Against his better judgment, the pilot relented. The logs and artists and baggage were all aboard when the pilot revved the engines. Slowly, sluggishly, the plane began to move. As it reached the end of the short airstrip, it lurched toward the lake and crashed.

Shaking the grogginess out of his head, Dave asked, "Where are we?"

Rick looked out the window. "Same place we crashed last year."

Remember *potentia*, the ethereal realm where electrons exhibit such *un*physical, free-to-choose-anything behavior. We aren't really "stuck" unless we think we are, or unless we refuse to learn. Then we land back inside the walls of the Brick Wall School.

The Value of Traffic Signs

Knowing that order rises out of chaos can help when everything seems to be going downhill. Sometimes we like the possibilities, and other times we fail to recognize them. Spiritual blindness is demonstrated by the case of the drunk standing outside the park, shaking the fence rails, and yelling, 'Let me out!' Only his delusion prevents him from seeing that he is free.[250]

My friend, Kurt, was managing a transportation business, but resigned after a set-to with the owner. He drove a cab for a while, but that was a dangerous job. He then bought a town car and built his own transportation business gradually, but the car needed repairs. All along, we'd talked about the nudges Spirit was providing, but this man who made his living by obeying traffic signs didn't act on the spiritual signs. Finally a woman ran a stop sign and plowed into Kurt's car, and because he landed in the hospital for a week, he lost his one-man business. Due to ongoing physical injuries, he wasn't able to care for his daughter, Cecilia, who left to live with her mother. Kurt lost his girlfriend, his home, and most of his possessions. Lamenting his refusal to heed the traffic signs of his spiritual life, he turned to liquor and drugs and repeated suicide attempts.

Thank goodness, Kurt's story didn't end there. When he had lost everything except the clothes on his back, he realized he was now free. Trusting in divine abundance, he found medical aid, a kind companion, and shelter, and his life took a different path than before the car accident. And all he had to do was to trust that he would receive exactly what he needed.

A tribe of Aborigines in the Australian outback lives in complete trust of the process of life. These tribes people pray every morning for "my highest good and the highest good for all life everywhere." They *know* there is abundance, even in their part of the world, and *expect* sustenance to cross their path—and they're never disappointed. Without crops, without supplies in the blazing desert, every day their needs for food and water are met. The faith, trust, and gratitude of these innocents keep them living "in the zone."[251]

What do we normally trust? Many place faith in physicians, when their bodies actually know how to keep perfect health, barring negative internal messages. I myself have faith that the sun will come up every morning, although I know that the Earth *has* stopped spinning at least once in human memory and started turning the other direction, as recounted in Pre-Inca records and in Joshua 10:13.[252] For the first time in two decades, I put my faith in an airline, and they lost my luggage, including a complicated sweater I'll never knit again. I trust various car mechanics not to overcharge (that's why there have been enough to call them "various"). I trust State Farm to be "a good neighbor," though they denied my claim when my basement flooded. We trust Rolaids to spell relief and our political system, as Abraham Lincoln said in his Gettysburg Address, to be a government "of the people, by the people, for the people." With all this trust and faith abounding in spite of glitches, why aren't we happier?

Reclaiming Our Own Power

Simply put, we have given away our power. How many times in the New Testament is Jesus quoted as saying, "Your faith has made you whole"? How many times did he heal because of the great faith the people had in him? Let's count:

1. Jesus marveled at the centurion's faith.
2. He saw the friends' faith and cured the man of palsy.
3. He spoke to the woman with the issue of blood: "*Thy faith hath made thee whole.*"
4. He spoke to the woman with the demented daughter: "O woman, *great is thy faith:* be it unto thee even as thou wilt."
5. He said to blind Bartimaeus: "Go thy way; *thy faith hath made thee whole.*"
6. He spoke to the Samaritan leper: "Arise, go thy way: *thy faith hath made thee whole.*"

Yet Jesus never claimed to be the ultimate healer; it was the people's faith in him, as their spiritual leader, that facilitated the cures, or their false beliefs that they were being punished for their sins, which Jesus healed by relieving their sense of guilt.

In all cases, the people healed allowed their bodies to resume their natural state of good health, which had always been an option, once their misconceptions were corrected. The power resides in our own bodies; they know how to maintain a state of wellness, of wholeness, when they are not commanded otherwise ("Both of my parents died of heart failure"). The power resides in *our* creative capability, not in Lourdes or charms or even Jesus, who served as a focus for the commoner's "doorway to the divine," an age-old spiritual practice which is still popular today with Jews and Muslims.[253] Our creative power is embedded in the Goodness, the Godness, that upholds all life. The power is in us and all around us—in the *whole* One—unseen but accessible when we become aware of our intimate residence within God. Spiritually, Jesus mended the divine/human separation that the afflicted felt. Physically, he may have healed by raising the frequencies of those ailing to match his own, so they once again resonated with the divine frequency.

> Imagine yourself as a sponge, absorbing the divine life that surrounds you every moment.
>
> Neil Douglas-Klotz
> *Sufi Book of Life*

However it works, we possess a creativity that can be used to prosper in all areas. Indeed, *prosper* literally means "to go with hope before us." We have faith in the Source that causes us to hope and, ultimately, to succeed. When we live mindful of the power within us (remember the trillion volts) and when we deep-in-the-heart trust that *goodness is all there is*, then goodness flows out of us and to us; the emission creates a vacuum that keeps us in a circulating current.

Our Own Personal Time (and Space) Machines

Einstein called space and our perceived flow of time illusions, characteristics of consciousness that can be manipulated. We can use time and space as easily as we use any tools, whether we choose a hammer or a pen (which, of course, can carry us into prehistoric ages or incredible worlds of the future). He illustrated the elasticity of time by pointing out that an hour spent holding your girlfriend's hand seems like a second, but a second spent touching a hot stove seems like an hour.[254] Another quick illustration of the elastic nature of time and space is—quick, now!—think of the dinosaurs. Now picture Frodo's hole on the movie set in New Zealand or the Great Wall of China. That was easy, wasn't it, to travel back in time and halfway around the world?

We experience the quantum quality of time when we go backward in time (memories) and forward (daydreams or fearful envisionings). In this way, we also demonstrate the quark's ability to be in two places at the same time! As Einstein mentioned, we unwittingly slow down time, like when we're dreading an upcoming test, or speed it up on joyous occasions, which we wish would never end. There is also the common experience of being so "wrapped up" in a good movie or a fascinating book that time seems to slow down or stop.

> If the 'present moment' elsewhere in the Universe depends on how you are moving, a whole span of 'presents' must exist, some of which will lie in what you regard as your past, some in your future, as seen by different observers. In other words, moments of time cannot be things which "happen" everywhere at once, in which only the unique present is "real." Rather, time is extended in some way, like space; which particular distant event any given observer regards as happening in the mysterious moment of "now" is purely relative.
>
> So does the future, in some sense, already exist "out there?"
>
> Paul Davies and John Gribbin
> *The Matter Myth*

These are examples of the psychological manipulation of time, but time itself is a slippery sort of element we little comprehend. When God proclaims, "Let there be light," the Hebrew word translated as "let there be" actually means "Let there have been light" because Hebrew has no present tense. The implication is difficult for Westerners to understand, but Hebrew connects the future with the past. If the "light *was*" in Genesis, then the future influenced the past, creating opportunities in our right-now.[255] This ancient Hebrew concept is pure quantum physics!

I thought about the future calling to the past, like full-grown plants calling to their seeds to grow into themselves. Or me standing at the top of a hill, where I put a soccer ball on the slope and it rolls downhill. The bottom of the hill is like the *future* attracting the ball to it. Wow.

Try It Yourself

Imagine driving a car down the road. You're not paying attention to the scenery; you just cruise along on "autopilot." When you look through the windshield, you see the future; when you glance in the rearview mirror, you see your past. Ahead on the horizon you spot an ugly thunderstorm, behind you've left a car wreck of a childhood, and at the moment, your love life's a total traffic jam. But what if you make a left turn onto another road? Now you're looking at a different probable future—*and* a different probable past.

Irwin Thompson
Pacific Shift

What it comes down to is, space and time are about as real as the words *space* and *time* printed on this page. They only make sense to someone who has an idea of what they mean, and they become real only *because* of this preconceived idea. As our concepts expand, the qualities invested in space and time also expand—because we determined what their attributes were in the first place and are now realizing that space-time is the stuff dreams are made of.

To me this means that, due to the mental maneuverability of time and space and the future's influence on the past, I can call on my best possible "future" self* to reach back to me and aid my progress, lesson by lesson, day by day.

I think poet Rumi understood the future's effect on the present when he wrote: "Grapes want to turn into wine."[256]

[*Not only my best possible future self, but also other selves. According to Hugh Everett's "Many Worlds Interpretation," every time I make a decision, the entire universe replicates itself and contains a different "me" choosing an alternate action. I sense that his theory is valid. When I was born two months early, the obstetrician stopped the nurse from administering drops of silver nitrate in my infant eyes, a standard practice in the 1950s. He said the drops would have blinded me. At that moment, the universe split into another where the nurse did apply the drops and that baby became blind. In another dimension, I have a blind self living out what has become *her* life. Although a dimension apart, my sighted-self and blind-self still affect each other, helping or hindering, and swapping talents.]

Seventeen

Miracles are the way life is meant to work all the time.

Each miracle writes for us in small letters something that God has already written in letters almost too large to be noticed across the whole canvas of Nature.

C. S. Lewis
Miracles

What If Paranormal is Actually Sub-standard?

One afternoon a man was sitting on his deck playing poker with his dog. Their neighbor leaned over the fence and watched them play a couple of hands. Finally she couldn't help but exclaim, "That's the most incredible thing I've ever seen, a dog playing poker. What a miracle!"

"Not really," said the man, raking in the pot. "Charlie never wins—he wags his tail when he gets a good hand."

Hebrew has no word for "miracle." The parting of the Red Sea was accepted as a normal part of life. I wonder when we westerners stopped viewing miracles—*magic*—as natural occurrences in our world.

> There are two ways to live your life. One is as though nothing is a miracle. The other is as if everything is. I believe in the latter.
>
> Albert Einstein
>
> We either see the evidence of God everywhere, or nowhere . . . let us regard life, not as an isolated miracle in an otherwise clockwork universe, but as an integral part of the cosmic miracle.
>
> Paul Davies
> *God and the New Physics*
>
> Nothing may truly be said to be a 'miracle' except in the profound sense that everything is a miracle . . . The so-called miraculous powers of a great master are a natural accompaniment to his exact understanding of subtle laws that operate in the inner cosmos of consciousness.
>
> Yogananda
> *Autobiography of a Yogi*

Often we fail to notice the miracles that light our lives because we're focused on the canceled game, the small pot in the kitty, the lousy cards from "the luck of the draw." We expect a miracle to be *deus ex machina*, Superman coming to the rescue or a divine event that supercedes natural laws, but miracles actually work "inside the system." Quantum God's system, that is. If miracles seem so, well, *miraculous* to us, it's only because we're operating on a substandard level, so that when we do experience normal Reality (with a capital "R")—which is our birthright—we call it "paranormal."

> A miracle . . . reminds the mind that what it sees is false . . . To you the miracle cannot seem natural, because what you have done to hurt your mind has made it so unnatural that it does not remember what is natural to it.
>
> *A Course in Miracles*

I was newly out of school, out of work, and out of food. I felt as if God had lost me, as if I'd slipped through a celestial crack and had fallen into darkness. I felt abandoned by God, and that feeling was exactly what was keeping me isolated in my "small self."

We can begin to accept our true Identity by not letting our minds be limited by the body and by suspending belief in the "laws" our bodies obey. For example, we believe our bodies are subject to disease and decline. We believe we need air to breathe as long as our feet are firmly rooted to the ground. Yet Trailanga was an Indian siddha who was born in 1601 and did not die until 1888—he lived nearly three centuries in perfect health, even after digesting poison. Hundreds of Hindus often witnessed Trailanga spending hours submerged beneath the surface of the Ganges River or days floating above it.[257] We are more than mere bodies.

In Reality, miracles occur as a matter of course. If we could see other dimensions, we might even find that everything is *dependent* on miracles. Whatever and wherever it is, miracles happen all the time to "plain" people in our familiar four-dimensional life on Earth.

THE QUANTA OF MIRACLES

What's so miraculous about miracles?

As depicted in Monty Python's *The Life of Brian*, Jesus wasn't the only miracle-worker of his time; people back then *expected* miracles. To the Jews, miracles merely indicated a beneficent God working in people's lives.[258] So why are people now so amazed when we hear of or experience a miracle?

Computer images from ones and zeroes. Self-healing DNA. Manmade diamonds. Remote viewing. Dogs who can detect cancer. Cats who alleviate their owners' illnesses. Are these scenarios not miracles?

Have we become so inured to Newton's out-dated clockwork cosmology that miracles *must* be seen as extraordinary events because they *seem* to contradict the laws of science we know? Well, science is changing, broadening our ideas of just what is possible, and yet there's so much we still do not know. We don't even know what questions are the best ones to ask.

When Einstein walked through Princeton, children would flock to see the old man waggle his ears at them. One day Einstein suddenly burst out laughing at a five-year-old. The boy's mother asked her child what he had said, and the boy replied, "I asked him if he'd gone to the bathroom today." Einstein hastened to tell the horrified mother, "I'm glad someone asked me a question I can answer."[259]

Quantum physics has shown us that *the questions we ask determine what we see*. So how do we define what falls outside the laws of nature?

The known laws of nature are (as of now) based upon quantum probabilities, and probabilities are drawn from a cornucopia of all possibilities. Yogananda said that people who know our world as "an idea in the Divine Mind" can do anything with the body, which is only condensed or frozen energy.[260] The yogi was standing on solid scientific ground, because one scientific definition of matter is light that's been trapped by gravity.[261]

Ordinary Miracles

A miracle is something we want to happen. The Kabbalah would call them coincidences arranged by Providence. I call them Miracles of Coordination.

> I think the real miracle is not to walk either on water or in thin air, but to walk on earth. Every day we are engaged in a miracle which we don't even recognize: a blue sky, white clouds, green leaves, the black, curious eyes of a child—our own two eyes. All is a miracle.
>
> Thich Nhat Hanh
> *The Miracle of Mindfulness*

What about "ordinary miracles?" It's a miracle to walk on the green earth, when we're feeling truly alive in the present moment. Another miracle is looking at life through a child's eyes, when we slough off the worries of adulthood and give free rein to our sense of playfulness and wonder. As Alice says in David Shannon's delightful book, *Alice the Fairy*, "With my wand, I can make leaves fall from trees." (She hits them with her wand.)

To Sister Mary Faith Schuster, OSB, *everything* she experienced was a miracle deserving of her awe and gratitude—even overcooked convent hamburgers, photographs cracked and yellowed by half a century's passing, and the stranger who offered her a needed ride back to the convent. She lived happily through each day because of the way she viewed life. We too can learn to look at our lives in the same manner.

I realized that if it were not for my mis-beliefs ("Life is hard), fears ("How can I support myself?"), and judgments ("If I get help, it'll have strings attached to it"), I would always be *aware* of the state of grace I live in. I would feel blessed and never afraid. I would be working with nature, with the Earth, with all species in a spirit of *biohood*, as partners and not as adversaries. (For a heartwarming story of cross-species bonding and love, see Christian the lion on youtube.) And I would be inviting synchronicities into my life.

Synchronicities, miracles, and answers to our prayers can *not* come to us if we're afraid of change. When her husband moved out, Carole slid into a depression that left her paralyzed. She lived through dull days and lonely nights, when it was hard to make decisions as small as choosing between peanut butter or tuna. Then one day she rushed into my kitchen exclaiming that she'd found a part-time job at a bookstore. She had also adopted a dog from the animal shelter, and she'd made new friends at work. "Isn't life wonderful?" she exclaimed.

I smiled, delighted at the turn-around, but also amazed at the thought that Carole's life hadn't changed—her husband was still gone—but she had changed how she responded to life.

At times the miracle is a change within us and our outlook on life; at other times it's something that does *not* happen that prevents a disaster. These "hidden miracles" result from a string of synchronicities orchestrated by divine management: The broken shoelace that causes us to run late, missing the car crash that occurred where we would have driven, had we left on time. The off-hand comment overheard in a crowd that gives hope to a stranger teetering on the brink of suicide. The man who stopped to have his eyeglass frames adjusted and so was not at his desk at the World Trade Center the morning of 9/11. The teacher (parent, friend, counselor) whose small act of caring causes a student to choose school over dropping out.

We used to call these miracles coincidences. Sometimes we'd hint at divine machinations and call them "providential," which gave a nod to divine intervention. Nowadays we use the term synchronicity. Synchronicities are noticeable miracles, although the intricate web of "happenings" that generate just one synchronicity is so detailed that it would be beyond our comprehension, even if we learned all the steps behind it.

Contrary to custom, I rose early one Saturday morning. Cecilia was getting married, and her best friend and I had volunteered to pick up the wedding cake and transport it to the chapel 90 miles away. The bakery was located in a part of the city we'd never visited before, but I followed directions, and we got the cake loaded in the back of the van. The entrance ramp appeared where it should be. And then I heard *ping, ping, ping.* "Do you hear that, Janelle?" I asked. *Ping, ping, ping.* The needle on the temperature gauge was ominously pointing to HOT. I bypassed the interstate and pulled into a gas station.

Well, no, not a gas station with a proper mechanic, only a convenience store. But a man came over and suggested adding antifreeze and then helped with the task. Needle upright, we returned to the road and pointed the van toward the highway. Again the *ping* sounded, and again I pulled off into a parking lot. And sent out an SOS. The bride's mother, Jeannie, dispatched a knight in a white Suburban; the ceremony went off without another snag. But how would we get back to the city, and would my van run?

We were assigned to a cousin . . . who just *happened* to be a *mechanic*. Without breakfast, without lunch, without a nibble of wedding cake, we left with Neil-the-mechanic right after Cecilia and Andy said "I do," reaching Kansas City just before sunset. Neil quickly deciphered the problem (a malfunctioning thermostat), drove us to the auto parts store a block away (still open at 7 p.m. on a Saturday night), offered to pay for the spare part, drove back to the disabled van, and changed out the frozen thermostat. Though hungry and spent, I nodded in appreciation of the string of synchronicities visited upon us that day: We could have been stranded on some remote stretch of the highway. The van might have overheated on the way home during the mid-night hours. Cousin Neil could have decided not to travel 300 miles to attend the wedding. Janelle and I might have stayed for the reception and missed the closing hour of the auto parts store. The cake could have melted. Rejoicing across the miles, we experienced one miracle on top of another, made all the more probable because "what we put our attention on is what we get more of"—because we had felt grateful every step of the long way there-and-back-again.

> What we call chance may be the logic of God.
>
> Georges Bernanos
> quoted by Donald Spoto in *The Hidden Jesus: A New Life*

Green Doesn't Always Mean Go

Sometimes we don't see the miracles coming. In the high heat of Kansas one June, I arrived at church to collect my daughter, Merrie Kate, and six other children: Chelsea, Janelle, Hadley, Sean, Cecilia and her friend. Bible School had run longer than usual, and the hungry children jostled for window seats in the station wagon. I wanted to rush the bickering children home, quickly feed them mac and cheese, and settle them all down for quiet time.

Rushing didn't work; a red light stopped us as soon as we left the parking lot. We were first in the left-turn lane to turn east onto a busy thoroughfare, but when the green arrow lit up, I hesitated. Suddenly, a truck and trailer coming from the east barreled through the intersection, running its red light.

A hush fell over the children as I explained in reverent tones that a miracle had saved all our lives. They were not too young to understand and to feel a sense of awe.

"Sometimes," I told them as we ate our macaroni, "we need to slow down and let miracles catch up with us."

A Course in Miracles affirms that one miracle is no harder to achieve than any other miracle, and this even applies to the aspect of time, because miracles are wrought outside the framework of time, undoing the past in present time.[262] Quantum physics supports this statement and has mathematically proven what is called "time symmetry," which confirms that time doesn't just go forward.[263]

The past only exists because of electromagnetic patterns in the brain, and these patterns change constantly.[264] Nevertheless, we define ourselves by time and space. "I'm 37 years old," we might say, or "I live at 5 East Main Street." Frequently we place ourselves firmly in the space-time system: "I'll meet you at the restaurant at Ninth and Central at 8 p.m." It works well enough in our day-to-day lives, but there is a deeper reality—or unreality—to space-time. Einstein wrote that "The past, present and future are only illusions, however persistent."[265]

> Beneath the regular inches and seconds that mark off everyday life, space and time ooze like mud—altering their appearance depending on the motion of whoever happens to be looking.
>
> K. C. Cole
> *Hole in the Universe*

As Radar explained to Frank Burns during "Mail Call" at the fictional MASH 4077, "By the time their now becomes our now, this'll be then." And Radar was only speaking of our normal conception of time, much less Einstein's radical notion of time.

Rewriting History

We make the distinction of future time, past time, present time; but in mathematical equations involving velocity, the figures do not distinguish between forward-moving time and backward-moving time. Whether the mathematician uses t or $-t$, the equation remains the same. Although we have never seen a shattered vase piece itself back together, mathematics shows neither space nor time exist for a photon.[266]

At the University of Texas at Austin, John Wheeler set up his Delayed-Choice experiment using photons or electrons that can pass through a particular apparatus in either of two different ways; one way would show the moving energy acting like a particle, the other would show the energy acting like a wave. The operator decided which path the photon would take *after* the photon had already passed through the double-slit system; the operator's decision was then reflected in actuality. The decision of the experimenter determined whether or not the light was behaving in the manner of particle or wave *in the past*.[267]

I mentioned earlier that I had suffered from a chronic bleeding kidney for all my adult life, and when the HMO lost my medical records, wiping out the physical paper record, it also wiped out the disease *in the past*, as far as I was concerned. Such an attitude is a regular procedure in China. Braden explains this process by reporting about the Chinese physicians who made a patient's cancerous tumor disappear, *simply by affirming that the tumor never existed.* With their repeated phrase "Already gone," in less than three minutes they completely eradicated a woman's tumor; on videotape we actually watched the tumor shrink down to nothing on the ultrasound monitor. How was this possible? The healers reached back into the patient's past to *rewrite history*.[268] At that time in the past before the tumor formed, they chose for their patient the possibility of good health that already existed.

Wheeler's Delayed Choice and Princeton's REG experiments, my personal cure and Chinese medicine prove in a spectacular manner how our actions in the present moment can affect the past, even back to how the universe looked billions of years ago.

> It is wrong to think of that past as "already existing" in all detail. The "past" is theory. The past has no existence except as it is recorded in the present. By deciding what questions our quantum registering equipment shall put in the present we have an undeniable choice in what we have the right to say about the past.
>
> John Wheeler
> John Archibald Wheeler and Wojciech Hubert Zurek
> *Quantum Theory and Measurement*

Twenty-five hundred years before we discovered quantum physics, the *Tao Te Ching* proclaimed, "The Tao . . . is always present within you. You can use it any way you want" (#6). Both mathematics and quantum mechanics show that new beliefs can and do alter the past (the memories of which change with us). We see "right before our eyes" the present affecting the past in the spontaneous disappearance of cancer, where new cellular memories replace old cellular memories.[269] Braden calls these reversals in the past "choice points" where the medical practitioners didn't try to heal the patient of the existing disease, but instead made a quantum leap to claim a reality that had been a "passed" possibility.[270] "Miracle" healings are merely demonstrations of not hindering nature.[271]

In other words, our bodies (and our entire reality) respond to what we imagine is—or was—real. We feel this for ourselves on mornings when we wake up tired, after having a dream where we were working hard. The action was located within the dream, but our sleeping bodies expended real energy while we were engaged in all that imaginary work.

Shaking Hands with a New-Old Star

In our participatory universe, the future and the past affect the present. In order to create an event, we need a wave traveling forward in time and a wave traveling backwards in time. For example, when we look at the clear nighttime sky and see a star 50 million light-years away, our act of seeing is *reaching into the past*, helping that star to exist 50 million years ago. The light wave from the star in its past moves forward in time, and the wave of our vision moves backward in time; together they create the star-to-us light.

We look up and expect to see stars. Our belief that stars twinkle in the night sky creates the thought, and the stars-in-the-sky thought travels at no-time speed and selects the possibility of "stars shining" from *potentia*. The actualized star then sends light forward to meet our eyes (or the tumor de-actualizes in the cancer patient), and we in the future have "shaken hands" with an object (or no-object) in our past.[272] The stargazer participates in the cycle necessary for a distant star's existence, which is completed by being observed. It is as if God caught hold of time and turned it back on itself to create eternity.[273]

These concepts turn our normal idea of cause and effect upside down and free us, individually and in unanimous groups, to decide beforehand what sort of event we choose to create. Child psychologists call this "foreshadowing." (So, when I feel a cold coming on, I immediately form the intention of *not* carrying that condition into the future, and turn my attention to what I *choose* to manifest; I claim my right to perfect health.) In his humorous manner, Douglas Adams wrote, "Very little of this is, however, at all comprehensible to anyone below the level of Advanced God . . ."[274] But Yogananda believed anyone is capable of making "miracles." He said that anyone who realizes the essence of creation is light is a miracle-maker.

> The impossible did not bother him unduly. If it could not possibly be done, then obviously it had been done impossibly. The question was how?
>
> Douglas Adams
> *The Long Dark Tea-Time of the Soul*

Unwittingly, our focus smushes light into the thing-forms of the universe—and our *awareness* of this procedure allows us to become deliberate miracle-workers. Real magicians. Masters. The night my energy partner spilled hot coffee on his hand, a nasty-looking blister formed immediately. After running cold water over the burn, I insisted we go into the healing room for a few minutes to pause, invite Spirit, heal, and "un-accident" ourselves. A couple of hours later I noticed with awe and joy that not only was there *no* blister on his hand but hardly even a pink spot to show where the burn had been! *We are miracle-makers.*

So there is a way to invite, to create miracles. We have heard that bad things happen to good people; on the flip side, good things happen to awe-ful people. Because we attract events at the same frequency we emit, the more often we're struck with wonder and stop to say, "Wow! . . . Thank you," the more often we'll find occasions to do so. Feelings of awe, appreciation, and gratitude perpetuate the cycle, so that we become caught up in a continuing circle of wondrous life.

Now is the time to claim our right to a higher standard of life, and when we do, miracles will literally become a matter-of-fact in our lives.

Eighteen

Let's do it—Now!

The rich man said to himself, "And I will say to my soul, Soul, thou has much goods laid up for many years; take thine ease, eat, drink and be merry." But God said unto him, "Thou fool, this night thy soul shall be required of thee . . ."

Luke 12:18-20 (KJV)

Living Now

My grandma Da—Frances Cain Baum to the rest of the world—used to tell us kids over and over again, "If you have something to do, *do* it!" Her corollary to this piece of advice was, "If you're going to do something, you might as well do it right the first time." And save yourself the trouble of having to do it again, she meant. It seemed that nearly every time I saw her when I was a teenager, Da would harp at me to get out into the yard and start pulling weeds. Well, Da, I've come to the point where I can't pass a weed, be it private, public, or corporate weed, without stooping down and pulling it. Pulling weedy thoughts out of the thoughts I habitually think is an ongoing process, too. One of the worst to get rid of has been "Life is too hard." The thistle of thought patterns for me.

The pilot addressed the passengers aboard his failing airplane. "I regret to inform you that we are going to crash."

A priest in the back row said, "Nothing can save us but God."

His seatmate said, "Yes, God can save us with a miracle!"

The plane continued to descend rapidly, and the layman grabbed the priest's arm. "Well, where's the miracle, Father?"

With calm eyes the priest looked at his distraught companion and held his hand. "The miracle is being at peace with what's happening, my son. Right here and right now."

How often are we at peace with what's happening? How often do we live in joy-filled moments? How often do we live this day as if it was the last day of our life? Da and my grandpa Rusty filled their days with fun and purpose and generosity. They used their time on earth well.

Go Wash Your Bowl

Are we spending our time as wisely as we spend our money?

> The concept of time is one of the great ways in which we are fooled. We believe that the past and the future are, as it were, more solid and of longer duration that the present. In other words, we live in a sort of hourglass with a big bulb at one end (the past) and a big bulb at the other end (the future); we are at the little neck in between, and we have no time.
>
> Alan Watts
> *Zen and the Beat Way*

We seem forever to "run short of time." We hang around "killing time," or feel the burden of "time on our hands." We "bide our time," take "time out," use "time-saving" appliances, and punch time cards. Without timing belts our cars won't run, and without setting our clocks to the correct time zone, our timetables would go kerflooey. We observe timeworn traditions and speak of eternal things as being "time out of mind." And yet, if we knew we were going to die in the next hour, would we regret that we had ever allowed time to drag by? Faced with imminent death, wouldn't we want to savor every instant? Smell new-mown grass one last time? See another dawn? Hug someone?

In her poem, "Speech to the Young: Speech to the Progress-Toward," Gwendolyn Brooks considered the way we "lose time" and advised her readers to

> Live not for battles won.
> Live not for the-end-of-the-song.
> Live in the along.

She meant to live *now*. Too often our minds are "there" and "then," but rarely are we thinking "right here, right now."

> . . . while you were looking ahead for something to happen, that was it! That was life!
>
> Clifford Odets
> quoted by Jessica Gribetz *in Wise Words*

We were experiencing one of the hottest summers on record, and I spent most of the time indoors. At first I completed projects, like recording shows off the DVR and putting together an alternative health guide, but the rest of my time was spent (wasted?) on television and computer MahJong.

How much time are we spending on self-evolution? How much time do we spend on activities we really enjoy? And are we having fun while we go about the business of living? One woman who had a near-death experience said that when she told the "being of light" before her that she had not danced enough, the spirit laughed and sent her back into her earthly body.[275]

The Kabbalah says that treating every moment as the chance to fulfill our purpose keeps us in the present, succeeding, and changing the world for the better.[276] What is our purpose? The basic Kabbalistic function of being a divine lucifer, a light-bearer and light-sharer, a beacon that strengthens the light in others, no matter how deeply hidden it may be? Each of us is only one person in the world, but we may be all the world to one person.

"I just arrived last night," a young monk once said to the master of the monastery. "What shall I do now?"

"Have you eaten your breakfast?" said Master Joshu.

The monk nodded.

Joshu said, "Then go wash your bowl."[277]

The master meant that even the most spiritual person must put his values to use within the world. Many of the people who have had near-death experiences say that after they traveled through a tunnel and were met by a being of light, they—not a judging God—reviewed their lives, and they were left with the question of how many times they showed love to others. The emphasis was on *how* they did the things they did. In their lives after the near-death experiences, they tended to touch more gently, speak more softly, act with more kindness, and live more vibrantly, more gratefully.

The Kansas City Star once asked its readers, "What would you do if you were God for a day?" I wrote the editor that a better question would be, "What am *I* doing?" God cannot end world hunger, put a stop to war, or totally alleviate human suffering without sabotaging our free will. But I can share a meal. I can refuse to participate in conflict. I can give someone a hug. I can stop feeling afraid. With even the smallest of actions, the intention to bless makes a difference in my own and others' lives.

I am often praying for others when I should be doing things for them. It's so much easier to pray for a bore than to go and see him.

C. S. Lewis
Letters to Malcolm: Chiefly on Prayer
quoted by Larry Dossey in *Prayer is Good Medicine*

Every Thought is a Prayer

> Throughout history, humans—whether through shamans invoking animal spirits or priests using the rites of the Christian church—have believed that the spirit world can influence events on Earth. Now, scientific studies are showing that our thoughts may indeed create our own reality. Bohr said reality was dependent on an "observer effect," that observation can influence events.
>
> *Curiosity*: "10 Biggest Questions Raised by Quantum Physics"
> at discover.com (September 4, 2011)

Some people believe that every thought we think, every word we utter is a prayer. Certainly, when we sigh, "Oh, God help me," or when we curse "Dammit!" we have used the name of God. And God's name cannot be used in vain; that is, *when we call, God listens*. We have a variety of prayers we use:

- Prayers of rote: "Now I lay me down to sleep . . ." and "Bless us, O Lord, for these, Thy gifts, which we are about to receive."

- "Let's Make a Deal" prayers: "Oh, God, if You help me through this, I'll never drink again." Dean Koontz's character, Odd Thomas, theorized that "You can con God and get away with it . . . if you do so with charm and wit. If you live your life with imagination and verve, God will play along just to see what outrageously entertaining thing you'll do next."[278]

- Prayers of supplication: "Please, God, bring her through this surgery." This type of prayer enhances our feeling of separation and disempowers us.

- Prayers of affirmation (usually unconsciously spoken): "Bless you!" after someone sneezes, or anytime we say, "I am . . ." as in "I'm going to climb that mountain!" or "I'm sick and tired of this s - - t." These "I am" statements are quite powerful, because we're declaring what we claim for ourselves.

- Mystical prayers: We become aware of being One with God.

- "Carrying an Umbrella" prayers: Like a playwright, we imagine a scene and write ourselves into it. Then we match our intention with action, like the woman who carries an umbrella during a drought. The monk Brother Lawrence believed that the time of business is no different than the time of prayer, that we are always in God's presence, and so our every action becomes a prayer.[279] The Buddhists refer to this state when they note that, although enlightened, we still have laundry to wash.

Even Jesus tended to dirty laundry; he ousted usurious moneychangers and championed women, slaves, children, and people ostracized by others, including tax collectors and lepers. He lived what he preached. So, too, did Nelson Mandela. And Mother Teresa, who roamed the streets of Calcutta, tending to the sick and the poor, and praying as she walked along.[280]

Yogananda was fond of saying that it was more difficult for the "householder," the ordinary person fully immersed in worldly life, to live a spiritual life than for the hermit who made a remote cave his home.[281] We're so busy! We're born. We live. We die (to this world).

The question is, do we live *consciously, intentionally*?

> Of so many great teachers I've met in India and Asia, if you were to bring them to America, get them a house, two cars, a spouse, three kids, a job, insurance, and taxes . . . they would all have a hard time.
>
> Pir Vilayat Khan
> quoted by Jack Kornfield in *After the Ecstasy, the Laundry*

During World War I, the students at the University of Berlin seized control of the campus. The faculty asked Einstein to help, and he and fellow physicist Max Born traveled through the irate coeds to mediate between students and the college officials. They were successful. These physicists who explored the secrets of the universe also put their time to practical use to save their university.

This was not the only time a scientist poked his head out of his laboratory to act as peacemaker. In 1933, when the Nazis declared a national boycott of Jewish stores, Erwin Schrödinger saw a gang of storm troopers beating some Jewish shopkeepers. The police were standing nearby, watching indifferently. Schrödinger (who was not Jewish) became irate and tried to reason with one of the storm troopers. What he got for his trouble was a beating himself, but he *tried*. He lived his humanity.[282]

Strange Numbers

No matter what large number we think of, we can add a 1 to it, then add another 1, and do this without end. The same goes for going backwards. Half of one is ½, and half of that is ¼, and so on. Numbers stretch to infinity. So there is no largest number we can plug into the t or $-t$ equation of time; time, therefore, is infinite.

Numbers are endless, and time too, but our physical bodies are not; sooner or later, entropy catches up with us. One nasty Iowa winter, a young woman in her first car, a light-weight Datsun, was edging along I-80 in zero visibility.

With the tail lights of the car ahead guiding her, she snaked through a full-blown blizzard—until her tires lost their tenuous traction on a strip of black ice and she slid into the ditch and snow four feet deep. The next week, she hit another patch of ice and ended up in a similar ditch. That young woman was me, and I came face to face with death and learned a lesson: I vowed to let the people I loved know how I feel.

We have to live before it's too late, before one small task grows into an overwhelming burden, an ever-growing heap of tasks that need to be done. A multitude of near-death experiences has been recorded, and they provide a "do it now" lesson for us. Without regret for the past, without worrying over the future, we are wise to stay in the present moment and to do it now—to dance and sing. To love and laugh. To blow the seeds off a dandelion, plant a tree, nurture a child, learn from an elder, share ourselves. With mindfulness.

In our society, remaining mindful and staying in the present can be difficult but not impossible, especially when we remember that 90% of the things we worry about never happen. Worrying sweeps us out of the present moment and plants us in a fearful future. In an episode of *All in the Family*, Edith comforts Archie with "Today is the tomorrow we worried about yesterday."[283] And today, her point was, that worry has not materialized. In the sixth chapter of Matthew, Jesus gives a poetic speech about why worry is unnecessary:

> Behold the fowls of the air: for they sow not, neither do they reap, nor gather into barns; yet your heavenly Father feedeth them. Are ye not much better than they?

> . . . Consider the lilies of the field, how they grow; they toil not, neither do they spin: And yet I say unto you, That even Solomon in all his glory was not arrayed like one of these. Wherefore, if God so clothe the grass of the field, which to day is, and to morrow is cast into the oven, shall he not much more clothe you, O ye of little faith? Therefore take no thought, saying, What shall we eat? or, What shall we drink? or, Wherewithal shall we be clothed? . . . for your heavenly Father knoweth that ye have need of all these things. But seek ye first the kingdom of God, and his righteousness; and all these things shall be added unto you. Take therefore no thought for the morrow: for the morrow shall take thought for the things of itself.

First we "seek the kingdom of heaven," because there *is* nothing else, really. Everything else is the illusion of the dream we're in.[284] How do we arrive at the kingdom of heaven? By cultivating a state of peace. Peace from worry, which sets up an energetic tangle of barbed wire, a barrier around us and the person or situation about which we're upset. Freedom from anxiety, which in fact amplifies disturbances in the energy field and reinforces the problems we're concerned about.[285] Worry and anxiety actually *feed* the problem, whatever it is. Remember, the energy of how we're feeling attaches itself to the outcome. As Tolkien's elves of Lothlorien told the Company, ". . . we put the thought of all we love into all we make." And their love imbued a kind of magic in the *lembas* and cloaks given to Frodo's group.[286] Peace, love, staying in the present, and trust are keys to the kingdom.

The power is within us, and *potentia* guarantees a host of opportunities. Whatever we do, we can be sure that if we do it in a way that's comfortable for us, we'll achieve better results than if we try to stuff ourselves into some pattern out of sync with our own nature. If "whatever works for you" were a keynote for our lives, it might keep us out of trouble when we're tempted (or suborned into) going along with the crowd.

Tolstoy once wrote a folk tale about *The Three Hermits*, friends who lived alone on an island. The local self-righteous bishop was worried about the hermits. He decided to travel out to the island to instruct them in proper prayers, for they knew only one: "We are three; Thou art Three. Have mercy on us!" The hermits respectfully listened to the bishop, who labored at his task. When he was finished and sailing away from the island, the bishop looked back toward the island and was amazed to see the three hermits walking across the waters.

"Father!" they called out as they approached the bishop's sailboat, "we've forgotten the prayers you taught us."

The astonished bishop humbly recommended the three men stick to their simple little prayer.[287]

If It **Is** *Broke, Fix It*

If what we're doing ain't workin', we gotta try something else. If our affirmation isn't bringing us health, wealth and happiness, maybe we need to look inside to see what beliefs are blocking the flow of Goodness. If we're not feeling peaceful, just what are we engaged in? Is the activity worth losing our peace of mind? It takes mindfulness to flip off the Autopilot switch and steer ourselves in another direction but, as Frost wrote, taking the road less traveled by can make "all the difference."

Sufis often begin a new activity by breathing the Arabic word *bismallah*, translated as:

We begin by remembering
the sound and feeling of the One Being,
the wellspring of love.
We affirm that the next thing we experience
shimmers with the light of the whole universe.[288]

This practice is rather like our common custom of saying grace before we eat a meal, when we feel grateful and bless the food and the company sharing it. We eat, drink, and be merry. We love and live and dance . . . now, before the opportunity has passed.

Anybody wanna waltz with me?

Nineteen

God-ing is a Multi-Level Process.

> Jesus said,
> "I am the way" (the *aum*)
> "the truth" (divine laws)
> "and the life" (life force).[289]

> John 14:6 (KJV)

Climbing the Stairs

Although Albert Einstein was a terrible student, he turned out to be a genius at math. Part of his talent came from his sense of wonder and his desire to discover what lay beneath the apparent world. When he was four or five, his father showed him a compass.

"Was ist das?" asked the excited little boy. "What is this? How does it work?"

Einstein called this encounter with magnetism his first miracle, and it made a deep and lasting impression on him. He felt that "something deeply hidden had to be behind things." [290]

There are four stair steps to that "something" in spiritual development.

- At the lowest level, we might complain, "It wasn't *my* fault!"
- At the second level, we take more responsibility: "I did it, but . . ." Following that "but" comes a variety of excuses: "The dog ate my homework" or "The other kids were doing it," or "That's how people get ahead—it's a dog-eat-dog world."
- When we climb to the next level, we see ourselves as a channel for the flow of divine or universal energy: "I am an instrument . . ."
- At the highest level, we know that we *are* what we desire. "I am _____." Peace. Compassion. Ingenuity. We become the embodiment of what we intend to manifest.

God designed our universe as a many-leveled creative process brimming with possibilities. For example, although a composer has only eight notes to an octave to work with, he still has as many octaves as the human ear is capable of hearing. The composer has various instruments she can include in her composition (including voices, clapping hands, stomping feet), and each instrument has its own certain tone or nature. Add to those possibilities the distinctive style of each musician, and the composer's options are almost innumerable.

Physicist Michio Kaku calls the universe a "symphony of strings," and says the mind of God is like "cosmic music vibrating through hyperspace." Sounds like Tolkien's creation-story, doesn't it? Kaku's scientific view coincides with the Vedantic picture of the Word, *Aum*, or the Holy Spirit being intoned throughout all we know.[291] Kaku adds, "Which raises another question: If the universe is a symphony of strings, then is there a composer?"[292]

The Principles of Orchestration

Imagine Quantum God (like Tolkien's Iluvatar) composing a symphony. First God creates the instruments and the musicians out of God's own all-pervasive substance, which maintains the elemental link of consciousness between Creator and Created. Then the musicians—the *godlings*—must mature, both in character and in talent so that, for instance, the violinists refrain from poking one another with mischievous bowing. Over the eons, God waits and watches, providing instruction here, encouragement there, without actually interfering with the individual musician's creative powers in the burgeoning symphony. God also shows discernment in withholding information until the best time, as in the conceit and manufacture of cannons, so the percussionists don't decimate the philharmonic with an ill-aimed cannonade.

The symphony is an on-going improvisation, created moment by moment and note by note, ever growing in harmony as each member learns to cooperate and resonate with or complement his neighbor, her section, and the rest of the orchestra. Through it all, God provides food, an auditorium for rehearsals, and temporary living quarters within the auditorium. Just like before the rehearsal began, God also provides, periodically, a vacation between the strenuous practices—a permanent Home where members once again become attuned to God's presence, since they tend to forget their God-connection and divine origin when they're so totally focusing their attention on the composition-in-the-making. (With this ultra-focus, some of the forgetful orchestra members decide that the auditorium exists without God's empowerment and that the symphony is *solely* a composition of their making. In spite of this misperception, it's only through the Life Force and the laws by which the Force acts that the instruments, musicians, and the structure are kept sound.)

Some of the laws are noticed by musicians, and some of the laws are still unknown. In fact, most principles cannot be discovered as long as the musicians in the auditorium forget their divine connection, the possibilities available to them, and their own unlimited creative abilities, all of which they remember when they return Home again.

In fact, few musicians realize until their Homecoming that other auditoriums also exist on other levels, and other symphonies. The instruments and costumes also come from another level and, from yet another level, the sheet music—blank pages, practice scales, and the hint of harmonies, which serve as inspiration—all of which are available to open-minded musicians.

The underlying organization was part of God's original layout, and it continues to provide for every possibility, every note and every rest, every coda and variation on a theme, so that when a cellist's C-string breaks, she "happens" to be sitting next to another cello player who has an extra set of strings to share. Or the clarinet player, who's beating himself up over a difficult passage, runs into a great master (lately returned from his stint with a touring company), who's delighted to mentor the promising young musician. God allows for any and every possible course of action, and *orchestrates* the synchronicities.

The cellist's life-lesson (the need to learn that help and friendship are only a neighbor away) initiated the very process that placed her in the best spot when her string broke. The clarinet player's unspoken desire to excel gave the Divine the green light to arrange a multitude of intricacies that enabled student and master to meet at the right time. But it was Quantum God Who *anticipated* these needs and desires, and Who laid the groundwork of that divine operating system outside space-time. It is our thoughts, desires, emotions, fears and worries, working on a physical level through energetic fields and frequencies that help or hinder God in our lives.

> With living systems, nobody would deny that an organism is a collection of atoms. The mistake is to suppose that it is nothing but a collection of atoms. Such a claim is as ridiculous as asserting that a Beethoven symphony is nothing but a collection of notes or that a Dickens novel is nothing but a collection of words. The property of life, the theme of a tune or the plot of a novel are what have been called "emergent" qualities. They only emerge at the collective level of structure.
>
> Paul Davies and John Gribbin
> *The Matter Myth*

Life is a multi-level process: We have a physical and a non-physical (quantum) system, both of which God designed and continues to power from yet another system. The following table shows how the Jews, Christians, Hindus, Taoists, and quantum science view the Multi-Level Process.

THE MULTI-LEVEL PROCESS

Judeo-Christian	*Hindu, Tao, etc.*	*Bohm's Order*
The Godhead *Ein Sof*[a] Mystic Abyss	Nirguna Brahman Buddhist Void (God without form) the *Tao* before it's named	holomovement (source-ground)
God the Father/[b] Mother Yahweh; Elohim	*Sat* Brahma(Creator)/ Vishnu (Preserver)/ Shiva (Transformer)/ Allah[c]	superimplicate (organizing level)
God the Son/ Messiah	*Tat* Christ Buddha avatars Tao's "ten thousand things"	explicate (unfolded order)
God the Holy Spirit[d] Shekhina (feminine indwelling spirit)	*Aum; logos; Tao* Christ- or Buddha- consciousness Brahman (cosmic consciousness/ Atman[e], the Self or soul)	implicate (enfolded order; *potentia*; morphogenetic fields beyond time)

---

[a] Cooper: Kabbalists teach that the very first line of Genesis has been mistranslated. Instead of "In the beginning, God created the heavens and the earth," the Hebrew words can be read as "With a beginning, [It] created God (Elohim), the heavens, and the earth." *Ein Sof* came first, and created Nothingness before creating God. *Ein Sof* is an ongoing process. (c.f. *Zohar* I:15a) The first line of the creation story can be represented in mathematical terms as a natural progression. Nothing precedes zero. Zero represents beginning. God is one, heaven and earth are two . . . space is three. Thus, *Ein Sof* precedes and must first create nothingness before the names of God. (Cooper, pp. 66-7, 310)

[b] Cooper: As long as we relate to God as Father and we as children, we sustain the dysfunctional paternalistic model in which Father knows best. We not only remain alienated with a sense of abandonment, we relinquish our personal sense of responsibility. We think that Father will take care of everything. (Cooper, p. 73)

Qualities	*Analogy*
all-inclusive spectrum of consciousness	Non-Being without form, but not Nothingness; *the Nameless*
One; Unity, (unmanifest organizer of *potentia* and all other levels	*ocean;* All-Being; All That Is (a pyramidal gestalt of consciousness)
"Only begotten" manifestation appearing as the separated "Many" (physical Creation)	*droplets*
the divine vibration that upholds all of Creation; (alive, conscious, joyful); the divine Ground; the Voice for God	*wave*

---

[c] Douglas-Klotz: The final H of *Allah* affirms . . . something not heard or pronounced, the life behind all life, without name and form and beyond all our ideas of the divine. As one Sufi writer commented, "Allah" is really not "god"; that is, Allah points to a being that is beyond humanly constructed images, ideals, and names. (Douglas-Klotz, *Sufi Book of Life*, p. 5)

[d] Elaine Pagels, *The Gnostic Gospels*: In the *Gospel of Thomas*, Jesus contrasts his earthly parents, Mary and Joseph, with his divine Father—the Father of Truth—and his divine Mother, the Holy Spirit . . . So, according to the *Gospel of Philip*, whoever becomes a Christian gains "both father and mother" for the Spirit (*ruah*) is "Mother of many." (p. 62)

[e] The Katha Upanishad: Atman, the Spirit, is smaller than the smallest atom, greater than the vastness of space. (Novak, p. 12)

Table information from: *Autobiography of a Yogi*, p. 144-5; *Bridging Science and Spirit*, pp. 69, 72; *Dialogues with Scientists and Sages*, p. 90, Wikipedia, and *A Course in Miracles*, pp. 67-69

All the "ten thousand things," including the book we're holding, the chair we're sitting in and the floor supporting the chair, the Force that created the things we know about, plus other unknown realms are beings that flowed out of the Godhead's state of Non-Being. But Non-Being is *not* nothing; It just has no form we can slap a label on.

To put it another way, let's suppose Lake Superlative is the source of the Bios River. The lake lies within the *implicate* order, the realm of the quantum wave function; it's a pool of possibilities outside of time. The Bios River flows from the implicate order into the *explicate* order, into our world and our progression through time. The lake was formed by Gaia, the *superimplicate* order, and by the condensation/evaporation processes that keep it full of energy—the laws that govern our universe. It is Quantum God (the *holomovement*) that has set up this multi-level system, and we—using our godlike creative energies—contribute to how and where the river flows. At some point, using imagination and intelligence, we might dig trenches that irrigate vast fields. At other times, smallness of spirit builds up eddies and dams that cripple but can never entirely cut off the flow; the current merely dives underground, without disappearing altogether.[293]

The Bios River also gives birth to many streams of consciousness, few of which we ever explore and some of which actually feed into other great lakes in parallel universes or totally different non-physical systems. But our focus on the physical traps us at the physical level; only Quantum God is large enough to oversee all the parts the holomovement encompasses.

God, however, *never* violates our free will. *We* make the choices—what notes to play, what dams to build—and our choices set in motion divine workings that coordinate details, manifesting everything in the physical realm. We are bobbing in quantum *potentia*.

We are always connected by non-local mind to the wisdom (which we may or may not heed) and to love and emotional support. Even when our choices lead us astray, here comes a detour at our dead end which, if we choose to travel it, puts us back on a spiritually progressive track.

Life is a Verb

Maybe the best way to think about God is a process of *God-ing*, and the best way for us to make progress is by *goding*.[294] Which is as easy as maintaining mindfulness and remembering that we are powerful creators and that we affect All. Why? Because Reality is a multi-leveled, multi-dimensional essence whose levels and dimensions and constituents influence one another.

What this means, for example, is that if two people come together in love, at that moment and at other levels . . .

- a hydrogen atom marries two oxygen atoms and gives birth to a molecule of water . . .
- an infant star flares out . . .
- the gravitational fields of two planets attract each other . . .
- two galaxies merge, and
- a black hole changes into a white hole.

And these are only *this universe's* possibilities. [295] Other universes, strange dimensions, alternate realities—everything in the Mystic Abyss affects everything else. The notes in our symphony shine like stars in other realities.

So what unseen off-shoot does a roomful of laughter produce in the ever-broadening psychological and spiritual levels of Quantum God? The music of the spheres. The song of the angels. The creation of new galaxies and other universes . . . The lives we live.

They're all a cooperative create-ing.

Twenty

Change is the only unchanging aspect of life.

If our senses were fine enough, we would perceive the slumbering cliff as a dancing chaos.

Nietzsche

Taxes Notwithstanding

Change is the only unchanging part of life (except, perhaps, for taxes, which appear a constant in our lives). Change is expressed in Japanese Zen as "Not always so." Zen says that once we realize everything changes, we attain the composure that places us in Nirvana.[296] Or the kingdom of heaven. Or the ever-flowing Tao. Nothing stands still, not even the immobile Royal Guards in front of Windsor Palace, for they are moving through the galaxy via our earthen spaceship.

We change moment by moment. Every seven years, almost all the cells in our bodies have renewed themselves. We grow new skin each week, and the air we breathe changes with every breath.[297] The brain's neurons live and die in nanoseconds, hormones change rapidly—even DNA, as we have seen, need not be permanent when we center ourselves in high-frequency emotions.

The boy Abraham wanted to find God. He looked at the sparkling stars and said, "You are my Lord." Then the clouds shifted, and out came the full moon, bigger and brighter than any star.

"You are my Lord!" young Abram told the moon. When the sun rose and the moon and stars disappeared, Abram cried, "Oh, Sun, how great you are! You are my Lord!" But he changed his mind with nightfall, when the sun disappeared.

"My Lord," Abram realized, "is the One who changes things and who brings them back. My Lord is the One behind all changes."

James Fadiman and Robert Frager
Essential Sufism

Everything changes, including Quantum God. As soon as I say, "God is
_____," God has already expanded in an ongoing explosion of creation.[298]
But God is perfect, I was taught, unchanging in perfection. With such a
portrait, however, are we not painting God in our own idealized image? If
this picture of a changing God violates our image of changeless Perfection,
maybe our definition of perfection on the divine level needs to be overhauled.
As humans, we consider perfection as the final step in a serial process, the
stage where "it can't get any better than this."

"Better" is a clue that we've reverted to mundane vocabulary and fallen
back on the polar definition of "good." God's goodness extends beyond
our comprehension and beyond any attempt to capture it in words, which
themselves are only symbols for our experiences. God-essence changes as
our understanding of God-in-our-image changes, and our idea of God matures
as we as a race grow into spiritual maturity. Moreover, the Aramaic word
translated as "perfect" also and more understandably means "all-embracing."[299]
God is all-embracing? Now, that makes sense.

Lose Something Everyday

Change is the only unchanging part of our lives, and how glad we can be
for that! While one joy may fade (making room for another joy to unfold), so
too can we count upon sun after storm, relief after disaster, and some sort of
aid any time we ask for it. In her poem, "One Art," Elizabeth Bishop writes,

> The art of losing isn't hard to master;
> so many things seem filled with the intent
> to be lost that their loss is no disaster.

Bishop's second verse advises us to "Lose something every day . . ."[300]
Loss is an ongoing theme for the spiritually wise, from Buddhists, who claim
that "letting go" is the key to happiness, to modern-day sages like Victoria
Moran, Deepak Chopra, and Dr. Wayne Dyer. Dyer wrote that being attached
to something is the surest way to guarantee you never get enough.[301] Bohm
believes that intelligent living means living as free from the past as possible.[302]
Jesus, too, spoke of attachment when he mentioned the rich man on his camel.
The eye of the needle was a small door in the large city gates that allowed
people to enter, but a camel—especially one laden with bags and wares—
would stand too tall and too wide to fit through the man-sized doorway.

In the walled city of Athens, Socrates often visited the marketplace, telling
his students he loved to see all the things he was happy without.[303] Without the
burdens of emotional baggage and fiercely grasped possessions, we become
light enough to *fly* over the wall. Spirit is light!

Sometimes our idea of what constitutes treasure needs refining. Once a wealthy man died and found himself standing outside the Pearly Gates, where he asked St. Peter if he could bring in his riches.

"No," said St. Peter, "you can't take anything with you."

"But I worked so hard," protested the man. "I earned everything I have."

"I assure you, you don't need your riches here."

"Now, look," said the wealthy man, "I insist—right down to the last gold ingot."

"All right, all right." St. Peter relented.

The man draped his jacket over his treasure and pushed a wheelbarrow through the gate. It was hard going over the lush grass, and he'd only made a little headway before he met a jogger.

"Welcome," he said. "What do you have there?" Before the rich man could object, the jogger peeked underneath the jacket. "Oh," he said, looking disgusted. "Paving stones!"

There's nothing wrong with using appliances and cars, valuing heirlooms, or cherishing people and happy memories; the danger comes only when we lose the ability to live happily without them. Desires are healthy motivators that move us from one level of consciousness to another, but they become addictions when they change our nature and make us obsessive.[304]

Jesus said wherever our treasure is, that's where our hearts are, and Rumi told us to look within if we want to find the greatest treasure.[305] Two thousand years later, one wise creature of our age, master Yoda, advised *Star Wars* fans to "Train yourself to let go of everything you fear to lose."[306] Thank you, George Lucas.

Making Sense of the "Bad" Things

So much for pleasant things—but what about unpleasant or downright nasty events? Well, I know that because I've gone hungry, I feel compassion for the 16 million people who die of starvation every year and I share whatever food I have. Because I was nearly homeless, I contribute to homeless shelters. Because I have lost people I love, I understand others who are grieving. Suffering may not be good for us, but it does teach compassion.

> The believer in God has to answer the question of why there is evil and cruelty in the world. But the atheist has a more difficult challenge. He has to explain why there is love, honesty, generosity, courage, and altruism in the world, and why it feels so good and so right when we let those qualities into our lives . . . they are things that we do, and when we do them, God is present in our lives.
>
> Harold Kushner
> *Who Needs God*

In the wake of the Asian tsunami in late 2004, the president of the Heartland Muslim Council was quoted in *The Kansas City Star* as saying, "There's a reason, but we don't always know what the reason is. You have to let go of the constant desire to try to control it and to know," and she added that the disaster caused us to focus our energies on helping one another.[307]

While changes may seem to be disasters or misfortunes, they do bring the chance to experience things we could not experience any other way. Life is not about what happens to us; life's only meaning is the meaning we assign to it.

After eighteen years in a Chinese labor camp, a Tibetan monk appeared before the Dalai Lama, who asked him, "Were you ever in danger?"

"Yes," the gentle man replied. "Several times I was in danger of losing compassion for my captors."

The monk, we think, would have been justified in feeling angry and bitter about his imprisonment and the way his warders treated him, yet he opted for a higher truth, an unprogrammed response. He must know that we can only be hurt by our own thoughts, and our thoughts determine how we choose to respond to any situation.

> Nothing can hurt you unless you give it the power to do so.
>
> Anger cannot occur unless you believe that you have been attacked, that your attack is justified in return, and that you are in no way responsible for it . . . What can be expected from insane premises except an insane conclusion?"
>
> You cannot *be* attacked, attack *has* no justification, and you *are* responsible for what you believe.
>
> Assault can ultimately be made only on the body . . . anything that is destructible cannot be real. Its destruction, therefore, does not justify anger . . .
>
> Teach only love, for that is what you are.
>
> *A Course in Miracles*

Naturally, there are times when we feel like grieving, or when we feel angry or lost, and those emotions must be acknowledged before they can fade. Lost love hurts. Cruelty tends to breed anger. And disregarding our connection to others and to the Divine leaves us feeling hopeless, helpless, powerless. Maybe the best way to ease pain, as when a child falls and skins his knee, is distraction. A joke, a hug, an activity—anything to *redirect* attention.

I was used to raising our sons when Merrie Kate came into our lives. Soon after her birth, a batch of little girls joined our childcare family, and I learned how girls' sensibilities differ from boys'. Teaching Sean and Tad not to go running into the street involved purple prose including two-ton vehicles, getting squashed pancake-flat, and blood oozing all over the concrete. Oh, but little girls require much gentler tactics.

Often Jenny or Cecilia would run inside crying, "Mama Chelle, I have an owwie," and she'd hold out a finger with a barely discernable pink mark on it. "I need a Band-Aid."

"Are you dripping blood?" I'd ask, kissing the finger. "You're okay." Then I'd engage her in washing green grapes for treat time or watching *Sesame Street* or *Teletubbies*. The key was to shift her focus from hurt to fun. And, eventually, to realizing that many of our hurts are imagined and short-lived.

Once a monk begged a master to become his teacher. The master agreed; he showed the monk how to meditate, and every day told him a wisdom to use in meditation—but every night the master beat the monk with a willow wand. After a month of beatings, the young man finally grabbed his master's branch and snapped it in two.

The master's face lit up with a broad smile. "You have done well," he said to the mystified monk. "You have finally learned that *you can stop the pain.*"

Suffering is not good for the soul unless it teaches you how to stop suffering. Instead of wallowing in sorrow, Candace Lightner, who lost her daughter to a drunk-driving accident, founded the organization MADD (Mothers Against Drunk Driving).

Much of our suffering, Buddhists and Taoists observe, arises out of attachment to "what is" or "what was," without allowing for change. A "helpful pain" will motivate us to make a change for the better. Change calls for acceptance, adaptability, and flexibility. Imagine a lump of clay dissolving in water. We can be like

- the water, which embraces all things;
- the clay, which adapts to its surroundings;
- a piece of iron that melts in a furnace, burning with passion or molding ourselves into a new creation, having passed through heat that tempers and strengthens us.[308]

Kahil Gibran felt we are the authors of much of our suffering. He believed we can choose our joys and sorrows before we experience them. How? Quantum mechanics. By deciding what we wish to experience *before* the event, we actually influence the direction of events.

Scrambling Broken Eggs

The ego hates change, so we shy away from difficult or chaotic situations, especially when we can't predict the consequences of our smallest actions (because of the Butterfly Effect and Chaos Theory).[309] Chaos and entropy seem constants in our universe, the working basis for life. However, with the application of additional energy into a disintegrating situation, entropy reverses into syntropy. Humpty Dumpty's fall from the wall is the essence of entropy. But when we apply a little heat, the chaos of Humpty becomes an order of scrambled eggs!

THE ADDITION OF ENERGY CHANGES ENTROPY TO SYNTROPY

We experience syntropy whenever a cut heals, whenever we clean house, when we rake fallen leaves; there is an order to our universe and syntropy we may fail to appreciate in our intricately changing lives.

Remember how $E = mc^2$ means matter vibrates slowly and light moves quickly, but that the equation is invalid for sub-atomic particles? That's how we know a faster-than-light realm exists, from which all physical matter is created. Now we come back to Quantum God, *potentia*, para-physical Power, heaven, and the frozen light that makes up matter.

The Science of Eternal Life

Energy can change form: Melting ice turns into water; heated water becomes steam; water condenses and falls to the ground as sleet (ice) or rain (water), or erupts as steam (a geyser). But no energy is ever lost—not the smallest quanta or photon or bit of star-stuff. Everything is made of light; our bodies composed of the energy of once-glowing stars, and energy never dies.

The Law of Energy Conservation says that energy cannot die. The energy that comprises the essence of every living being ultimately returns to Source. So the Law of Energy Conservation is the scientific term for life after death! The continuum in field theory, too, provides scientific support for life after death.[310]

> Don't confuse me with death.
> I offer you a new country
> to walk into . . .
>
> Phil Miller, "The God of Autumn"
> *The Kansas City Star*, Poets Corner (November 2, 2003)

In *All in the Family*, when Archie is declared dead because of a computer error, Edith learns the name of the man who did die and remarks, "I don't want nobody to be dead." Archie replies, "Edith, somebody's gotta be dead—that's life!" We are, however, more than our bodies; we're conscious energy systems. As Archie proclaims with wry insight, "Everybody's scared of death until it hits you. After that, you never give it another thought."[311] In fact, we discover that we who worried about dying wasted our energy when we could have been dancing.

Why do we fearing dying? Moses and the Hebrews lived on the border of the land of abundance, allowing fear to keep them in the wilderness for forty years. The Hebrew word usually translated as "death" (*mawet*) merely means a transition from one state to another.[312] Even this, which seems to be the most startling change for us is merely a change in form. Most people who have had near-death experiences go on to live without feeling afraid of dying.

> Some waves are high and some are low. Waves appear to be born and to die. But if we look more deeply, we see that the waves, although coming and going, are also water, which is always there. Notions like high and low, birth and death can be applied to waves, but water is free of such distinctions. Enlightenment for a wave is the moment the wave realizes that it is water. At that moment, fear of death disappears.
>
> Thich Nhat Hanh
> *Living Buddha, Living Christ*

While we tend to fear the unfamiliar or unknown, every part of life, including death, was considered a blessing by Tolkien's elves; they viewed death as a *gift* given to humans by Iluvatar.[313] As for non-fictional people, the Oglala Sioux Indians believe every object in the world has a spirit they call *wakan*, and because of this spirit, nothing is ever born and nothing ever dies.

In India, the *Bhgavad Gita* explains that at death people merely pass into another kind of body, comparing our bodies to garments we put on and take off. We are truly en-*light*-ened when we realize there is nothing to fear. Our existence is a bio-psycho-spiritual experiment in Practical Humanity, and our bodies temporary clothing for this earthly field trip we're attending for our soul's education. But our spirits are indestructible.

An ancient story from India tells about Nachiketa, who confronted the Lord of Death. Since Nachikita was kept waiting, the Lord graciously offered him three wishes. Nachiketa's first wish was for forgiveness, and it was granted. His second wish was for inner fire: spiritual passion, energy, and courage. That wish was granted. After some thought, Nachekita finally asked to know what is immortal, and the Lord of Death handed him a mirror.[314]

Playing Cosmic Hide and Seek

A "koan" is a Zen teaching technique for which there is no one right answer. Quantum physics, too, has many koans ("Imagine a massless particle") but it seems to have solved the Zen koan, "What is the sound of one hand clapping?" The answer may well be "Nothing." Nothing is physically "real" unless it has been seen, measured, heard, tasted, touched—processed by one of the five physical senses. The reality we know has been filtered and heavily processed as electrical signals by our brains.[315] The flip side of the physical process—the sixth sense, our conduit for non-local mind—is more real than two hands clapping.

A student once asked, "How do I seek identity with God?"

"The harder you seek, the more distance you create," answered the teacher.

"But what can I do about the distance?"

"Understand that it is not real."

The student thought about this and then asked, "Do you mean that God and I are One?"

"Not one. Not two," replied the wise man. "Look at the sun and its light, the ocean and its wave, the minstrel and his song: not one, not two. Close your eyes and look within, at that which cannot be seen."[316] The wise man's words sounds like "*neti, neti*: not this, not that." Or, simply, "We are all One."

> One Hindu myth teaches that the Self or God sees life as a form of play. But since that Self is all that there is, there's no one else to play *with*, so he plays a cosmic game of hide-and-seek [*lila*] with himself. Like an actor, he plays the roles of people like you and me, forgetting who he really is. Eventually, however, the Self stops dreaming and remembers his true identity, the one eternal Self who never dies.
>
> Reginald Horace Blyth
> *Games Zen Masters Play*

Our contact with the eternal (the whole) is hampered by our focus on the physical (the diverse). Quantum physics, remember, has proven that what we focus on determines what we experience. Too much of the time we focus on darkness, which Kabbalists see only as an absence of light and Taoists call the "gateway to understanding."[317] In fact, Nobel laureate Leon Lederman nicknamed the Higgs boson, a piece of vibrating empty space, the "God particle."[318]

Quantum physics proposes that what appears to be the darkness of space is actually filled with "dark matter," because that "empty" space *does* have weight.[319] It's heavy! What we call outer space Bohm identifies with space beyond time, or the implicate order.[320] Only 4% of the universe is made of the atoms and particles we're familiar with; the remaining 96%—a huge figure—comes from "dark energy," which Kaku likens to the Force.[321] Dark energy could well be called divine or universal energy. The stuff of magic. The magic of miracles.

Dark energy is the stuff we're made of. Although the manipulation of energy in techniques like Feng Shui, Attunement, and Reiki healing work with universal energy on the physical level, the magic does not lie in a special technique or natural crystal or lucky charm. The magic isn't in the mantra or the meditation, the ringing bell or tapping drum; we use these only to get to the *feeling* place of prayer.[322] Neither is it summoned by a certain posture or recited prayer or even the sacredness of a place, for all prayers have an effect and any place is made holy by its inhabitant. The magic resides in:

- how we feel—a literal real-ization of our identity in God;
- a knowledge of the way life really works—how goodness (or grace) flows through our lives;
- a deep knowing of and faith in the nature of God—goodness—and
- an unflagging trust; confidence that we're always a part of that Go(o)dness.

It is interesting that the Aramaic word, *haimanuta*, usually translated as "faith," also means the confidence a person feels from being part of "Sacred

Unity," or God.[323] Miracles are made possible through confidence in our own truly divine essence.[324]

One night a woman heard her kindergartener singing the alphabet at bedtime. The mother peeked into the room and saw her daughter with her hands clasped and her eyes closed as if in prayer, yet she was singing the ABCs.

"What are you doing?" the mother asked.

"Oh, hi, Mama," replied the little girl. "I didn't know what to say to God tonight, so I'm saying all the letters. God will know what to do with them and make the right words."

Some say it's the silence between the notes that creates music and the spaces between words that create language. Certainly an atom would not be an atom without space for the electron to race around in, any more than a room would be useful without empty space inside. And while we can eat a donut hole (or three or four), a doughnut is not a true doughnut without the nothingness of its missing hole.

Silence. Space. Nothing. If "nothing is bothering us," we feel blessed. When we think about it, we realize that *nothing* is nothing to sneeze at. Scientists have discovered the emptiness of outer space teems with bits of energy that flash in and out of existence like the light of fireflies dancing on a June night's breeze. Cultivating and maintaining a silent space in which to do nothing is important, for if we carry that quiet place inside us wherever we go, we have an ever-present refuge, a place where sparkles of hope blink on. In a crowded subway car, at a noisy convention, or as an alternative to feeling lonely. Developing an inner sanctum takes discipline and mindfulness, but it can be done.

> You must go beyond all your imagery, beyond your thoughts, into the divine darkness. That's where you meet God. You know, in a Hindu temple the inner sanctuary is always dark. You go through the courts of the temple, which are filled with light, the figures of the gods, but when you come to the inner sanctuary you come to the heart, the inner center of your own being, and you encounter God in the darkness. God without form.
>
> Father Griffiths
> quoted by Renee Weber in
> *Dialogues with Scientists and Sages: The Search for Unity*

We create our lives. We live in a perpetual state of grace. We need fear no evil, for everything works toward the manifestation of growing Goodness. Light or dark, *shem* or *hoshech*, it's all a vital part of Quantum God.[325] It is, in fact, darkness that defines the value of light.

The dark matter that makes up so much of the universe (and of ourselves) may well be light that vibrates beyond our ability to perceive it. When we come to understand *maya* as *maya*, in that instant *maya* doesn't exist for us any longer.[326] We've awakened from our dream, claimed our seemingly magical ability to "make miracles" (which is merely using our creative power consciously), and turned away from the shadows on the wall. Maybe enlightenment is nothing more than remembering that the light is inside us, along with the power to do more than just survive—the power to create every bit of our lives in this very moment, despite any apparent darkness.

Is our world but a shadow? Maybe, but—according to *any* sort of science—there can be no shadows cast unless there exists a great light beyond the darkness. Ultimately, All is well.

PART TWO

With this prayer I am making up a God
Who answers prayer, responding like the snow
To footprints and the wind, to a child in snow
Making an angel who will speak for God.

. . . God, I am thinking of you now as snow,
Descending like the answer to a prayer . . .

Mark Jarman
Unholy Sonnets, "The Word, 'Answer'"
Sarabande Books

How Do We Begin to Live These Principles?

For decades I waited for my hair to turn to the salt-and-pepper my grandpa Rusty had worn, the grandpa I loved so much. Now silver adorns my head, trophies I earned across the space of half a lifetime. I wear them proudly. Here, too, are the crow's feet I'd waited for. These laugh-lines at the eyes are a welcome sight. But the lines at the corners of my mouth—where did they come from? Where is that smooth, full face of the twenty-year-old woman I feel like? Did marriage change it? Child-rearing? Struggling and trials? What created the harsh-planed landscape of the face I wear now?

The following image shows both a young woman facing back and left and an elderly woman facing forward left. It's funny how no one ever pictures himself as an old man.

No one contemplates the changes time will etch into a woman's face. But, I think, does it even matter, these external constructions, if I still feel like a twenty-year-old inside?

Of course, our feelings lie to us, just as sight or hearing does, like when we hear bumps in the night which, though they're harmless house-settling or tree-talking noises, may frighten us. If we can't trust what we see or hear or feel, that means many of our experiences act as false prophets. "No," we think, "I've never been able to do that, so why even try?" Genetics tells us we must die as our parents did; American medical science tells us we must decline as we age, and pharmaceutical companies reach into deep pockets to remind us every day of every way our bodies can betray us—*if* we buy into their propaganda. *We are so much more than our bodies.*

We are energy. Every thought, every emotion, every object and animal and person is energy. Rabbi David Cooper's definition of God as a Verb expands on this idea; now Quantum God is energy-in-action.

The Hindus honor a thousand gods; they differ from Jews and Christians with their idea of One God only by embodying each attribute of God individually, as do the Muslims with their Ninety-nine Names of Allah. The Taoists may come closer to the truth. The guiding light of Taoism is simply called "The Way," the process. If we are in harmony with the Way—if we're "in the flow" or "going with the flow"—then we're doing okay.

The fact is that God is to each of us whatever we *think* God is . . . and more. God is a concept, a Force, the Process of manifestation, communication, and life. God is any name we use . . . and more, always more. Even saying "God is Love" limits God to our personal idea of love. To some, love hurts; love is a slap or a slur. Love can mean a house, a status. Companionship or a hug. A relationship at least, and now we move another step closer.

Walt Whitman wrote, "I am large. I contain multitudes." Fair enough. We might think Whitman's statement would cover just about everything—and yet, "everything" is only a word, a symbol for a thought, and *any* thought is necessarily limited and limiting. To *experience* God carries us beyond simple concept, and yet Quantum God is so complex, so large and ever-growing that even the experience of cosmic consciousness cannot behold all of God in entirety, for God must be beyond human comprehension. Mystics—who are *ordinary people like the rest of us*—have felt this cosmic Oneness and still find it difficult to describe their singular experience in words.

The masters say enlightenment, like the Tao, cannot be described. Nonetheless, we share our experiences so others can avoid some of the pitfalls and boulders and hells we have tripped over, crashed against, and lived within. From every race, creed, and philosophy come documents that provide clues for knowing enlightenment—or, ultimately, God. But enlightenment is not the end, it's the means.

The East usually walks the path toward God through transcending the self. The West seeks enlightenment through *via positiva*, the way of laughing, singing, dancing, and telling jokes.[327] Indeed, Vivekananda said one of the signs we're becoming more spiritual is that we become more cheerful.[328] Just look at the Dalai Lama. Cheerfully we strive for self-realization, for recognizing and honoring the divinity contained in the greater self, which contains some part of All.

No matter what our path or how we think of God, our home is something we carry inside us. Literally. "Home is where the heart is." The following practices contribute to a heart/mind/spirit-healthy diet.

> Only you can deprive yourself of anything. This is a crucial step in reawakening.
>
> *A Course in Miracles*

1. *We are willing to change.*

The following is an alleged transcript of a radio conversation between the British and the Irish off the coast of Kerry, Ireland, in October of 1998, released by the Chief of Naval Operations.

IRISH: Please divert your course 15 degrees to the South to avoid a collision.

BRITISH: Recommend you divert your course 15 degrees to the North to avoid a collision.

IRISH: Negative. You will have to divert your course 15 degrees to the South to avoid a collision.

BRITISH: This is the Captain of a British Navy Ship. I say again, divert *your* course.

IRISH: Negative. I say again, you will have to divert *your* course.

BRITISH: *This is the aircraft carrier HMS Britannia, the second largest ship in the British Atlantic Fleet. We are accompanied by three destroyers, three cruisers, and numerous support vessels. Demand you change your course 15 degrees north or countermeasures will be undertaken to ensure the safety of this ship.*

IRISH: We are a lighthouse. Your call.

How can we hope to change the world for the better if we're not open to change? Self-improvement requires our willingness to do so, beginning with who we are at this moment.

In the mid-1970s, a woman once visited a chiropractor. She didn't know how he could help her because she had been diagnosed as having multiple sclerosis and had been confined to a wheelchair for the last 17 years, but she was willing to try an alternative medical treatment. What happened? After that first realignment, she *walked* out of the chiropractor's office.

Physically, we change moment by moment. The atoms and cells of our bodies are constantly changing, dying off and being renewed; every seven years, we're a totally different person physically. From moment to moment hormones, emotional-electromagnetic energy, and air in our lungs change. We don't pay attention to these changes, so we don't worry about them.[329] But changes in character, mood, and philosophy deserve all the time and effort we choose to give to them.

> When I complained to my abbot Ajahn Chah, considered by millions to be a great saint, that he didn't always act as if he were completely enlightened, he laughed and told me that was good, "because otherwise you would still be imagining that you could find the Buddha outside of yourself."
>
> Jack Kornfield
> *After the Ecstasy, the Laundry*

We have to start where we are to get to where—and who—we choose to be. A well-known adage states, "If you meet Buddha on the road, kill him." We need to get rid of our "Buddha-concept" in order to experience Buddha directly. The point is, neither Buddha nor Christ, the Messiah nor enlightenment is found outside ourselves. *What we're looking for is what we already are.*

In John 6:8, Jesus is quoted as saying, "And ye shall know the truth, and the truth shall make you free." *Just because we believe something wholeheartedly doesn't make it true. We must be willing to believe that some of the facts we've accepted as truth are nothing more than mistaken ideas, and that any thought that holds us back or harshly judges us is a false belief.* We're still fleeing from the Garden, shrinking from the responsibility entailed in our divine nature. This defection makes us feel ashamed, leads to the imagined need for sacrifice and atonement, and opens us to being exploited by religious leaders.

As Rev. Duke Tufty observes, the Ugly Duckling made a horrible duck but a beautiful swan; *he was at his best when he was being what he was meant to be.*[330] Marianne Williamson expressed it this way:

> Our deepest fear is not that we are inadequate. Our deepest fear is that we are powerful beyond measure. It is our light, not our darkness, that most frightens us. We ask ourselves, who am I to be brilliant, talented and fabulous? Actually, who are you not to be? You are a child of God. Your playing small doesn't serve the world. There's nothing enlightened about shrinking so that other people won't feel insecure around you. We were born to make manifest the glory of God that is within us. It's not just in some of us; it's in everyone. And as we let our own light shine, we unconsciously give others permission to do the same. As we are liberated from our own fear, our presence automatically liberates others.[331]

Willingness to change is essential, but self-evolution does not require that we trip over every boulder we encounter, fall into every pothole, bang our heads against every brick wall, or beat ourselves up while we're learning.

You must learn from the mistakes of others. You can't possibly live long enough to make them all yourself.

Sam Levenson
quoted by Jessica Gribetz in *Wise Words*

A feeling of inadequacy is one of the flaws mentioned in Louis Tartaglia's book, *Flawless, The Ten Most Common Character Flaws and What You Can Do About Them.* We attain mastery one mistake at a time. When Einstein fled from Nazi Germany, he became part of Princeton's faculty. An official showed him his office and asked what he needed, besides a desk and chair. Einstein told him he needed a large wastebasket to throw away all his mistakes.[332]

We make mistakes because we're not perfect, and if we were perfect, how boring we would be! The Hebrew language has two tenses, but neither of them denote the present tense. Hebrew understands actions only as having been accomplished or not having been accomplished; verbs indicate past or future action.

What makes this quality of Hebrew so interesting is that in Exodus 3:13-14, where God of the burning bush speaks to Moses, *"Ehyeh asher Ehyeh,"* it's usually translated as "I Am That I Am." This rendering in the "present" turns God into a static, inactive and unchanging essence. But with a more correct translation, we see a better picture of a dynamic Force: "I am not yet Who I am not yet." God has not accomplished being all God can be, and in this aspect, too, we are like God. The fact that Hebrew has no present tense gives hope to all of us for our "becoming."[333]

A nomad was once asked why he believed so strongly in a god he could not see. "If you see camel tracks in the desert," he replied, "do you have to see the camel before believing it exists?"[334] The reflection we see in the mirror is but a small part of the entity we really are.

We are what we *believe* we are (although that's not our whole identity). Change for the better is not as simple as making "I get what I think" or "I reap as I sow" our mantra. Our goal is a sense of well-being, and that may require improving self-image, thought management, and an upswing of habitual feelings.

To help us redefine our self-image, saying, "Hi, beautiful!" or "You're wonderful!" whenever we catch our reflection in the mirror does wonders for building self-esteem. Or we can replace how we look with a new picture; it might be as simple as placing on the frig or bathroom mirror a magazine cut-out of a slim/plump/healthy/happy person taped below our own head snipped from a photograph. Whatever image we choose, it must be reasonably believable—for someone weighing either 89 pounds or 450 pounds, a cut-out of J Lo's or Arnold Schwarzenegger's body won't help us believe that we can change.

Recently, Hollywood has given us a slew of superhero movies. Why? Because our world now is bereft of Spencer Tracy, Gregory Peck, and John Wayne; we're missing FDR and Churchill, Gandhi and the young Kennedy brothers, Anne Frank and Helen Keller, Golda Meir and Princess Diana, Salk and Schweitzer and John Paul II, and Jackie Robinson.[335] We love heroes, whether it's a fireman who braves a blazing fire to rescue a pet or a miner rescued from a collapsed shaft.

We love Santa for his cheerful generosity and Robin Hood for redressing injustice. We cheer for the underdog in sports, politics, and even in crime: Columbo, the bumbling detective, or Don Westlake's hapless thief, John

Dortmunder. We're glad when the lion frees the mouse, and wave a knowing finger at Leo when his tiny friend gnaws through the netting and saves the King of the Beasts.

But how many of us realize that each of us is, has been, or shall be a hero in someone's eyes? Dog owners know this. You feed your dog, you give her love and affection, and the dog waits impatiently for you to return home, and greets you with wagging tail and doggie kisses and romping around. That dog considers you a hero. He believes in you.

Echoing Jesus, who said we are gods, Yogananda taught his listeners to believe in themselves, and encouraged us to believe in what we thought was impossible.

> You are all gods, if you only knew it. Behind the wave of your consciousness is the sea of God's presence. You must look within. Don't concentrate on the little wave of the body with its weaknesses; look within. Close your eyes and you see the vast omnipresence before you, everywhere you look. You are in the center of that sphere, and as you lift your consciousness from the body and its experiences, you will find that sphere filled with the great joy and bliss that lights the stars and gives power to the winds and storms.
>
> Yogananda
> *Sanctuary of the Soul*

When we are willing to change and ready to loosen the limiting ideas that have kept us from changing—growing—then we are ready to believe . . . in our *becoming*, but also to *celebrate ourselves as we are in this moment.*

2. We believe in "six impossible things before breakfast" and live without fear.

Obert Skye writes about a fictional *potentia*, where "possibility is eternal . . . and *impossible* is a whisper spoken only by the souls who have just accidentally stepped in." He says that this place "between the possible and the impossible is a place your mind enjoys keeping from you, yet it is as real as a thick patch of goose bumps or as any strong nagging notion. It exists within the minds of everyone, because without it there would be no room to dream or hope. It was created at the beginning of time so mankind could aspire and imagine. It is an entire realm hidden in the folds of your mind."[336] How do we reach this place? Not through Orbitz or Travelocity. If it is an intangible, *thoughtful* place, then one of the first steps leading to this realm is to suspend our usual beliefs and whisper, "Maybe . . ."

A fabled king once gathered together the wisest men in his kingdom to write about the nature of reality. The sages labored for twenty-three years and finally produced a thousand-page document.

"I haven't time to read this," said the aging king. "Go back to work. Shorter."

The learned gentlemen returned to their study and, after seventeen more years, presented the king with one page about reality.

"Still too long," said the king, whose eyesight was failing. "One word. Just one. That's what I want."

Again the wise men returned to their study and debated and deliberated until they had come to a unanimous decision. With a quivering hand, the wisest of the wise men approached the king on his death bed and held out a small sheet of parchment on which was written the single word, "Perhaps."[337]

What potential resides in the word, *perhaps*! Matthew 25:14-28 recounts the parable of the talents. This passage implies that the master would have rewarded even an unsuccessful attempt at investment, as long as the servant had tried. Although the third servant showed caution with his master's property, he allowed fear to rule him and failed to make any use at all of his buried talent. (The English word *talent* in this case is highly appropriate. What talents do we have that are lying latent, buried by the density of doubt?)

> "You mustn't let the fear make the decision for you."
>
> Dr. Sydney Freeman, *M*A*S*H*, "Pressure Points"

We are only afraid of the things we think we cannot do. If, however, we were to approach each event or possible event in our lives with the preface "perhaps . . .", well then, *perhaps* many more pleasant things would blossom into being. As a child, I didn't learn the phrase "I can." What I learned was, "I can do better." So I always felt as if I was letting everyone down. Now I'm working on replacing that old thought-pattern with "Maybe I *can* do this." Or, indeed, trying to skip the thought process completely and just jumping into the challenge instead.

We have two supports for making "I can!" a permanent part of our vocabulary. The first relates to the way cells function; although they become limited to a specialized purpose—like, for example, the eyes functioning as organs of sight—this specialization is not absolute. In the 1960s, the Soviet Academy of Science studied a Russian peasant named Rosa Kuleshova, who was able to see and read using her fingertips. Not Braille, but real photographs and printed materials. The cells in her fingers functioned as eyes![338] The second support involves the non-local (morphogenetic or Akashic) library of knowledge available to all living beings. If anyone at all has ever done something we'd like to do, that ability is just waiting to be claimed again. For instance, great athletes show us what our bodies are capable of.

> If a piece of steel or a piece of salt, consisting of atoms one next to the other, can have such interesting properties; if water—which is nothing but these little blobs, mile upon mile of the same thing over the earth—can form waves and foam, and make rushing noises and strange patterns as it runs over cement; if all of this, all the life of a stream of water, can be nothing but a pile of atoms, *how much more is possible?*
>
> Physicist Richard Feynman
> quoted by Christopher Sykes in *No Ordinary Genius:*
> *The Illustrated Richard Feynman*

In 1970, John Lennon wrote the song, "Let It Be." On the University of Iowa campus appeared the sign, "LET IT BE," to discourage foot traffic across the quadrangle's green lawn. But "Let it be" means more than "leave it alone."

"Let it be" means "allow it to exist." In peace. In accordance with its nature. It can also mean, "Let it go."

Or the statement can mean, "Let it be done," as in the command, "Fiat lucem! Let there be light!"

One summer my foot was bitten by a brown recluse spider. After two days, I woke with the bite swollen to silver-dollar-pancake size and painful to the touch. It even hurt to move my foot. Reluctantly, I limped into a free health care clinic.

"No appointments open today," the woman at the reception desk told me.

They didn't have time to see a person with a deadly spider bite?

Uncharacteristically, I lost patience and replied, "Fine. I'm a healer. I'll do it myself!" The Inner Self, I meant, with a capital S, and with that determination (*command*), my Self went to work. I limped home, took naproxen for the pain and ibuprophen for the swelling, then propped my foot up and forgot about it. I let my body handle it, with faith that it would heal.

It did. By noon that day, the pain and swelling and danger were gone. I had allowed to reappear and flourish the condition of good health that I believe is my divine heritage.

The Bible contains 62 references where we're told not to feel fearful. In Luke 12:29-32, Jesus says, "And seek not ye what ye shall eat, or what ye shall drink, neither be ye of doubtful mind." Don't worry, he means. "For all these things do the nations of the world seek after: and your Father knoweth that ye have need of these things. But rather seek ye the kingdom of God; and all these things shall be added unto you. Fear not, little flock; for it is your Father's good pleasure to give you the kingdom." Happiness and fear cannot occupy the same space in our minds or hearts—and we can choose which to feel. Care-free.

When we trust that we'll get what we need, we live a more carefree life—and, accordingly, attract events into our lives of higher frequency. Remaining carefree is, in fact, both a necessity for and a result of Presence of mind. And what is there to fear or fret over? We are not waiting on the universe or a whimsy-driven god to grant our wishes or deny our dreams.

The system underlying this life is set up so that we *are manifesting* exactly what we believe in, what we desire without desperation, what we expect is possible. Now that I have been living more fearlessly, I am not just attracting but creating more pleasant circumstances. How cool is that, to see the result of no-fear so clearly and quickly out-pictured in my life?

We can believe, as Lewis Carroll said, in "six impossible things before breakfast." Six impossible things before breakfast. Not too tall an order, once we shift our thinking into the *Maybe* mode, thinking, "I can" and "Nothing is impossible." Or, as Rod Serling wrote in a *Twilight Zone* episode, "If you don't believe . . . it won't be true. That's the way magic works."[339] The combined magic of quantum mechanics, fearlessness, and Spirit.

3. We maintain our own self-esteem.

Of course, if we always remembered that we *are* the essence of Light, Love, and Creativity, we'd never feel anything but joyful, but most of us have not attained that level of awareness.

> I'm not afraid that God will ask me, "Zusha, why have you not become an Abraham, Isaac, or Jacob?" But I am afraid that God will ask me, "Zusha, why have you not become what Zusha was *intended* to be?"
>
> Rabbi Schachter-Shalomi
> quoted by William Eliot in *Tying Rocks to Clouds*

Cultivating a healthy self-esteem keeps us closer to an enlightened level while we learn and grow in spiritual stature. Many of us learned that unless we put others first, we would become egotistical and selfish. We were taught to "love your neighbor as yourself." But did we ever learn to love ourselves?

Tao Te Ching states: "We shape clay into a pot, but it is the emptiness inside that holds whatever we want" (#11). We often crucify ourselves; low self-esteem, anger, and blame nail us to a cross. Feeling good comes out of self-love and peace of mind. The *Tao Te Ching* adds that a master "never loses touch with who she really is. In the midst of joy or anger or sorrow, she remains imperturbable."[340] We can't depend on getting someone else to cheer us up; we must be our own best cheerleader. And cheerfulness is more determination and discipline than it is natural disposition.

Cheerfulness comes when we *love ourself.* Is there any one of us who has never felt a huge emptiness inside or believed that there burns inside us a small, flickering light we hoped someone else would fan into bright flames for us? Is there anyone who hasn't felt as if he or she were half a person, just ripe and ready for joining with a partner to make one whole? But two broken people together don't make one whole; they make a mess! It's true that a caress or kind word when we're feeling sad may help us feel better for a while, but the feeling is fleeting.

Our personal and spiritual transformation depends on opening up the heart chakra, the energy vortex centered near the heart. And if the only person we can hope to change is our own self, where better to begin than with the heart? In the last twenty years of our marriage, my (ex-) husband often told me, "I love you." I would reply, "But you don't *like* me." Maybe he didn't like himself, either. Learning to like ourselves is critical, for that is the foundation on which we stand.

To learn to like ourselves, we . . .

♦ *Smile at our reflection in the mirror every day.* In "The Zoo Story," the character Jerry says, "It's just that . . . it's just that if you can't deal with people, you have to make a start somewhere. With animals! Don't you see? A person has to have some way of dealing with something. If not with people . . . something. With a bed, with a cockroach, with a mirror, no, that's too hard, that's one of the last steps."[341] But a mirror is actually the first and best place for us to begin. Smiling at our reflection in every mirror we see is like a slow-working miracle. I found that my self-esteem and sense of well-being has increased with each smile.

♦ *Find one thing to appreciate.* I learned, when I found my train of thought going in a direction that wasn't self-affirming, to immediately switch to thinking about something I appreciate. Appreciation and gratitude are high-frequency emotions, and we know that when we put out high-frequency vibrations, that's what we get back.

♦ *Make a list of all our accomplishments.* This is a good list to review when we're feeling a little blue.

♦ *Spend time with people who make us feel good about ourselves.* Obvious, but how often do we actually make time for *fun*? How much time do we spend with happy people? As a student of the Brick Wall School, I've finally learned to avoid being around or talking with people who are "downers." People who drain me (literally, of energy). People who carry anger inside of them or focus on the negative. The boss who yells. The friend who talks about how the country's going downhill. The father who sees me as a failure. Which leads to the next suggestion.

♦ *Don't let the world set our standard for success.* If we try something new, we *have* succeeded in mastering our fears. As the artist Bob Ross was fond of saying, "We don't make mistakes, we just have happy accidents." Ross, the eternal optimist, viewed accidents in painting as well as in life as opportunities. Another artist, the Chinese potter, believes in "the controlled accident" when he or she allows the glaze to run.[342] Not every ceramic piece turns out beautiful, but out of every batch, odds are that at least one exquisite work of art emerges from the kiln. As for the field of science, many advances have been discovered by accident, like penicillin.

Living by our own standard is "being true to" our own self. And when we're being authentic, we find unlooked-for blessings. There was once a young man whose tuition to medical school had been paid by all the inhabitants in his village. When the young man returned to the village, he hung this sign outside his office door: "Dr. V. S. Krishna, M.D. Failed, Calcutta Medical College." In spite of failing to pass his final exams, the young man offered whatever medical help he could—and his office was always busy![343]

We are not all accomplished artists or professionals. My mother has always maintained that she can't draw a straight line. Yet this woman creates Easter treasures, May baskets, and valentines for those who would otherwise not receive any. She celebrates birthdays, cooks for sick friends, and goes out of her way to do countless small favors. She herself is the masterpiece she creates every day.

♦ *Define ourselves by our strengths, not our weaknesses.* If we get what we think about all the time, why not concentrate on what we're good at? In fact, the more we imagine doing something "impossible," the more possible it becomes. There was a study done with two groups of basketball players. The first group held regular practices for shooting free throws. The second group *imagined* themselves shooting and making baskets—and their scores improved significantly! It's also important to remember that there will be days when we don't feel particularly brilliant or talented. When the best we can give is only 75%, or 52%, or even 38%, that amount *is* our 100%.

A corollary to this suggestion is, *Refrain from comparing ourselves to anyone*, not even to the "Ideal Me." (The INFJ's ongoing, ever-elusive, and often daunting plight.) We only need to strive to be better than we used to be, remembering that we are all "becoming."

♦ *Eliminate our need for others' approval.* I'd like my poetry printed in *Norton's Anthology* and my screenplays made in into movies or TV serials. Am I going to feel bad, to doubt my ability, just because this hasn't happened? No!

> Care about people's approval, and you will become their prisoner.
>
> *Tao Te Ching #9*
> Stephen Mitchell, translator

If I feel good when someone gives me a thumbs-up, I'm probably going to feel bad with a thumbs-down. Being authentic, or true to one's self, requires "self-referral." That quality is in play when we feel autonomous; that is, *we are free of old hurts or new fears*, and we depend on no one outside ourselves for telling us, "You're okay."

♦ *Don't take criticism personally.* Autonomy helps here, too, to keep us from feeling hurt or depressed by disapproval and criticism. Einstein paid no attention to his classmates who called him *Biedermeier*. (That's "nerd" to us.)[344] And look what happened to the youngster whose headmaster predicted that he would never succeed. Einstein went on to become *Time Magazine's* "Person of the Century."

I once let my father's label of "failure" send me spiraling down into depression, even though I knew that, just as orange juice comes out of an orange, angry words are spoken by an angry person.[345] In fact, using unconscious projection, someone on a rant may actually be describing him- or herself and not us at all.[346]

This is because what we dislike about ourselves we often see in others, and then we feel threatened by those behaviors "outside" ourselves. Projection is a common psychological defense that the projectors usually don't recognize as part of their own behavior. For the person targeted by these low-frequency emotions, love and forgiveness are the best gifts we can offer.

> Fear and misunderstanding are the root causes of much illness, distress, and suffering in the world. Often, when we are functioning in the lower aspects of our awareness, we are blind to our own fears and we project them onto the world, when in fact the problem lies within. The key toward dissolving and healing these fears is to release the blockages of the heart chakra and to operate from a position of love and forgiveness.
>
> Richard Gerber
> *Vibrational Medicine: New Choices for Healing Ourselves*

Writers learn not to take rejection personally. They preserve their sense of self and confidence in spite of editors' rejection or acceptance. So, too, does the mother who continues to love the child who screams in a fit of defiance, "I hate you," just the same as when the child shows her affection. That image of basic (true) self is vital for a sense of well-being.

♦ *Update our vocabulary.* I'm trying to eliminate the word "but . . ." and phrases like "I can't" from my vocabulary. Whenever a "but" sneaks into my speech, it drives one of my friends crazy, and he immediately jumps on me. He's taught me that seeing two sides of an issue is okay; using "But I can't ____" when I'm talking about doing something is a recipe for failure, when I haven't even tried.

♦ *Breathe!* We stay this side of death by a single breath! The increased oxygen from a few moments of slow, conscious breaths does wonders for the racing mind and anxious heart, and also helps to slow down the aging process; mammals tend to breathe about 200 to 600 million times during a lifetime, with their hearts beating about a billion times. Giant tortoises breathe only four times each minute, and they live for 200 to 300 years![347] In light of this fact, anger (which quickens our breath rate), and fear (which strains the heart) are emotions that take a heavy toll on our bodies.

For thirty-five years, the Bavarian Catholic Therese Neumann lived on Spirit alone. Neumann ate and drank nothing for all those years; her fast was documented by a doctor.[348] The point is that we can live on less if we breathe with awareness, knowing it is universal energy—or God's own blessing—we're incorporating with every breath we take, and if we bless our water and food before consuming it. (See techniques for breathing under "5. Practice Joy," and in the Exercises at back of book.)

♦ *Be persistent.* At the beginning of their career, the Beatles were rejected by Decca Recording Company, Theodor Geisel's first Dr. Seuss book was rejected 27 times, and J. K. Rowling's first Harry Potter book was rejected by 12 publishing houses. None of these people were afraid to persist. They didn't give up.

Babies don't give up. They never feel like a failure when they miss their mouth and stick a spoonful of strained peas in their hair, their eyes, or the dog's nose. With a laugh and a bounce, they try again. Toddlers fall down and get up and try again. Children may feel a little afraid, once they've fallen off their two-wheelers, but they don't give up, either. They climb on the bike and practice till they've found their balance and confidence.

For most of my life, I've been afraid. Afraid of bullies. Afraid to speak out. Afraid to dance at senior prom. Afraid to live. And that fear did something for me—it got me raped. Robbed. Isolated. But even in my isolation, I believed in the Goodness that upholds everything. I persisted in knowing that I was blessed, and little by little came to wonder why I had ever felt afraid. PB&J means peanut butter and jelly to a child, but PB&J also stands for the life skills of persistence, blessing, and joy. We just have to hang in here long enough to figure out how to see the blessings so we can live in joy.

> After a thousand, or several thousand, experiments that did not produce the result he was seeking, Edison would just say, "Well, we're making progress—we know a thousand ways it can't be done. We're that much closer to getting there."
>
> James D. Newton
> *Uncommon Friends: Life with Thomas Edison, Henry Ford, Harvey Firestone, Alexis Carrel, and Charles Lindbergh*

♦ *Live with passion.* People live in quiet desperation when they have nothing to feel passionate about. We have to figure out what makes our hearts sing, without over-thinking or overanalyzing. *Quick, write down five things that make your heart sing.* Hmmm. My list might be:

1. Working with children and the elderly.
2. Editing and layout work, and helping others to see their works in print.
3. Chocolate—and sharing it!
4. Living in an Arts and Crafts bungalow with the love of my life.
5. The ocean, streams, forests, thunderstorms—anywhere with flowing water and green, growing things.

Well, that's five things off the top of my head that make me feel alive, that help me live with purpose, that make me feel like my Self. Knowing my self, my nature, is the beginning. Now I have to be open to opportunities, recognize them when they come, and then jump on them!

Trusting that opportunities will come is basic, but I also have to act. Take the teaching job. Create the webpage. Buy the chocolate and make a ganache cake, and then share it with someone. Drive out to the woods, or save up money to vacation in the beautiful northwest. So, in a nutshell: Feel. Know. Trust. Act.

♦ *Be a light unto yourself,* said the gentle Jesuit Anthony De Mello.[349] We cannot love ourselves without self-respect, and one of the ways we earn our *own* respect is by keeping our word. I promised I wouldn't let my grandma live in a nursing home, but four times she landed in a convalescent center, and four times I brought her home again. That is one of the things I'm most proud of in my life. I *like* myself.

We know from quantum physics that the energy of light is what everything is made of. What we need to persist is to remember that we *are* light. Each of us shines uniquely and offers the world something no one else can.

> It is easy to be light, if light is what you are.
>
> Rev. Karyn Bradley, Unity Palo Alto

Nurturing our own inner light was illustrated in a *Twilight Zone* episode. The main character, Mr. Bevis, "believes in a magic all his own. The magic of a child's smile, the magic of liking and being liked, the strange and wondrous mysticism that is the simple act of living. Mr. B. W. Bevis . . . who has his own private and special" heaven. Though unemployed, broke, and homeless, yet still Mr. Bevis remained optimistic and kind. Without him, Serling said, "without his warmth, without his kindness, the world would be a considerably poorer place."[350]

4. We "spend what is in our purse." (Or our heart.)

When Paul Newman and Joanne Woodward were on location in Kansas City for the filming of *Mr. and Mrs. Bridges*, Newman visited a Brookside ice cream shop one afternoon. While he was waiting his turn, the customer standing at the cash register recognized him and became flustered. She paid for her ice cream cone, crammed the change in her purse, and left, only to return immediately.

"You forgot to give me my ice cream cone," she complained to the clerk.

Paul Newman turned to her and said, "Pardon me, ma'am, but I believe you put it in your purse."

> Once Jesus was walking through the marketplace with his disciples. Some Israelites insulted Jesus, who merely blessed his taunters. The disciples were offended and asked why Jesus hadn't gotten angry and cursed the men.
>
> "I can only spend what I carry in my purse," Jesus replied.
>
> Compassion abided in his heart, and compassion was what he had to give away.
>
> James Fadiman and Robert Frager
> *Essential Sufism*

Each of us has a gift to share. Each of us *is* a gift. Some have material resources and some have talents, but we all have a responsibility to share, and how we do it is of utmost importance. The Bible tells us to be a cheerful giver, sharing gladly and without a feeling of obligation. Why? Because the energy attached to the action influences the outcome, as quantum physics proves.

There are two ways to spend well: by giving up anger and resentment, old pain, grudges, and possessions, and by gladly giving and gratefully *accepting*, which keeps us in the loop of circulating abundance.

Dr. Hunt says that anger serves us well when it's like a "shot in the arm," prompting us to take constructive action, as it did for Jesus with the corrupt moneychangers, or Roger, who was erecting a shed in his backyard. He slipped on a sheet of plywood lying on the hill, got up, and slipped a second time when the sheet slid out from under him. Rising again, again Roger slipped on the same wood. Taxed beyond patience, he rose shaky and swearing, grabbed the big sheet of plywood, and flung it onto the burning pile. Two minutes later, however, Roger was back at work and humming a cheerful tune. His short spurt of expressed anger hurt no one, released pent-up frustration, and energized him toward the end of his long workday.

It takes a lot of energy to stay mad, and prolonged anger or resentment results in an emotional state that wreaks havoc on every part of our biological and psychological system.[351] During her teaching career at a boy's school in Texas, each year Reverend Karyn Bradley gave her fourth-graders a memorable assignment: They were to carry a five-pound sack of potatoes everywhere they went. They slept with, went to the bathroom with, and ate potatoes for a solid week. The youngsters gained a real feeling for the burden of holding onto emotional baggage.

Try It Yourself

Fill an empty milk container with water, then carry it around with you for ten minutes . . . for an hour . . . for a day. It seems to grow heavier, the longer you carry it, doesn't it?

When we let go of judgments, grudges, resentments, and even small irritations (a form of mild anger), we have more room in our purse, wallet, and heart for emotions that make us feel good. Any time we get rid of negativity, we create a vacuum where more compassion, love, and understanding can rush in.

If, however, we give grudgingly or just to "stay in the flow," it's fear of lack that's motivating us, so we actually increase the feeling of lack within us. When good cheer and the sense of "I have plenty!" accompanies our donation, we create a space for good things to flow into, like the lock system at the Erie Canal.

Every so often, a friend of mine tells me I'm living at the edge of poverty, but I have given tips that amounted to as much as the bill for my food because Vicki, the owner of the diner, needed it. When we share *because* we feel prosperous, abundance is what we attract. Giving *and* taking forms an exchange that is an integral part of Bohm's projection from the explicate order (the world we know) to the implicate order (*potentia*) into and back again to us.

Let go! Two monks once came upon a river where they saw a girl dressed in fine clothes. Without hesitation, the larger of the monks carried the girl piggyback through the water and set her on the bank. "Surely it was wrong to touch a woman," said the smaller monk, and he kept nagging about his friend's breach of right behavior. Finally the other monk said, "I set the woman down by the riverside, but you are still carrying her."

At the coming of each new year, congregations at Unity churches participate in letting go through the Burning Bowl, a symbolic ritual of writing what we wish to release on a piece of paper and then burning the paper. Another way to let go is by de-cluttering. Sometimes our possessions seem to breed, expanding into all available space! There comes a point where our stuff owns us, rather than the other way around, and our possessions become more burden than pleasure. Garage sale time! Of course, I'm usually happy if I make enough at my garage sale at least to cover the cost of the ad, but there are other rewards.

Roxie was organizing a garage sale and wanted me to sell my paintings. I knew it wasn't the right venue but I love my friend, so I lugged three heavy boxes over to her house. Nothing sold . . . until the last afternoon, when a woman stood before a small landscape partnered with a narrative of my hapless journey through life:

> . . . It's mostly my own fault I chose wrong turns
> or tumbled into traps before I knew
> I'd tripped the spring or snapped the cord or threw
> the counterbalance off weight. You'd think that I
> should be quite wise by now from what I learned
>
> of all the different ways you sabotage
> yourself as you go blundering through the years,
> spending little on laughter and much on tears . . .
>
> It's not so much a matter of regret
> nor yet of wishing vainly on a star,
> this being discontent with where we are;
> it's more of being what we're *meant* to be
> that rankles deep inside, as if to bet
>
> against experience, against all odds
> that God intended humans to be gods.

The woman read the entire poem. Stood speechless. Turned. She had tears in her eyes.

"That painting needs to go home with you," I said.

"I can't afford it."

I asked if she could pay for the frame. The woman smiled in delight. That was my reward.

Almost forty years ago, I let my little sister drive my very first car, and she ran that shiny new Datsun into the only post in the entire parking lot. While she was apologizing, I laughed. "Nancy," I said, "it's only a thing."

Throwing away, giving away, putting away, and not worrying too much about our stuff cuts down on clutter so the energy of abundance can flow freely. Just as the mathematical principle "Occam's Razor" recommends adopting as few assumptions as possible in an equation, fewer possessions leads to the beauty of the simple life.

Neighbor: "What is the secret of life?"

Thoreau: "Simplicity, simplicity, simplicity."

Neighbor: "One 'simplicity' would have been enough."

The Kabbalah maintains that human beings influence the direction of creation. Every time we use free will in giving, we are in co-partnership with God and we raise the consciousness of all creation. Many people act like a beneficial presence, improving the lives of the people around them, even when they have no idea what goodness has occurred in their wake. In this way, the Kabbalah says, we transform the flow of creation.[352]

During World War II, a woman was seated in the back of a Munich bus when SS storm troopers boarded and began rounding up Jews. The woman began to cry.

"*Was ist los?*" asked the man seated beside her. "What's the matter?"

"I have no papers," she whispered. "I'm a Jew. Those soldiers will take me away!"

Immediately her neighbor screamed at the woman. "You're so stupid," he hollered, and he kept yelling curses at her until the soldiers asked what was going on. "My wife!" the man said scornfully. "She does this all the time, forgetting her papers! I don't know why I married her!"

Laughing, the soldiers got off the bus. And because of the generosity and quick thinking of a stranger, the woman lived to tell this tale, though she never learned her benefactor's name.[353]

We can give away our stuff or we can share the essence, the wisdom, the treasure of ourselves. We don't have to do a lot to be a Good Samaritan. Sometimes the best gift we can give is listening, without feeling bored, without planning what we are going to say next.

> If a person is anxious to give charity, the Holy One will furnish the money to do so.
>
> The *Talmud*
> Rabbi David Cooper, *God is a Verb*
>
> Your smiling in your brother's face is charity.
>
> The Islamic *Hadith*
> Philip Novak, *The World's Wisdom*

The easiest gift to give is that of blessing indiscriminately. A woman sneezes, and we say, "Bless you." A reckless driver zooms past our car and we whisper a blessing in his wake, for his safety and that of other drivers along his path. A dog approaches, tail wagging, and we spare a kind word for its warm welcome. We think of someone in need, and mentally surround the person's image with light. Learning to bless indiscriminately brings peace and gladness into our lives.

Giving, forgiving, and receiving—all are necessary to the cycle of flowing abundance. Allowing others to minister to us gives someone else the opportunity to be generous. And there is nothing wrong with asking for help. Indeed, we might be surprised at the goodness that finds us when we invite it with a simple and humble request.

Basically, generosity demands an outlet, like the Tao of a river flowing home to the sea. Following its own nature, love flows outward from its source to Source and back again to self, surrounding and eroding all obstacles in its path. Generosity of spirit shines in this note, found on a child's body at the liberation of the Ravensbrück concentration camp in 1945:

> O Lord, remember not only the men and women of good will, but also those of ill will. But do not remember all the suffering they have inflicted upon us—remember instead the fruits we have bought, thanks to this suffering: our comradeship, our loyalty, our humility, our courage, our generosity, the greatness of heart which has grown out of all this. And when those who have inflicted suffering on us come to judgment, let all the fruits which we have borne be their forgiveness.[354]

Gandhi believed the greatest gift we can give is to live well. We are at all times living examples for the people around us. When we live with joy and kindness lighting our days, how can we help but make a difference in this world?

5. *We practice joy.*

> Angels fly because they take themselves lightly.
>
> G. K. Chesterton

For many of us, living is a serious business. We tend to forget to laugh and have fun. We forget to focus on "what is going right." If you stopped now and made of list of all the things you do to have fun, would you be writing furiously or thinking hard? I would have trouble making that list, and I *know* the value of laughing every day.

When we take life with a grain of salt and laugh, laugh, laugh, our laughter raises the vibratory level of everything that exists! In Jerry Spinelli's book, *Loser*, main character Zinkoff is "an all purpose laugher." The boy "laughs as naturally as he breathes."

Laughing every day is more beneficial than the healthiest diet. In the 1950s, Norman Cousins used a generous daily dose of humor, along with love, faith, hope and vitamin C, to cure him of heart disease. Laughter strengthens the immune system, improves eyesight, can cure heart disease, helps with depression, pancreatitis, and bladder infections, relieves stress and toxicity, and protects against illnesses as diverse as anemia, bunions, blood clots, cancer, dementia, diabetes, leukemia, phlebitis, vascular disease, and viruses. Laughing every day is the best medicine.

The *Talmud* says, "A person can be judged by how readily he laughs with others and at himself."[355] And being able to laugh at our own follies results in our being bothered less often by the stupid things other people do.

Becoming an "all-purpose laugher" like Zinkoff is helped along by feeling grateful. In the 1997 movie *Con Air*, ex-Army Ranger Cameron Poe accidentally kills a man threatening his wife and lands in the penitentiary. "Here I am," he writes Mrs. Poe, "in maybe what seems like the worst place on Earth, and I feel I'm the luckiest man alive." People who feel grateful also feel loved and supported and blessed.

> Every time I hold a bowl of rice, I know how fortunate I am. I know that forty thousand children die every day because of lack of food and that many people are lonely, without friends or family.
>
> Thich Nhat Hanh
> *Living Buddha, Living Christ*

The air we breathe and the fact that most of us need not labor over the process of breathing—is that not a blessing? Even a deliberate and mindful fresh "breath of air" can help us ward off depression. Indeed, Jane Roberts wrote that "The very air about you sings with its own joyful consciousness. It does not know the same kind of burden of consciousness that often oppresses you."[356]

I know a lot about depression. At 17, a minister surprised me by stating that I had a right to be on this earth. At 22, when I walked and slept and worked with a darkness surrounding me that was almost tangible, there was one thought I could not ignore: *There's always hope.* At 25, after being raped more than once, the revelation that saved me was that I couldn't be happy in a romantic relationship until I was able to be happy on my own. Twenty-some years later, at the Marianas Trench of my marriage when my husband and I were both suffering from severe depression and I did *not* want to live, my friend Kurt told me, "Michelle, if you really wanted to die, you'd be dead." That concept clicked, because I knew if I'd *really* wanted to die, my Self would have arranged some fatal "accident." Besides, I was a healer; I believed I could heal myself.

Three years later, I was divorced, felt I'd been resurrected, fell in love in an impossible situation, and once again despair tapped me on the shoulder. Repeatedly. Again I felt it would be so much easier just not to be alive. On top of that, a whole slew of unfortunate things happened, until I realized I was *attracting* these events through the vibrations of lack and loss and grief I was putting out. Then Spirit reminded me of my ultimate goal: to be so great a light that I could stand on a cliff over the Pacific Ocean and guide lost souls through a stormy sea. But how could I become such a light if I couldn't shine for myself through my own internal darkness? Yes, I know about depression. I've learned techniques to cast it aside, and learned to be guided by synchronicities.

Interpretation of Synchronicities

Opportunity	may mean	accept.
Information		pay attention.
False accusations		stop trying to impress.
Easy transitions		you're on the right track.
Embarrassments		inflated ego.
Same old problems		work on yourself.
Betrayal		relocate your trust.[357]
Loss		let go of attachments.
Accidents		slow down and "ground out."
The onset of illness		give yourself time to rest and pamper yourself.

Remember the Necker Cube, which changes direction depending on our viewpoint? Almost anything can be a blessing if we look at it from a different angle. Counting our blessings and feeling grateful are quick ways to change our vibrational frequency. There is a tale about a traveler who came upon a man sitting beside the road. "I'm so poor!" wailed the weeping man. "I have nothing to call my own. Everything I own is in this one little bag."

The traveler frowned, wondering how he could help. Suddenly, he swooped down and grabbed the man's bag, then sprinted down the lane and around the bend up ahead.

Jolted out of his self-pity, the poor man rose and chased the robber. As he turned the corner, he saw his bag was setting in the middle of the road, intact and undamaged.

"Thank God," he cried. "I have my possessions back, lucky man that I am!"

How rich he felt, once he'd lost and regained all. Prosperity isn't about hard work and struggling, it's about how we *feel*. The year my "angel card" was *Gratitude*, I found that the more often I felt grateful, the more often I had something to be grateful for. Gratitude produced a snowball effect.

Sometimes we have so many trials and responsibilities that we forget to count our blessings, and we forget to have fun. For the Hindus, the creation of the universe is not work for God; rather, they call it the *play* of God, the *Vishnu-lila*.[358]

Many modern sages advise us to discover what makes our hearts sing, because the best accomplishments come from a cheerful heart, and doing something just for the fun of it cultivates a joyful attitude.

Try It Yourself

When was the last time you did something fun? When did you laugh so hard your ribs hurt? Are you making sure you get a daily dose of anti-coronary/anti-cancer laughter?

Question: What's long and yellow and seldom rings?

Answer: An unlisted banana. (Thanks, Dick van Dyke.)

Think that joke needs help? Stop and find some jokes right now that make you laugh out loud.

Rabbi Cooper recommends that we adopt the habit of inviting joy, just as we would any guest, and by doing so, we can cultivate joy so that we keep feeling joyful longer.[359] For times when we need some help, here are some techniques for regulating moods.

1. Physical exercise, of any sort, increases the endorphin level: housecleaning, car waxing, Frisbee with the dog; walking barefoot in the grass literally "grounds" you.

2. Breathing exercises:

   • Take three deep breaths, smiling all the while.

   • The yogic alternating nostril technique: Place a finger on one nostril and exhale, then inhale. Do this two more times, then switch nostrils. This exercise helps to balance the brain, emotions, and psyche.

   • Inhale to the count of *x*, hold that breath to the count of *x*, exhale to the count of *2x*, and no breath for *half-x*. This exercise contributes to intuition and long life.

   • Breathing the negatively charged night air promotes general good health. Other sources of negative-ionized air are mountain air, air around the ocean or any running water, and salt lamps.

   • Sitting before flaming candles or a hearth or campfire has much the same benefits for us as basking in sunlight has for flowers.

3. Certain foods: Carbohydrates like oatmeal allow tryptophan to enter brain cells, where serotonin, a calming chemical, is then increased. Tryptophan, the "happy hormone," is also found in eggs, turkey/poultry, chocolate, dates, milk, yogurt, cottage cheese, red meat, fish, sesame, sunflower, and pumpkin seeds, and peanuts. Dark chocolate, a mood enhancer, increases endorphins (and aids blood flow, decreases blood pressure, reduces cardiovascular disease, and has the most of antioxidants of any food).[360] Omega-3 fish and blueberries counteract stress; sunflower seeds produce pleasure-inducing dopamine, and foods containing folate and spicy foods also help. On a more subtle level, the foods we consume are basically energy, and all energy possesses some degree of consciousness. Therefore, there will be a huge difference between eating the eggs of a free-range chicken and a cooped-up hen, and between eating lovingly grown and freshly gathered vegetables and vegetables reaped by poorly paid migrant workers and shipped to be sold later.

4. Posture: Straightening the spine allows for the free flow of energy. Slouching tangles up the flow of the main physical channels and contributes to our feeling of being "in a slump."

5. Redirecting our attention. Think a different thought!

6. Doing activities we're good at, and breaking out of the routine to do something new. If our forte is baking, we can bake up a storm—our friends will be glad we did—and try a new recipe, too. If crunching numbers is our thing, we can give ourselves an imaginary million dollars and then plan the best methods of spending or investing it.

7. Doing something nice for someone else. This action removes our focus from our own worrisome "Me-Story" and forges another link in an ever-lengthening chain of passed-on kindnesses.

8. Laughing: reading a funny book or watching a funny movie.

9. Time for feeling grateful.

10. Foot massage, bubble bath, grilling out—whatever works!

11. Ayurveda. (See Appendix.)

12. Yin and yang balancing. (See Appendix.)

> The man who looks only at himself cannot but sink into despair, yet as soon as he opens his eyes to the creation around him, he will know joy.
>
> Elie Wiesel
> *Souls on Fire: Portraits and Legends of Hasidic Masters*

Sometimes *joy* is too great a stretch; it is then that *we try for an emotion a step or two higher than where we are.* For example, on the rare occasions when I feel irritated, I explore understanding. And if depressed, I shoot for blessed—thinking of reasons I feel grateful.

On the other hand, *many of us have learned to distrust feeling good!* I have noticed that when I'm flying high, I'm also liable to feel afraid that the happiness is going to disappear. With mindfulness and practice, however, we can learn to lighten up, relax, and enjoy life.

6. We go for a walk on our Path.

As children, we only watched television before bed and on Saturday mornings. All the rest of the time, we were playing outside. In the heat of summer, the sleet of fall, the blizzards of winter, we were out riding bikes, running through the sprinkler, climbing on swingsets, or building snow forts. It's never too late to run out and play! Or, like Elvis, we can leave the building and take a walk. Physical exercise contributes to good health and wards off depression and apathy.

> The journey of a thousand miles starts with the first step.
>
> *Tao Te Ching #64*

Sir James Jeans compared the motion of atomic particles to the dancers in a cotillion, and Bohm compared them to an improvisational dance, so what is more natural than to dance and sing?[361] Skip down the street!

Admire the late spring lilacs or wade through piles of autumn leaves. Make a daisy chain along the way or chant a silly song. Walking in the grass or working with the soil of the Earth grounds us and helps us stay emotionally and energetically balanced. And even if we've hit rock bottom, at least we're standing on good, solid ground. Where better to regain our balance?

Gardeners are usually both level-headed and visionary, for staying close to nature helps relaxes us and opens us to divine inspiration. When we're walking or taking a bath or on the verge of falling asleep, our brainwaves change; the "monkey mind" quiets down, and inspiration slides into consciousness. I still remember stopping dead in the middle of a field to jot down what would be one of my best poems.

Mental problems like working crossword puzzles or writing a poem help to keep our intellectual and emotional bodies balanced and in good working order. In fact, I've learned a lot about life from crossword puzzles.

Along with physical and mental exercise, making time for spiritual exercise keeps us strong and confident. Both the Kabbalah and quantum science agree that each moment is a new beginning; because of this, when we become aware of our journey, no matter what we've done before, we start out fresh again. Every day is a new day!

> What saves a man is to take a step. Then another step.
>
> C.S. Lewis

Along the way, there are signposts that mark even the vaguest of paths. Spiritual signals alert us that it is time for us to grow, and the signs are anger, depression, and anxiety. Any thought, feeling, or attitude that does not feel good is a sign of imbalance. This is when we need to stop and take time to remember that *we have a choice in how we feel and what we think.*

I had to practice disciplining my thoughts, and to "practice living." Soon I began practicing joy, doing small things that made me feel good. Six months later, because of two lovely ladies, Polly and Jeri, a pleasant job fell into my lap and I once again ventured out into the world—into the land of the living—just when I was ready to make the next psychological step. Then I came across a children's book by author Obert Skye, which had a time-stopping message.

"I am who I am," I read, "because I have made myself so."[362] What made this statement momentous was what it implied: *If I am who I am because of me, then I can be anything I want to be.* The thought sank deep into my bones, and I am trying to claim it as my own.

CROSSWORD LOGIC

Give yourself the gift of time: An hour of solitude with a crossword puzzle is soothing. (Puzzle-solving with a partner is fun, too.)

Brainstorm: Lightly fill in possible solutions.

Dare to be wrong: Being able to accept that you might have made a mistake allows the correct answer to come to you.

Make room for the best answer: It's often amazing how, after the wrong letter has been erased, the correct solution flows into the resulting vacuum.

Allow for a spectrum of solvers: Different sorts of puzzles accommodate people with differing tastes, talents, and developmental levels, but the people who work *The New York Times* Sunday puzzles refrain from making fun of those who do giant-print *Find-A-Word* games.

Unfocus to see the larger picture: Leaving an unfinished puzzle overnight allows missing information to come to you the next day. When I return to a puzzle that was begun the night before, I'm less focused on individual clues, and it's easier to see the bigger picture. For example, in accordance with the language patterns of English, "T _ E" in an almost full line of blanks will probably fill out to "the."

Look for a good fit: A certain answer may make sense in a certain place, but if it doesn't fit in with the larger solution, toss it out and look for a different solution.

Keep at it: The more puzzles you work, the more you learn. The more you read, study, and live, the more you know.

Look for synchronicities and blessings: Some puzzles have general patterns or themes.

Learn from experts: When people who use ink to work puzzles speak, it might be a good idea to consider their advice.

Don't despair: Even the most difficult puzzles come with answers.

Though the path may be dark and though I may have to step blindly, I am learning to trust that the Path lights up before me as I walk (or stumble) along. Even for the masters, enlightenment is a moment-to-moment achievement, like a series of stop signs.

- *If you don't feel good about yourself, stop!* You *are* good.

- *If you have prejudices or feel better than or inferior to someone else, stop.* Along with the Kabbalah and other spiritual philosophies, the tantric mysticism of Tibet believes that everything is an expression of Spirit, a shape of God expressed in differing degrees.

- *If you have regrets, stop!* Forgive yourself and let go of the past.
- *If you feel anxious about the future, stop!* Everything is in divine order, and God will provide.
- *If you think you must have something in order to be happy, stop!* Concentrate on what's "right" in your life. When a tire on your car goes flat, it's hard to see just what's going right—but what's going right is the other three, unflat tires![363]

When we go dancing, we don't dance in order to get somewhere; we just move to the rhythm of the music. When we walk a spiritual road, we remember that the destination is less important than the journey itself. How are we feeling, what are we giving, *when* are we in the present moment? What are we loving and learning and reveling in? *How* we get there is more important than *where* we end up.

Besides, where we're going is no farther away than right here; that divine essence we really are is right now.

7. *We make personal peace a priority.*

We can make peace a top priority in our lives. How? By taking time to be quiet. One summer afternoon I laid our sons down for naptime. "You don't have to sleep," I told two-year-old Sean and toddler Tad, "but I want you to be quiet," and I settled myself in the living room. Quite a bit of time passed before I realized I'd heard no sounds coming from the bedroom situated a mere fifteen feet away from my chair. *Too quiet,* I thought, and I rose to check on my mischief-makers.

One step into the hallway, I trod on a chunk of something. Something strange. Something mushy. Squishy but solid. And here was another. I raised my head from the bewildering hunks of—of foam rubber?—and stared into the boys' doorway. And gasped.

Pieces of crib mattress littered the floor. The crib was upended. At what was now the bottom of the structure, Sean lounged beneath a sheet he'd strung through the bed rails to create a tent. He beamed up at me. For three full seconds his gaze held mine, before I raised reluctant eyes to behold Tad—small, cuddly, barely walking Tad, sitting above my head on top of the crib.

This child who could hardly toddle across the kitchen had climbed the ladder-like rails and was sitting, unafraid, on his perch close to the ceiling. As a scream struggled through my throat, Tad giggled and waved. And Sean continued to lounge.

"Maybe Sean will work in construction when he grows up," John said later that night. We had hauled the remains of Tad's crib out and were now making up two pallets on the floor. "A building contractor." Our son's mischievous grin appeared on his father's face. "And what do you want to be," John asked me, "when you grow up?"

"An empty-nester!"

As a young mother, I judged that peace surrounds empty-nesters, but when all the children moved out, I found living alone to be a traumatic change.

> Let not your heart be troubled; neither let it be afraid.
>
> John 14:27 (KJV)

Peace comes from not making judgments. Sometimes we lose a friend or possessions because we're no longer resonating at a mutual frequency; the mutual vibrations have gone out of synch. That means we don't *need* them anymore. Or it may be a case of our out-picturing our vibrations, as when my weeping caused the foundation to leak and water pipes to burst; I was supposed to *learn* what my emotions were creating and stop judging my loss as a loss.

A Taoist story illustrates the value of non-judgment. An old peasant was barely able to eke out a living as a farmer. One morning a horse wandered into his small field.

"Now you have a horse to plow your field," exclaimed his friends from the village. "How fortunate you are!"

"Maybe," replied the old man.

That afternoon the horse galloped across the field and disappeared into the woods.

"What a terrible loss!" cried the friends.

"Maybe," replied the old man.

The next morning, the farmer rose and discovered the wild horse had returned, bringing with it a whole herd of Mustangs! Suddenly the farmer was a wealthy man.

"How wonderful!" exclaimed his friends. "How fortunate you are!"

"Maybe," replied the old man.

That afternoon, the farmer's son mounted one of the wild horses, intending to tame the creature, but the horse bucked and the young man fell and broke his leg.

"Now you have no one to help with your crops," mourned the villagers. "What a tragedy!"

"Maybe," replied the old man.

On the following day, strong-arms from the local warlord rode into the village. The soldiers forcibly gathered all the young men, conscripting them into their army, but they had no use for the boy with the broken leg.

"Oh," cried the villagers, "how fortunate you are!"

The old farmer smiled. "Maybe," he said.

The farmer trusted the Tao, believing wholeheartedly that everything works to the good of All. The same rain, for example, that ruins our picnic waters the corn growing in the field on the other side of the park. Yes, there are eddies, sinkholes, and undertows that don't move at the same rate as the main current, but they are still part of the water, part of the flow, and the current will eventually even them out.

Try It Yourself

To gauge your spiritual strength, over the course of one day, keep track of how many times you become disturbed and lose your serenity.

Anthony De Mello

Less than one hundred years ago, humans were exposed to 600 bits of information each day from other people, newspapers, and the environment. In our modern world we are bombarded with 60,000 bits and bytes of informational stimuli in one day's time, what with television, Internet, e-mail, faxes, cell and land phones, radio, billboards, and people talking. If we didn't distinguish what to allow in and what to let slide by our consciousness, we would be overwhelmed by external stimuli. The difference between judging—which always involves "judging against"—and discernment is that discernment merely directs the focus of our attention.

In our busy days, it is the "I see," "I hear," I touch" that keeps us sane—but this sense of "I-ness" also keeps us feeling separated from all the "not-I" people and things of the world. We can regain a sense of wholeness if we center ourselves in the "I Am Becoming" self in meditation or prayer, or just quiet but *aware* solitude. (For more on meditation, see next section.) Peace is precious.

One of the secrets of peace is acceptance, and acceptance lies in knowing that *every situation changes over time*. Time, patience, and inspiration help us focus on solutions and serve us well in interpersonal relationships. Instead of arguing with someone set in his or her opinion, we might mention our idea and then allow time for it to germinate.

The great physicist, Max Planck, tried to share his vision of peace by meeting with Adolph Hitler in May of 1933. At their meeting, all Hitler did was to rant against the Jews. Planck said, "I failed to make myself understood . . . There is simply no language in which one can talk to such men." No matter what the outcome of his attempt, though, he probably gained some sense of peace because he had tried.[364] Planck knew that arguing with an angry person is futile, and reciprocating with anger explosive. He also knew when to "make himself scarce." Watching out for ourselves sometimes means stepping to one side to avoid being run over.

Peace can be found at any time, at any place and, as Jesus so often found, peace more easily comes with solitude. However, with discipline and an "I can" attitude, a moment of quiet solitude is possible in the middle of a traffic jam or at a crowded school cafeteria. It was, in fact, during a summer of afternoons spent at the swimming pool with kids yelling and music blaring from the overhead speaker that I learned how to concentrate, no matter what was happening.

Sometimes, however, we have too much solitude while we focus on the wrong thing. Once a man named Chris was shipwrecked on a desert island. He spent a long time asking, "Oh, God, why did this happen to me?" Eventually, he went exploring and found a pond of fresh water, and he knew he wouldn't starve because coconut trees circled the beach. He spent the rest of the day constructing a lean-to and bed made of palm branches. The next day he labored over a driftwood table, which he placed beside his bed. On it he set his only family photograph. Beside the photo he lit a rolled up moss candle with one of the four matches that hadn't been ruined by saltwater. After uttering a prayer of thanksgiving, he went out to look for food.

Chris searched along the beach but soon noticed a column of smoke was rising from beyond the trees. "My God," he exclaimed, "my home! My picture! They're on fire!" Sure enough, everything he'd built was charred, and there was no trace of the family photo. Half the night Chris ranted against God and life and his bad luck.

The next morning Chris woke and for a moment thought he was still dreaming, for he heard the sound of an engine. An engine! Quickly he sprinted down to shore, where a dinghy had just beached; beyond the reef lay an ocean liner. The crew of the launch helped him aboard and ten minutes later Chris was standing on deck, being greeted by the captain.

"You saved me! Thank you, thank you," he said, shaking the captain's hand. "But how did you know where I was?"

The captain replied, "We saw your smoke signal yesterday."

In this fable, how much time did the shipwrecked man waste on how unfair his life was? Both the Kabbalah and the *Talmud* say that because our world is not perfect, neither is it fair or unfair. Time and space are like a blackboard on which we write and draw as well as we are able, but when we begin exclaiming, "Why me? It's not fair!" we are operating in victim-mode, singing the blues about how we've been wronged while others are leading more perfect lives. To guard against feeling this way, Talmudic teachers taught their students not to pray for a lighter load, but for a stronger back.[365]

Try It Yourself

Imagine you're a pebble thrown into a body of water . . .

Effortlessly, you as the stone sink through the turbulent surface waters . . .

Unattached to anything, you fall until you find perfect rest at the stillness of the bottom . . .

Having let go of everything worrisome, you now are not pushed or pulled by anything, and you are at peace.

Thich Nhat Hanh
The Miracle of Mindfulness

Positive results (and lower blood pressure) come from a state of peace and, like learning of our innate enlightenment, peacefulness takes practice. When I was worried about Valdi consulting an oncologist because he was coughing up blood, every so often I would have to take myself in hand, calm down, and refocus on sending him beneficial energy. But after not hearing from him for two days, I grew worried again, which popped me into the old programming that I could not live through another heartbreak, and life is "too hard." What happened? I was stopped for mindlessly driving over the speed limit. Metaphysical translation: Control my runaway thoughts! Outcome: a warning ticket.

The benign citation was the first of a series of blessings to come that evening in answer to my unspoken prayer. Merrie Kate brought home my favorite dinner. My friend, Lisa, came over and shared joys and concerns, homemade chocolate cake Roxie had shared with me, and prayers of thanksgiving. By the time I went to bed, I was feeling joyful. Then, before sleep descended, when my heart grew hot and I knew Valdi was thinking about me, I checked the computer and found he had emailed me that very minute with the news of *no* cancer. Like shipwrecked Chris, I had wasted time and peace of mind worrying.

Peace is more accessible when we remember the Chinese character for "crisis" also represents "opportunity." A Middle Eastern story tells about a falsely imprisoned man. His friend brought him a prayer rug, even though what the prisoner really wanted was a hacksaw. He railed a while at the injustice and cursed his friend, but after the emotional storm passed, he decided, "Why let the rug go to waste?" He began using the rug in his daily prayers, and the more he used it, the more he puzzled over the unusual pattern in the weave. He looked closely and discovered that the pattern diagrammed the inside of the lock on his cell door. He'd had the means for freedom with him the whole time, if only he'd been calm enough to notice![366]

Of course, simple little activities also lay the groundwork for feeling peaceful, like popping bubble wrap. It's fun, too.

8. *We DECIDE to be happy (and then we stop trying so hard).*

The author of books for young adults, Jerry Spinelli, wrote about Nazi-occupied Warsaw, telling the tale through the eyes of an orphan. The youngster, Misha, asks his friend one day what "happy" is. His elder replies, "Did you ever taste an orange? . . . Were you ever cold, and then you were warm?" He taps his chest and adds, "That was happy. Happy is here. Here . . . Inside." [367]

Buddha believed a tamed mind brings happiness. From the *Essene Book of The Teacher of Righteousness* comes "For to weigh thy happiness according to that which may befall thee is to live as a slave." (Note that Jesus himself was an Essene.) This sounds like Confucius, who said, "To be elated at success and disappointed at failure is to be the child of circumstances; how can such a one be called master of himself?"

One trait that allows us to be unshaken by things outside ourselves is faith or, as Jesus said, *haimanuta*: remaining centered within Sacred Unity.[368] What they all mean is that happiness is a decision we make while centered in peace, and we choose our feelings by choosing our thoughts.

We *can* control our thoughts and by doing so choose which emotions we will feel. An example of this is someone who's just ended a relationship. Sitting around worrying or listening to sad songs will almost certainly bring depression, while guarding against loneliness by calling a friend or taking a walk can bring a measure of relief. And conditions tend to be self-perpetuating, so if we choose to be cheerful, that mood is likely to carry us through dark times.[369]

Setting apart a short time every day or night when we refuse to worry about anything benefits our general outlook. The Bible warns us to beware of false prophets. What are false prophets? Thoughts that do not serve us well. "Let every tree that does not bring forth good fruit be hewn down and cast into the fire." If worries or emotional hurts keep badgering us, we might imagine popping each one like a bursting balloon, or giving that weedy idea a tug, yanking it out by its roots, and replacing it with a more pleasant thought.

Emotion literally means to "move out of," and unless we resist, emotions *do* move and change. This is hard to remember when we're feeling bad, but that is when the mantra "This too shall pass" helps. We are *not* what we feel. We are spirit wearing a coat of flesh.

At the same time, denying what we feel, whether it be depression, anger, resentment, or shame, won't help at all. First we have to *acknowledge* the emotion, without judging against the feeling (which makes us feel worse and strengthens what we'd rather let go of). We need to feel that emotion and then let it move out of us. To cry when we're sad. To punch a pillow when we're angry. To let it out, without acting like a human Mount St. Helens. And all the while, to keep in mind that our moods change.

Even in the darkest of times, we can decide how we are going to feel in any situation. Holocaust survivor Elie Wiesel has written about Jews who were walled inside ghettoes and those who lived in death camps. "In the shadow of the executioner," he says, "they celebrated life. Startled Germans whispered to each other of Jews dancing in the cattle cars rolling toward Birkenau."[370]

There are ways to remind ourselves of how we have been blessed, like adopting the mantra, *Whatever can go right, will,* making time daily to be *aware* of what's going "right" in life, and pampering ourselves for a few moments every day or night. Meditate. Have a bite of chocolate. A foot massage. A warm bath. Whatever works (and does no harm to others).

Ultimately, however, *nothing outside ourselves has the power to make us happy.* Remember how prosperity is more an attitude than what we possess? Happiness is a commitment to look at life in a positive way. Think of the "clouds with silver linings" our mothers taught us about. Happiness is a natural part of each of us. For example, babies cry when they need something, but otherwise, they don't feel shame and they don't worry. They laugh and coo and snuggle and play with their toes, exploring as much of their world as they can reach, never doubting themselves.

The trouble with trying to make the right accident happen is that it won't.

Douglas Adams
*Mostly Harmless: The Fifth Book in the Increasingly
Inaccurately Named Hitchhikers Trilogy*

We can take a lesson from babies. Sometimes we get along better when we stop trying so hard. Intense concentration or the attempt to force an issue hampers alpha waves, which are the brain waves associated with higher consciousness and inspiration.

When we try to force an outcome, we actually push it away from us, energetically. If we wake in the middle of the night and *try* to go back to sleep and cannot, we get frustrated and the frustration prevents us from relaxing, which would naturally lead to sleep. If, on the other hand, we accept the fact that we're awake, and we lie still and quiet, peaceful in wakefulness, sleep usually overtakes us. (For insomnia relief, see Breathing and Attunement section.) Another example is when people try not to smoke. They try really really hard *not* to smoke, which places their attention on what they don't have, and they get more of what they are focusing on—the craving to smoke.

The feeling of contentment is real wealth. I thought it was interesting that the word "wealthy" comes from an Old English word (*wel*) that meant well-being. "Being well." It even sounds good, but how do we access it? One way is through moderation, to lessen the behavior of wanting more, more, more. The Middle Path of Buddhism allows for polar opposites but doesn't get caught up by either extreme, so that while life may include suffering, life is also filled with blessings, with beauty, with grace.

> If you realize that you have enough, you are truly rich.
>
> *Tao Te Ching # 33*

"Moderation in all things" is the Western adage that expresses this Buddhist ideal, and is also advocated by Christian, Islamic, and Zen writings:

- "And every man that striveth for the mastery is temperate in all things." (1 Corinthians 9:25a, KJV)

- "People of the Book, do not go to excess in your religion." (*Koran: Women [al Nisaa']* 171)[371]

- "Although gold dust is precious, when it gets in your eyes, it obstructs vision." (Zen)[372]

Too often we go looking for happiness, for pleasure, for companionship, for material goods that we think will bring us happiness, and the farther away our goal seems, the more frantically we search for it. We try harder. We try so hard we wear ourselves out, when what we really need to do is to pause and breathe and look inside ourselves. We work too hard at trying to force the outcome. It's interesting to note that in the New Testament, the root of the Greek word usually translated as "evil," *paneros*, means "to toil."

The East has a philosophy of "effortlessness," or *Wu-Wei* in Chinese, also translated as "not forcing." Effortlessness is a natural state for most living creatures. A rose, for example, doesn't *try* to be a rose, it just *is*. Spontaneously. *Wu-wei* is more about not struggling than about inaction or passivity: The toned, trained, resilient athlete has a better chance in competition than an overweight couch potato. And the inspired writer has probably spent many years reading, studying, writing, and reflecting.

An athlete moves into "the zone" when reflexes come from instinct and intuition, what Zen calls "no-mind." For a poet, the zone is verses flowing from muse to paper, whole and wholly pleasing and needing little revision. To the Aborigine in Australia, the zone is accessed through trust and knowing that the universe will provide what they need. To the Taoist, non-doing allows events to occur naturally, but it isn't sitting on the couch while waiting for good fortune to knock on the door.

A joke tells about a man who wanted to win the lottery, so for a week he rose five minutes early to say extra prayers. When this didn't work, he spent the next week rising an hour early for more time in supplication. When he arrived at the end of the third week and twice-daily prayers he cried out, "God, help me!"

"Look, Floyd," said a strange voice, "help Me out here. Go buy a lottery ticket, will you?"

Neither does effortlessness mean staying in a toxic relationship or remaining uninvolved when a mugger grabs an elderly lady's purse. *Wu-Wei* doesn't condone laziness or non-caring.

Effortlessness calls for adapting to what is taking place around us, and we have the ability to do it well; humans must be one of the most adaptable species on earth. I grew up with Ozzie and Harriet, Rob and Laura Petrie, the ever-elegant Loretta Young, and Dionne Warwick singing about wives being lovers. So, for nearly thirty years at five o'clock every night, I would brush my hair and put on lipstick and perfume . . . and after the divorce, I sorely missed having a reason to do so. Years have passed now; I have adapted to a new schedule (which often includes evening hours providing eldercare). But I can still wear lipstick and perfume—anytime I like!

Hungry? "Go cook your rice," a master might say, adding, "and when you cook your bowl, do it cheerfully. Make everything you do a *light* experience."

> I kept continuing now to play with [the problem I had been working on] in a relaxed fashion . . . and it was just like taking a cork out of a bottle—everything just poured out, and in very short order I worked the things out for which I later won the Nobel Prize . . . So I decided I'm going to do things only for the fun of it.
>
> Richard Feynman
> quoted by Christopher Sykes, *No Ordinary Genius*

Zen master D. T. Suzuki said that what happens to the enlightened person looks like luck to the rest of us. My friend, Marie, just *knew* she would find a job, and she refused to let unemployment hinder her generosity. As for myself, when my friend, Polly, introduced me to office manager Jeri, who was looking for help, the secretarial job fell into my lap. I could call it luck, or synchronicity, or trusting that I'd get what I needed (which was a job), but I hadn't panicked over being unemployed or wasted energy applying for positions I wasn't qualified for—I had "networked," however, and that brought about my good fortune naturally.

Often we look for good fortune in the wrong place. When our house was ready to be put on the market, most of our belongings got boxed up. But the house didn't sell, so I decided to unpack my art supplies and start painting again. The only problem was, where were my paints? I looked under my bed. Not there. I looked through boxes in the storage room. Not there. My daughter offered to help in the search; we shifted boxes, opened boxes, tripped over boxes, and still no paints. I began to cry. Four hundred dollars' worth of paints and brushes packed away. Or stolen? Or forgotten at someone's house after a dogsitting job? Gone, at any rate. All gone, I feared.

Patting my back, Merrie Kate observed, "Mom, they must be where we haven't looked."

"But we've looked everywhere!" I said. "We've looked everywhere they should be."

She rolled her eyes and left to create her own art project, an ice cream cone.

Downstairs I went, to the storage room once again. *Somewhere we haven't looked.* I took myself in hand and sent out a wordless plea to the universe, to God, to Grama Zelma, our family's personal saint for locating lost items . . . and then calmly walked to the farthest corner, stuck a blind hand through a small opening between boxes, and felt the fabric of the suitcase holding the art supplies.

So often when we're searching for something, we look where it should be. Then we look again because it *should* be there, even if it isn't. Even when, in despair, we broaden our search, we still look in places we're *likely* to find the lost item. It was not until I cultivated peace within myself—slowed down to allow inner light to shine—that I found what I was looking for, and I found it somewhere I hadn't looked before. I stopped listening to my ego *should* me, I stopped being afraid, I stopped feeling desperate. It was then that I was centered in a different kind of light.

Struggling along while searching in the wrong place guarantees that we'll never find happiness. Effortlessness also involves not wasting energy to fight or judge against something we cannot change. Happiness is an "inside" treasure. A light in the darkness. As Walt Whitman declared, "I am myself good-fortune."

> The mistake of looking for Buddhism, for Zen, for truth, reality, God, apart from this thing at this place at this moment is so ineradicable as to make us think sometimes that perhaps after all God is up there in the sky, and reality is a big block of Something that we must nibble at, and the truth something that must be sought with shoes shod with iron. But as Stevenson said of the touchstone, "What if it was in his pocket all the time?"
>
> Reginald Horace Blyth
> *Games Zen Masters Play*

Christ consciousness, Buddha mind, messianic consciousness, God Mind—in a word, en*light*enment—doesn't usually happen in one great cascade of complete wisdom. More often, spirit-growth acts like a constant drip of water that ever so slowly erodes solid bedrock. Little by little, awareness of god-ing creeps into our systems, and enlightenment blossoms like quanta harmonizing into a uniform laser beam. Once formed, the harmonic light must be nurtured, for no light ever eliminates all the darkness, outside or inside an enlightened person. No, light works *with* the darkness, because without an area of un-light, light wouldn't be recognizable!

When we recognize that spark of the divine within, we have to remain patient with ourselves over any lapses and gently nurse the light along. But we keep trying, moment by moment, and keep choosing to be happier in the *present* moment.

All my life I've been riding a train bound for the town of Happiness. At each station I told myself, "No, at the next station I'll find Happiness." Towns on either side of the tracks have come and gone: College. Marriage. Children. It's time for me to get off the train and stop looking down the road. How true is Jon Kabat-Zinn's warning, "If you miss the 'here,' you will likely miss the 'there,' too."[373] Marie told me many years ago, "You may be unhappy now, but you know there will be a time in the future when you are happy again, so why waste all the time in between?"

> If we cling to our idea of hope in the future, we might not notice the peace and joy that are available in the present moment. The best way to take care of the future is to take care of the present moment. Practicing conscious breathing, aware of each thought and each act, we are reborn, fully alive . . .
>
> Thich Nhat Hanh
> *Living Buddha, Living Christ*

If we have "enough" *right now* (and maintain a reasonable notion of what constitutes enough), that is when we live contentedly; it is then that we have *chosen* to be happy.

9. We accept things as they are (but make them shine brighter).

In 1970, blacks were marching down Pennsylvania Avenue, students were protesting the Vietnam war, dissidents were burning the flag, and women were seeking liberation. It was a time when advertisers told us that blondes had more fun and, in order to experience some of this fun, we women—blondes, brunettes *and* redheads—needed to "lift and separate." Or so advised Playtex. Weighing in at less than 100 pounds, I mourned the fact that small breasts adorned my small frame. I was already lifted and separated, so I figured the Cross Your Heart bra would be perfect for me.

I crossed campus and walked into the department store. On the second floor I found the Playtex display, chose the smallest bra, and closed the curtain to the fitting room. Began to undress. Wrangled into bra straps. Awkwardly managed the hooks . . . Then I raised my head to look straight at the mirror, to gaze at the manufactured marvel that was going to bring me fun and popularity.

What I saw in the mirror left me humiliated. That smallest of bras was still too big for me! It bagged. It puckered. It looked ghastly. Hastily I cast aside the Cross Your Heart and figuratively burned my bra. (Studies have since proven that women benefit from wearing bras no longer than necessary, as the strictures that tight bras place on the lymph nodes can contribute to breast cancer.)[374]

American merchandizing had thrust me into Women's Liberation via the back door. True liberation came more slowly, as I let go of my dream of large breasts and learned to appreciate my body and my own well-matched, never bound-in and never sagging bosom. Now, cross my heart, I like me. But what about other people?

Acceptance contributes to our happiness. Acceptance. Respectful non-judgment. Unconditional love. These are all part of the same attitude, and they involve accepting people without expecting *them* to change. Being happy doesn't mean everything's going perfectly. Happiness comes when we rise above the imperfections of the moment.

Think about how falling in love feels—the other person is probably far from ideal, but his or her imperfections just don't matter. The love we feel expands to include our surroundings; it seems as if "God's in His heaven, and all's right with the world." Actually, it is we ourselves who are residing in heaven at that moment. When we begin to lose that all-inclusive feeling is when we begin to notice differences, and we slap labels on this and that. Uh-oh. Whatever we label, we've judged, and whatever we judge we set apart from "me," lessening our power to understand it and to make constructive changes. We can only begin to understand a situation or someone with whom we feel a connection; *whatever we embrace, we can hope to heal.*

The story goes that a mother once came home to find that her 14-year-old daughter had cleaned her bedroom without being asked. Amazing, thought Mom, and then she saw the note on Samantha's pillow. "Oh, God," she muttered, and she sat and read:

> "Dear Mom, I'm eloping with Chase, but don't worry. Chase says we'll be really happy in his tent in the woods, and he helped his ex-girlfriend have her baby so he'll know what to do when our baby is born. I know he'll be a good provider because he's super at making crystal meth. It might be hard with him having AIDS, but I just know they'll find a cure for him. So don't worry. Chase will take good care of me . . .
>
> p.s. None of that is true. I just wanted you to think about stuff worse than my report card. (I got a D in Civics.) Call me at Jo's house when I can come home. Still love you—Sammy"

The cultivation of an accepting attitude is a vital part of practicing non-judgment and "Carrying an Umbrella." We can, in general, accept things as they are, both the yin and the yang. Although our world is full of polarities, things that need improving, and people (most of us) who need to grow spiritually, nothing that was created is not good, and what is not good was *not* created by God.

This leaves us with two possibilities. The first is that our perception of bad or evil must be false, that bad is the lower end of a spectrum, a small part of the larger picture we cannot see. Our definition of "bad," therefore, must be based on faulty information. The second possibility is that what we're seeing is part of our own nightmare and is only an illusion, real enough while we're participating in the daily dream-earth existence, but as a whole simply a communal dream (or nightmare) our souls are conjuring up. Taoism and the Kabbalah support the first premise, and *A Course in Miracles* advocates the second premise at great length, as does Buddhism.

Whether we're dreaming or whether we're mistaken in what we perceive, changing our vision of ourselves changes the way the world looks. The Baal Shem Tov maintained that absolute evil doesn't exist because of the divine spark that resides at the core of every living being—which the ego often fails to recognize.[375]

When the great Tao is forgotten, goodness and piety appear.

Tao Te Ching #18
Stephen Mitchell, translator

When the legendary Adam and Eve ate of the Tree of Knowledge, they gave birth to the human ego. The ego is the faculty that judges everything and everyone, and judgment always involves rejection and condemnation. Before the ego's development, humans accepted every part of their human nature and Nature itself and "saw that it was good" (if they thought about at all).

When we're not operating at the level of the divine, that's when we start tagging things with "good" and "bad" labels, which in turn generates fear and guilt. Ultimately, Satan and hell became involved in the ego's plan for an iffy sort of salvation, for if we feel condemned, then we also feel the need to be saved. But saved from what? These are manmade distinctions and manmade outgrowths of *fear*. A standard that transcends our idea of justice does exist.

> The moment we left paradise and fell from grace was the same moment we attached the idea of "good" to one thing, and "bad" to another. This created something to fear.
>
> Richard Dupuis
> *From the Mouth of God*

In God's eyes, everything is *still* holy and wholly good. Of our own making are hell and evil and the doing of evil, which becomes more profound as we feel more separated from God and more sinful by nature. The moment we believe in our holiness, the moment we believe that everything God created is sacred to and beloved of God, that is the moment enlightenment comes and our feeling of abandonment begins to dissipate, like the illusion (or bad dream) it really is.

Like most people, I'm inclined to resist "what is." When my family invited my 90-year-old grandma to move into our house, the upheaval began immediately. Quite some time passed before I accepted that Grama Zelma was not going to change; due to a hearing disability, Grama's speech would always sound too loud. Doors would slam and drawers would bang and her metal walker would thump across the floor and I, a light sleeper, was going to hear every shout, every slam, every thump, and every bang in my sleep. Not good, not good! It wasn't until I realized that Grama had the right to be quite as annoying as any other member of our rambunctious family did I lighten up, laugh at myself, and begin learning how to sleep in spite of external noises. (The sound of a deep-humming fan helped.) A new attitude of acceptance allowed me to discover the joys my grandma brought to our home.

A Course in Miracles is emphatic in its insistence that spirit-based humanity is sinless in nature. John 8:1-12 tells about Jesus' refusal to condemn a woman. Had the woman actually sinned? Maybe "sin" has been mistranslated; she certainly made a poor choice, and it landed her in trouble. But the crowd was just as human as the woman they wanted to stone. We inhabit the kingdom of heaven (or Eden) when we decide not to assign labels, not to polarize our existence—in short, when we practice acceptance.

> In mythology, Sisyphus was condemned to rising each morning and returning to his unending task of rolling a large boulder up a steep hill. He was a strong man, and with great effort he accomplished the task—but the boulder always rolled back down the hill.
>
> Sisyphus accepted his fate without using his head. Had he been solution-oriented, he would have saved muscle-power in the long run by chipping off a piece of boulder each morning before putting shoulder to stone. Eventually, his burden would have vanished into the gravel underneath his feet.
>
> Rev. Duke Tufty, Unity Temple on the Plaza

Accepting "what is" doesn't mean we can't work to change it. Sometimes we work to improve inhumane conditions, but we have to be careful that our judgments and even our compassion don't cripple us, if we see sickness and suffering and fall to the level where a feeling of uselessness overcomes motivation for constructive action. (Feeling hopeless and helpless is a result of the ego's denial to accept our god-nature.)

HAPPINESS

Buddhism—Dalai Lama: If you want others to be happy, practice compassion. If you want to be happy, practice compassion.
—Buddha: Thousands of candles can be lit from a single candle, and the life of the candle will not be shortened. Happiness never decreases by being shared.
—Thich Nhat Hanh: Sometimes your joy is the source of your smile, but sometimes your smile can be the source of your joy.

Christian—Helen Keller: When one door of happiness closes, another opens, but often we look so long at the closed door that we do not see the one which has been opened for us.

Islam—Habib Bourguiba: Happy is the person who can laugh at himself. He will never cease to be amused.

Jewish—He who is rich is one who is content with his lot. (*Ethics of Our Fathers* 4:1)

Modern Sages—Leo Buscaglia: What we call the secret of happiness is no more a secret than our willingness to choose life.
—Deepak Chopra: Happiness is a continuation of happenings which are not resisted.
—Jacques Cousteau: The happiness of the bee and the dolphin is to exist. For man it is to know that and to wonder at it.
—Malcolm Forbes: When what we are is what we want to be, that's happiness.
—Louise Hay: When we really love and accept and approve of ourselves exactly as we are, then everything in life works.
—Princess Di: Nothing brings me more happiness than trying to help the most vulnerable people.
—George Santayana: Knowledge of what is possible is the beginning of happiness.
—Albert Schweitzer: Happiness is nothing more than . . . a bad memory.
—Red Skelton: Live by this credo: Have a little laugh at life and look around you for happiness instead of sadness.

Sufi (Mystical Islam)—Hazrat Inayat Khan: Happy is he who does good to others; miserable is he who expects good from others.

Taoism—Throw away holiness and wisdom, and people will be a hundred times happier. Throw away morality and justice, and people will do the right thing. Throw away industry and profit, and there won't be any thieves. If these three aren't enough, just stay at the center of the circle and let all things take their course. (*Tao Te Ching #19*)
—Zhuangzi: Happiness is the absence of the striving for happiness.

Buddhism and **Vedanta**—Suffering comes from being attached to a person, place, thing, or attitude ("My way or the highway").

Vedanta (Hindu)—Our nature is happiness.
—Vivekananda: Neither good nor bad, neither life nor death—only the one infinite Brahman exists . . . When a man has arrived at that perception, he has become free . . . [and] he alone can say, "I enjoy life, and I am happy in this life." . . . If all my pleasures are in myself, I must have pleasure there all the time because I can never lose my Self. ("Practical Vedanta")

The *Bhagavad Gita* urges us to remain centered: "One who has control over the mind is tranquil in heat and cold, in pleasure and pain, and in honor and dishonor; and is ever steadfast with the Supreme Self." In other words, the same in suffering and in joy—content always.

What? Wait a minute. I'm supposed to be content in poverty? Content in abuse? Happy that my son Matt, a gentle and kind healer, is in prison for a crime he did not commit? But there wasn't much I could do in this situation, and feeling sick and railing against injustice did not help him. It was tough, but I had to accept his situation and think about the ways I *can* help and encourage him. Happiness—or at least efficiency—requires accepting our circumstance at any given moment, whether it's a joy we revel in or a situation we intend to change as soon as possible. In any case, *whatever we focus on is what we're going to get more of.* Scientifically, it's a case of mind over matter—if we don't mind, it doesn't matter!

One Saturday, Mr. and Mrs. McDaniels went out for breakfast and listened as the waitress told them about the Senior Special—two eggs, bacon or sausage, hash browns and toast—for $4.95.

"I'll have the Special," said Mrs. McDaniels, "but without eggs."

"Oh?" said the waitress. "Then the price is $6.49. You see, if you change the Special, then it's not the Special anymore, it's à la carte."

Mr. McDaniel began to protest, but his wife patted his arm. She accepted the situation, decided to be practical, and told the waitress, "All right, dear, I'll have the Special, with my eggs raw and in the shell in a to-go container."

The woman accepted the situation and, working "within the system" thought of a clever solution. *She went with the flow.*

It is the ego that rejects, while the spirit accepts. We hardly realize what we're doing when we say, "Oh, no, not really," in the face of a compliment. If we, as a rule, brush aside compliments, how can we accept blessings when they come our way? How can we manage anything that "comes at us"? How much harder is it to interact with someone we'd really rather not be around, to say "Namaste" and mean it?

We accept someone by honoring the divinity that is inherent in him, by letting go of any remembrance of her past mistakes, by remembering that we are One. We may learn from past experiences, and yet both physics and metaphysics say there is *no past*, only this moment right here and now. Certainly, only in this moment do we have any power. Yes, Hitler, for example, committed atrocious crimes against humanity but, although there was probably little chance for his redemption, it remains that we are One. One quantum soup. One Being. All connected. When we fail to allow for the possibility of divinity in any person, *we harm ourselves,* damage our peace of mind, and limit our power to work for positive change. Zen says, "No ego, no problem."

Remember the Babemba tribe, who live without rules and without crime because they actively affirm the goodness of one another? A path like theirs seems like a sure road to happiness. Affirm. Forgive, or take no offense in the first place. Speak kindly. Touch softly. Bless indiscriminately. By doing so, each of us becomes a bright light that shines into our world and makes it better.

The ego was not created by God. It is a product of the human mind and, for the most part, the manufacturer of our nightmare. We are not small, not helpless, not weak, not bad. Everything our eyes can see is a distortion. Accepting a new vision based on what we *cannot* see reminds us just how powerful we are, and enables us to make changes so that "what is" becomes "what shines even brighter."

And to help us look at the larger picture, mystics remind us that the sharpest stones beneath our feet may be diamonds.[376] Rock on!

| Allow "this" to be, because it is, anyway. |
| Jon Kabat-Zinn |
| Unity Temple on the Plaza, Kansas City, Missouri, |
| January 30, 2005 |

10. We place ourselves in win/win situations.

"Live long and prosper," Mr. Spock often said. For most of us it's easier to prosper when we're in win/win situations, like the Sufi, Ali, who boasted that he could see in the dark. "Then why," asked his friends, "do you carry a lamp at night?"

Ali quickly answered, "I only use a lamp to keep other people from bumping into me. Right?"[377]

Well, yes and no.

The word *Allah* means *yes* and *no.* The word comes from the root *AL* (or *EL*), meaning the sacred Something—the ultimate Yes—coupled with the root *LA* (or *LO*), meaning the sacred Nothing—the ultimate No. People in the Middle East have used some form of this name for at least 4,000 years: the Hebrew *Elohim*, the Aramaic *Alaha* (used by Jesus), and the Arabic *Allah*, used now by both Muslims and Arabic-speaking Christians.[378]

Knowing when to say "No" is just as important in choosing win/win situations as knowing when to say "Yes." If, for example, I were to go snow skiing, I'd start on the bunny slope rather than the expert run. Having said no to the slalom course, I'm sure that even the bunny slope would earn me bruises, but it would still be a winning situation because I tried something new, even if my first effort ended in what seemed like failure (ouch!).

Too often I've set myself up to fail: visiting the grocery store when I was hungry. Attempting a full-length dress for my first knitting project (yes, a success—Mom wore it as a nightgown). Expecting my young children to behave a certain way without having first explained in vivid detail what I expected. Allowing myself to feel overwhelmed by a To-Do List, the nightly news, the plight of the starving, my own hell. The feeling of being overwhelmed is pure ego, keeping me small, frightened of and "safe" from new experiences in my familiar comfort zone.

> Life is either a daring adventure or nothing.
>
> Helen Keller

Sometimes we've won, though we may not realize it. Merely moving out of our familiar routines is an accomplishment. Like Captain Kirk, whose mission was to "boldly go" where no one had gone before, physicist Richard Feynman loved traveling to places off the beaten track.[379] He was a great adventurer because he didn't measure his life by success or failure, but pushed ahead with a passion for learning, and doing whatever he did playfully. Success and failure are less important for Sufis than "standing still," which they believe is the greatest misfortune.[380] If I quit standing still, I guess that at least gets me out of the losing situation of not moving at all.

We may remain in our comfort zones because we're afraid of the unknown, or because we strive for perfection. Either way, we miss out on chances to grow. Katherine was a very bright nine-year old who shied away from new activities because if she couldn't do something right off the bat, she preferred to fall back on the things she could do well. She'd forgotten there was a time when she didn't know how to read or jump rope or play the piano. Knowing when to keep trying is essential in mastering a skill or creating something new. When we think of Thomas Edison, we recall his successes—the improved light bulb, the phonograph, waxed paper and tin foil, and the primitive forerunner of the television tube—but those triumphs required taking a chance on something new and repeated trials.

Trials seem like losing battles, but in those times strangers often touch us briefly, appearing at need and then quickly fading from our lives. They are special blessings, like the pretty coed who paused to ask after me when I was sitting outside St. Mary's, grieving for my late father-in-law, Joe. I may not have learned the name of the Girl with the Blue Backpack, but her kindness I shall never forget. Only a moment it took for her to touch my shoulder and ask if I was all right, but my gratitude for that kindness has lasted the rest of my life.[381]

Another way we place ourselves in win/win situations is by displaying a basic courtesy toward everyone and everything we encounter. (Remember, we reap what we sow.) A person great of heart treats subordinates, children, strangers, and animals with special kindness.

There is a well-circulated (but probably untrue) tale about the consequences of disrespect. In the mid-1880s, a man and his wife walked into the outer office of Harvard University's president. Because the lady was dressed in a gingham dress, the secretary pegged them for "nobodies." The couple waited a long time before the secretary told President Eliot about the visitors. He was too important to give his time to someone wearing gingham, but he allowed them into his office.

"Last year," the wife said, "our son died of typhoid fever. My husband and I would like to erect a memorial to him. We'd like to donate a building to Harvard."

"Do you know much a building costs?" Eliot scoffed. "Five million dollars."

"Really?" she said. "Leland, we could start our own university."

Within six years, the railroad baron Leland Stanford and his wife opened the doors to Stanford University "for the children of California."

Another way to create win/win situations is by being understanding. Two-year-old Jenny was sitting at the lunch table on her booster seat—no, she was *bouncing* in her seat—when her silliness caused her to tip over a bowl of rice and creamed tuna. With a stricken expression, she looked across the table at me.

I smiled and said calmly, "You know what to do."

The little girl jumped down, ran to the kitchen for a wet rag, and cleaned up. Then she happily refilled her bowl and settled down to eat. I understood that happy children bounce and shriek in delight and do silly things (me, too). The children understood that "we clean up our own messes." It was a win/win situation all around.

But no matter how understanding, how lucky, how thoroughly in the zone we are, we can't always win. Let's think about failure as a possible blessing in disguise: When the air conditioner's running, along with the washer and dishwasher and ceiling fan, turning on the microwave blows the fuse. If, however, the circuit breaker hadn't tripped, the overloaded wiring could have started a fire that would burn down the house. And cracks in sidewalks—did you know they are deliberately designed stress points that protect the concrete squares from cracking?[382] Things like these are the *rewards* of failure!

> To appreciate beauty and find the best in others; to leave the world a bit better, whether by a healthy child, a garden patch, a redeemed social condition, to know even one life has breathed easier because you have lived, this is to have succeeded.
>
> Ralph Waldo Emerson

Ralph Waldo Emerson linked success with generosity and creativity. And John Cleese of *Monty Python* fame associates creativity with

- quiet space ("an oasis of quiet"),
- time without responsibilities or racing thoughts,
- time for many ideas to come rather than merely the easiest solution,
- confidence that you won't make a mistake while you're playing with silly or absurd ideas ("Nothing is wrong . . . and any drivel may lead to the breakthrough"),
- having a positive outlook and surrounding yourself with positive people,
- and playfulness and humor (which lead to being open to new ideas).

Indeed, Cleese interspersed his lecture with jokes, like "How many psychiatrists does it take to change a light bulb? . . . Only one, but the light bulb really has to *want* to change."[383]

From an open, calm mind and a loving, *light*, and confident heart come the win/win events of success: well-being, compassion, peace, and constructive creating—heaven itself.

May we create joyfully and mindfully, and remember that we are blessed.

> You don't have to worry about me. I always look both ways—Dean
>
> Stuart Hample and Eric Marshall
> *Children's Letters to God: The New Collection*

APPENDIX

Ayurveda

People in India follow a system called Ayurveda, which determines a person's body type and personality traits and then recommends specific activities and foods to eat. Like Chinese medicine, ayurveda also considers the wisdom of the Five Elements. Most people are more than one dosha, and the elements of every dosha are required for well-balanced health and psychology.

Vata doshas are usually slight of build, enthusiastic, and energetic. Because they are quick in their movements and thinking, they may suffer from insomnia or irregularity, overexert themselves and tire easily, and worry a lot when the dosha is unbalanced. They dislike cold. They represent the elements of space and air.

Pitta doshas have more fiery temperaments, even down to red hair and freckles. They are intellectual, intense, passionate, and precise, and tend to be leaders who may also be workaholics. They dislike sun and hot weather. They represent the elements of fire and water.

Kapha doshas are built solidly, have a slow digestion, a steady energy, and a relaxed and peaceful nature. They are sweet, brave, forgiving, and slow to anger and slow in moving, but tend to suffer from respiratory ailments. They represent the elements of water and earth.

To rebalance too much Vata:

When the Vata dosha is out of balance, people suffer from cold hands and feet, chills, anxiety, impatience, fatigue or restlessness, an overactive mind, cramps or gas, an irregular heartbeat, high blood pressure, and low back ache, among other things, and they may waste money and energy. *If the Vata element of an individual is not balanced, neither the Pitta nor Kapha elements will be balanced.*

Establish regular mealtimes and habits, make quiet time, drink fluids, decrease stress, get enough rest, stay warm, and have a sesame oil massage.

Eat chicken, seafood, turkey, and dairy; oats, rice, and wheat; carrots, green beans, and onions; ripe fruit, including apricots, cherries, grapes, melons, nectarines, oranges, peaches and pineapple; tofu and chickpeas, and any nuts (almonds are best). Use any sweetener and oil (especially sesame oil), and hot or sweet herbs and spices.

Eat less red meat; broccoli, celery and leafy greens, mushrooms, peas, peppers, and potatoes; apples, pears, cranberries; corn and rye grains, and dry oats; all beans bur chickpeas; parsley and coriander.

To rebalance too much Pitta:

When the Pitta dosha is out of balance, people suffer from fiery ailments like hot flashes and heartburn, ulcers, heart disease, anemia, and rashes and other skin inflammations (among other things), and they feel more feverish, critical, resentful, impatient, argumentative, or angry. Delays and heat will make them irritable, and overwork will disturb the ability to sleep well.

Use moderation, stay cool, do leisure activities, get outside, and balance rest and activity.

Eat Oriental foods; chicken, shrimp, turkey and egg whites; milk, butter, and ice cream; barley, oats, wheat, and white rice; asparagus, broccoli, leafy greens, mushrooms, peas, potatoes, and sweet peppers; apples, sweet cherries, grapes, mangoes, melons, oranges, pears, plums, and prunes. Use cilantro, cinnamon, dill, mint, and any sweeteners except honey and molasses; pumpkin and sunflower seeds.

Eat fewer Mexican foods, processed foods, and red meat; seafood; sour foods, sour fruit, and fermented food like yogurt; brown rice and tofu; corn oil, honey, barbeque sauce, ketchup, mustard, and black pepper. Drink no alcohol.

To rebalance too much Kapha:

When the Kapha dosha is out of balance, people suffer from asthma, colds, or congestion, weight gain or bloating, allergies or hay fever, sinus headaches, drowsiness or wanting too much sleep, lethargy or depression, and painful joints. They may also procrastinate, feel overly attached to things or people, and feel better by overeating.

Exercise regularly, have a variety of experiences, and stay warm and dry.

Eat light meals, including raw vegetables and fruit (not sweet or sour), spicy Oriental foods, and baked, broiled, or grilled foods; chicken, shrimp, and turkey; barley and corn; corn, safflower or sunflower oil; raw honey; pumpkin and sunflower seeds. Drink hot beverages rather than cold.

Eat fewer sweets; cold and oily, fast foods; red meat and seafood; high-fat dairy; avocadoes, bananas, dates, melons, oranges, peaches, and pineapple; oats and wheat; salt.[384]

Yin/Yang Balancing

T he Chinese also recommend ways to bring harmony into your life, as all diseases are caused by yin/yang imbalances and interruptions to the meridian flow.[385]

Yin is affectionate, receptive, nurturing, serene, devoted, compassionate, and intuitive.

Excessive yin is clinging, timid, smothering, lazy, a martyr, hypersensitive, and superstitious. *Indications of excessive yin* are cold body/limbs; slow metabolism; low immune system; weak or diseased organs, blood vessels, ears, genitals, brain, lungs, bones.

Yang is assertive, active, enduring, logical, goal-directed, analytical, and powerful.

Excessive yang is dominating, hyperactive, stubborn, calculating, blindly ambitious, cold, and cruel. *Indications of excessive yang* are hotness; high metabolism; hyperactive organs; weak or diseased skin, hair, nails, eyes, nose, teeth or mouth, joints, muscles, ligaments, breasts.[386]

All disturbances in the body are primarily yin- or yang-related.. In the human body *yin* is deficiency, stasis, cold, dampness, and dull aching pain. *Yang* is excess, movement, heat, dryness and sharp pain.[387] The natural law of duality states that yin equals expansion, and yang equals contraction. Arthritis involving calcium deposits in the joints is yang; rheumatism, which involves degeneration of joints, is yin. Solid tumors are yang, and blood cancers yin. But, although symptoms may indicate excessive yang/deficient yin, *most illnesses today are caused by a yin imbalance.* (What appears to be excessive yang may be masking a yin deficiency.)

Globally, we have become extremely yin through exposure to ionizing radiation, electromagnetic pollution (cell phones, computers, etc.), toxic chemicals, fertilizers and pesticides, use of refined wheat and sugar, illegal and prescription drugs, and the importation, packaging, and cooking of many foods. *Most illness today is very yin.*[388]

The symptoms of an internal disease will be more yin (pain in the abdomen, nausea, vomiting, and diarrhea). *External diseases will be more yang symptoms* (sharp pain in the extremities, joints, or head; sweats; constipation; thick mucus, etc.). Internal refers to an illness that has settled in the organs. External refers to an illness that is still in the meridians. *When a disease is on the move in the body, it will cause intermittent chills and fever.*[389]

To increase yang:

♦ Eat [hot, salty] cereals, legumes, root vegetables including carrots, onions and garlic, seeds and nuts, meat, eggs, goat cheese, salty fish;[390] butter, and the spices basil, black pepper, cloves, ginger, oregano, thyme.[391]
♦ Avoid caffeine, alcohol (extremely yin), drugs, table sugar and sugary drinks, preserved foods including white flour, preservatives, chemicals, pesticides.
♦ Drink fewer fluids.
♦ Do strength/aerobic exercises, and run, play tennis, go horseback riding, learn karate, or go sailing.
♦ Meditate at mid-day.
♦ Rise early.
♦ Spend a lot of time outdoors.
♦ Wear red, orange; bright shades, and have these colors in your home.[392]
♦ Use dry heat: dry saunas, ginger, fasting, and sun and red-lamp exposure (which also helps liver, kidneys, and adrenals).
♦ Get plenty of sleep and sunshine; eat cooked root vegetables and meats; avoid sugar, most fruit and juices, green tea, high doses of vitamin C, and victim-consciousness.

Note: Toxins are mostly yin. Use yang therapy.[393]

To increase yin:

♦ Eat [cold, sweet] citrus, soft vegetables (like tomatoes), dairy, frozen foods, refined oils, most fish;[394] raw fish and vegetables, rice, tofu, chili peppers, and spices curry, parsley, salt, soy sauce, and sugar.[395]
♦ Consume sparingly: caffeine, alcohol, drugs, sugar, foods processed with white flour; these foods are extremely yin.
♦ Drink more fluids.
♦ Do stretching exercises like Tai Ch'i, swimming, yoga, and walking slowly.
♦ Meditate in the evening.

- ◆ Listen to music.
- ◆ Stay up late.
- ◆ Spend a lot of time indoors.
- ◆ Wear blues, greens, and pastels, and have these colors in your house.[396]
- ◆ Yin therapy includes the cool and moist: raw food, cool and Epsom salt bathing, homeopathy, visualization, surgery and radiation, and most drugs, supplements, and herbs. While *juice fasts and vegetarian diets may eliminate tumors*, yin therapy will not re-energize a yin body.[397]

Meditation

LADY O' THE BRAE

"Be still," recommends Psalms 46:10, "and know that I am God." Deep internal silence helps us become aware of the divine Presence that upholds all life. Jesus knew this; he made a habit of retreating from crowds and friends alike.

Besides the time to regroup that seclusion brings and easy access to the Ethernet, meditation holds many benefits for those who practice it. Regular meditators feel the effects in their everyday lives, meeting whatever comes at them with a greater sense of tranquility than non-meditators. Meditation opens and aligns the chakras more quickly than devotion and prayer.[398] It also lowers cholesterol levels, decreases the possibility of heart disease and malignant tumors, and helps decrease dependence on drugs.[399]

> Meditation should be an opening of ourselves to all the possibilities.
>
> Lama Govinda
> Renee Weber, *Dialogues with Scientists and Sages*

Where we meditate can make a difference to our experience, for trees are deeply rooted in the essence of Mother Earth. Resting against different tree trunks in a forest while they meditated, a group of people sensitive to energy currents studied how the shapes of living trees organize the air patterns in their immediate environment. They found:

- Old apple trees and crooked timberline pines cause the energy to spiral gently upwards.
- Tall pines sweep energy upward, causing meditators' consciousness to soar.
- Rows of trees planted in a symmetrical grid produce a jumbled pattern of energy that leaps back and forth.[400]

THE "CHAKRA TREE," CANNON BEACH, OREGON
This tree just outside Canon Beach (in Klootchy Creek County Park,
off U.S. Highway 26 about 2.5 miles southeast of the U.S. 101 junction)
has the immediate effect of opening the crown chakra, cleansing the system,
and sweeping you out of your "small self."]

Several years ago, my only exposure to meditation was limited to my husband regularly yelling that the house full of children trying to be quiet had disturbed him while he was meditating. This, it seemed to me, was not the effect Transcendental Meditation was supposed to engender! Master meditator Jon Kabat-Zinn recommends that we "meditate without judging what sounds you do or don't want to hear. Be with the experience without labeling" the distractions.[401] Meditation isn't about wiping the mind clean, like deleting documents from a file folder. It's about not getting hung up on any one thought. While meditating, we will have a more beneficial experience if we remember that any noise we hear is an expression of the vibrating cosmos. The crying baby and the barking dog have a right to exist. Indeed, if we interrupt our meditation to soothe the crying infant or pet the barking dog, we will have carried one of the purposes out of our solitary experience and into the world, putting our meditation to work for us and others.

Lama Govinda said, "A meditation which cannot prove itself in action is useless . . . In the Tibetan tradition, for instance, people go about their work: they fill their day, they cook their meal, they do their tasks, they clean their rooms, and make all these actions a part of their meditation . . . Whatever they do, whatever they think, whatever they experience—all belongs to the state of meditation."[402] This makes the task of doing something as mundane as washing dishes a spiritual experience. The time spent doing normal humdrum activities is no different than the time when we utter our most somber prayers. The same spiritual laws are at work, whatever we happen to be doing.

If we have time to breathe, we have time to meditate. A variety of meditations follows. Please use, combine, or adapt any of them to a *meditation that works for you; there is no right or wrong method.* For all meditations, first quiet yourself, breathe slowly, and center in peace. And—surprise, surprise!—if you take time to yawn several times, according to neuroscience, your brain will be better prepared for quiet contemplation, and you will alleviate stress and feel more compassionate.[403]

> Peace is all around us—in the world and in nature—and within us—in our bodies and our spirits. Once we learn to touch this peace, we will be healed and transformed. It is not a matter of faith; it is a matter of practice.
>
> Thich Nhat Hanh
> *Living Buddha, Living Christ*

BASIC MEDITATION
1. Sit or lie quietly with spine straight.
2. Concentrate on taking slow breaths.
3. Refrain from deciding there are sounds you don't want to hear; allow any distractions to become part of your meditation.
4. If you find you have followed a thought that takes you out of the present experience, simply return your attention to your breathing.

MINUTE MEDITATION
1. Stop periodically through the day.
2. Breathe deeply.
3. Smile.
4. Feel grateful.
5. Be here now, without worrying.

MESSIAH MEDITATION
Rabbi Cooper asks us to imagine what would happen if the Messiah were to enter the room where we are.

1. Imagine the Messiah or Christ came into the room.
2. How would you feel?
3. Think about a challenge you have faced. How would you have acted, had the Messiah been there?
4. Finally, imagine that you yourself are the Messiah. This is, in fact, a tenet of the Kabbalah: the Messiah is none other than ourselves. Now how would you behave as a general rule? Would you feel more peaceful? Strive to radiate peace? Would you feel more powerful? More confident?[404]

MEDITATION for CHAKRAS
We are connected to the divine by invisible vibrations, which Ayurveda calls primordial sound.[405] The vibrations flow in and out through chakras, energy centers in our bodies. There are seven main physical chakras (referred to in Revelation as "the mysteries of the seven stars" and the "seven churches.")[406]

These are the sounds associated with each chakra: [407]

7. *Om*—Crown of Head
6. *Sham*—Third Eye/Brow
5. *Hum*—Neck/Throat
4. *Yum*—Heart
3. *Ram*—Solar Plexus
2. *Vam*—Gonadal
1. *Lam*—Base (of Spine)

ARABIC MEDITATION
Chant the phrase, *"La illa-ha il Allah-Hu,"* which means, "There is no God but God."

TO FEEL CONNECTED
1. Breathe slowly and deeply.
2. Slowly bring your arms together in front of you, forming a circle. Hold within this circle those with whom you feel connected.
3. Allow the circle to expand, so it includes all of humankind and nature.
4. Allow your circle to grow as large as possible. Through vibrations, you are connected to everything within this circle.
5. Feel the limitless power and vision that in-forms you now.[408]

ANGEL MEDITATION
You may feel a pressure, presence, tingling, vibration or temperature change as you slowly recite the names of the angels. [409]

1. When you are quiet and still, repeat: "May Michael be at my right . . .
2. May Gabriel at my left . . .
3. May Uriel stand in front of me . . .
4. Raphael behind me and . . .
5. Above my head, the *Shekhina*, the Divine Presence." At this point, imagine a benevolent light above your head that descends, surrounds you in peace, and cradles you in safety and kindness.

AhL-LaH MEDITATION TO INTEGRATE FRAGMENTS
1. Place your hand over your heart; feel your chest rising and falling with each breath.
2. Say "yes!" and notice how your heart and breath respond to this word. Notice any images that come to mind.
3. Say "no!" and notice how your heart and breath respond to this word. Notice any images that come to mind.
4. Repeat the syllable "*AhL*" several times. Affirm your part in the Sacred "yes."
5. Repeat the syllable "*LaH*" several times. Affirm your part in the Sacred Void. Which syllable is more comfortable?
6. Repeat the entire word: *AhL-LaH*. Be both the yes and no, the wave and the particle.
7. Release all misconceptions about yourself, and breathe with the sound and feeling of *Allah* in your heart. (Does it give you a goosebumpy, bubbly sort of feeling?)

HEALING MEDITATION
1. Center within your heart.
2. Cup your hands before you, as if offering your heart to be healed.
3. Pretend your heart is a mirror, and wipe it clean with your breath.

MEDITATION FOR PEACE AND POWER
1. Center within your heart.
2. Breathe. Realize that with each breath, the Divine is re-creating the universe.
3. Feel this power reside within you. Nothing is outside this power, and nothing can oppose it.
4. Breathe the strength of this peace with your whole inner self.[410]

TO FEEL BALANCED AND SUPPORTED
1. Imagine God saying, "I bless you with every breath you take."
2. Be aware of your breathing: In . . . out . . . in . . .
3. With each inhalation, know you are breathing in universal energy.
4. With each exhalation, feel the tension or irritation flowing out of your self.

TO ACCESS ABUNDANCE
1. Meditate with hands lying open, as if ready to receive.
2. Think of reasons to be grateful, and let thankfulness fill you.

MAHAYANAN BUDDHIST MEDITATION
1. Breathe in others' suffering (gray). (Include the names of people you dislike).
2. Breathe out peace and blessing (light).

Know that their hurt *cannot attach itself to you* when you are in an egoless condition.

METTA BHAVANA (LOVING HEART) MEDITATION
1. Center calmly in peace. Feel the warmth of love in and around your heart.
2. Say "May I be well and happy" (or whatever intentional phrase works best for you).
3. Think of someone you love. Repeat the phrase, surrounding the person with love light from your heart.
4. Think of someone you dislike. Repeat as above.
5. Think of your neighborhood . . . town . . . country . . . world . . . universe . . . All That Is, expanding your love light to shine and embrace each, and repeating your intention.

Breathing and Attunement

M indfulness is all-important. With mindfulness of breathing, a person can feel like an island of tranquility in a sea of chaos.

When we apply mindfulness to breathing, when we pray "in Jesus' name" or follow the Tao, and when energy healers facilitate a balance within their recipients, what is happening is *attunement* with the energy of Mother Earth and the Divine.[411] We align ourselves with the energy that operates at the physical and para-physical level. True healing, however, occurs from correcting the idea that we can become sick in the first place. Each of us possesses healing power, because each of us is based on a non-physical blueprint for perfect health.[412] Healing does not supply what is missing, but rather evokes awareness of our innate nature, which is firmly founded upon good health, wholeness, and the spirit of love.

Remember how my chronic kidney dysfunction was erased when my medical charts were lost? We are *all* energy workers; we work with energy *all* the time—and our own beliefs and intention shape or taint the energy that passes through us. Healers who channel energy impart learning to recipients, a simple re-awakening to their basic holiness and wholeness and their place in God Whose nature is not subject to humanly conceived concepts of sickness.

Breathing is important in part because the more oxygen you give your brain, the more peaceful you feel and the more memory power your brain has. The more flexible your spine and the more active (oxygenated) your brain, the more flexible your life.[413]

It is interesting to note that the religious or yogic posture of "praying hands," with palms together and thumbs against chest, serves the practical purpose of completing an energetic circuit within our bodies.

The following practices help calm or energize us, and balance chakras and the energies that flow through meridians.

> Speaking about his time as a young monk in Vietnam: "Each village temple had a big bell . . . Whenever the bell was invited to sound (in Buddhist circles, we never say 'hit' or 'strike' a bell), all the villagers would stop what they were doing and pause for a few moments to breathe in and out in mindfulness."
>
> Thich Nhat Hanh
> *Living Buddha, Living Christ*

The most difficult part of adopting a new regimen is remembering to do it! Some people set their watches or cell phones to beep once every hour. Another man who was already rich would always pause whenever he found a penny lying on the ground. For him, the copper coin didn't mean ". . . and all the day you'll have good luck" as much as that it represented the good fortune he was already enjoying, and he stopped to gaze at the motto "In God We Trust" imprinted on the front. Whether a penny found, the chiming of church bells, or a beeping alarm, reminders like these can help us flip off the Autopilot switch and reclaim our rightful and constructive place in the universe.

Rabbi Cooper believes that with each step we take, the Divine steps with us, and with each breath we draw we are connecting with the breath of the universe. Deep breathing also has healthy physiological effects: It cleans out our lungs, soothes the heart, calms the mind, and acts as a deterrent to the aging process. It also helps constipation, eyesight, nicotine withdrawal, and pain and stress relief.

Note: "Dominant hand" means the right hand if you are right-handed; your left hand, then, is the "non-dominant" hand.

TO FEEL PEACEFUL
1.　Breathe in and think, "Calming."
2.　Breathe out and think, "Smiling."
3.　Breathe in again and think, "Now."
4.　Breathe out and think, "Wonderful."

Hanh maintains that practicing this way helps us touch peace immediately, without having to wait for anything around us to change.[414]

TO CALM THINKING
1.　Ground yourself: Grow "roots" out of your feet and base of spine, sink them into the earth, and breathe through roots.
2.　Place your non-dominant hand at side of neck and dominant hand at brow (the pituitary gland).
3.　Breathe in and out of solar plexus chakra.[415]

TO CHANGE/LIGHTEN MOOD AND BALANCE BRAIN
(Yogic Breathing)
1.　Breath in.
2.　Hold one nostril closed with a finger.
3.　Begin with exhaling to a count of $2x$.
4.　Repeat twice more. Switch nostrils.

A SIMPLE METHOD FOR CLEARING AND BALANCING THE CHAKRAS
1. Ground out and center first (growing roots into Mother Earth from base of spine and soles of feet, and expending all negative energy).
2. Starting at the base, breathe into and out of each chakra. (All chakras except base and crown have access at both the front and the back of the body, throat, and brow.) Spend more time/breaths with any chakra where you feel resistance or denseness.
3. Breathe into the base chakra; hold; then move the energy upward and out through the crown with the exhalation.
4. Breathe down through the auric field and into the crown; hold; push the energy downward and out the base chakra with the exhalation.

FOR INTUITION and BETTER GENERAL HEALTH
1. Sit or lie with straight spine, chin in, chest out, arms straight.
2. Rest backs of hands on knees (if sitting cross-legged), with index finger under thumb and other fingers straight (active gyan mudra).
3. Deliberately slow breathing; breathe long and deep, with abdominal muscles relaxed.
4. Fill bottom of lungs, then middle, and top last, taking three seconds.
5. Hold for three seconds.
6. Release your breath, from top to bottom of lung, over three seconds.

The Kundalini yoga teacher, Nirmal Kaur Khalsa, recommends that we begin with three minutes' practice and gradually build to eleven minutes, working up to 20 seconds per breath/20 seconds to hold/20 seconds to release. This exercise should increase intuition because it helps the pituitary gland to secrete and balances the endocrine gland system, when we have progressed to 8 breaths a minute or less.[416]

TO CALM AND RELAX BODY (and for INSOMNIA and DIABETES)
Place your dominant hand over heart, and the other hand over liver (base of right-side ribcage). Soon you will have a warm and fuzzy feeling. Since this technique also cleans the blood, it is a good exercise for diabetics.[417] For insomnia, accompany the hand positions with *only* the thought, "In" as you inhale and "Out" as you exhale. If your mind wanders, simply return to "In" and "Out." This works for me 99% of the time (especially if you have eaten turkey before the exercise).

TO RE-ENERGIZE LIFE FORCE
The exercise simply involves breathing in and out through the medulla oblongata, located at the back of the neck just below the notch at the bottom of the skull.[418]

FOR LONG LIFE
1. Breathe in to (x) count.
2. Hold for (x) count.
3. Exhale to (2x) count.
4. No breath for (½x) count.[419]

TO REFRESH and FEEL CHEERFUL
1. Breathe deeply three times while smiling.
2. While continuing to breathe, imagine breathing in divine or universal energy and breathing out stress, doubt, resentment, tension, etc.

TO ACTIVATE THE PREFRONTAL BRAIN
FOR RESILIENCE AND HAPPINESS
Dr. Joan Borysenko recommends the following exercise: Breathe in through your nose, and breathe out through pursed lips as if through a straw. Breathe all the way out. The next breath through your nose will be a little deeper. The next breath that you breathe out through that straw is going to take a little bit longer. Only three to four breaths per minute changes neuroactivity (activates the prefrontal cortex) and calms the limbic system (the emotional brain). [420]

EXERCISES
One: Moving the Energy from Feet to Pelvic Area, and Loosening Lower Back

1. Lay on your back, with arms bent and palms down over navel.
2. Turn toes in toward middle as far as possible.
3. Turn toes outward as far as possible.
4. Point toes at your head; point toes away from head.
5. Raise right knee, planting right foot at the level of the left knee, and keeping left leg flat on the ground.
6. Lay right leg over left leg, without moving right foot off the ground.
7. Repeat with left leg.
8. Raise both knees, feet on ground, and bend to left side and to right side.
9. Raise both knees to chest.

Two: To Bring Energy into Solar Plexus, and Relieve Middle Back Pain

1. Lay on your back and push your butt into the floor.
   (The lower back will form a natural arch.)
2. Arch your back up and off the floor.
3. Do a crunch-like stretch, starting from just below the ribcage.

Three: To Bring Energy into Heart, and Relieve Pain Between Shoulderblades

1. Lay on your back and push down with your shoulderblades.
   (Middle of back will form a natural arch.)
2. Roll shoulders forward as far as possible.

Four: To Bring Energy into Upper Chakras, and Relieve Neck Pain

1. Lay on your back and bend your head, as if to touch the back of your head to your shoulder blades. (Upper back will form a natural arch.)
2. Move head to touch chin to chest.

For the next set of stretches, stand with your feet shoulder-width apart. Move slowly and gently. Do ten to fifteen reps for each exercise.

Five: To Move Energy Up from Root Chakra

1. Turn your knees inward until they touch.
2. Rotate pelvis in large, clockwise circles.
3. Rotate pelvis in large, counterclockwise circles.

Six: To Move Energy Up from Solar Plexus

1. Lean back slightly, feeling a pull right below your ribcage.
2. Rotate clockwise.
3. Rotate counterclockwise.

Seven: To Move Energy Through Upper Chakras

1. At the base of the back of your neck, place a thumb on either side of the vertebra and push in gently.
2. Rotate your head clockwise.
3. Rotate your head counterclockwise.
4. Continue up each vertebra.

TO BALANCE THE MERIDIANS
Tap, brush, or imagine yourself running your hand:

- Back over the crown of your head
- Down the spine
- Down the outside of your legs
- Off the toes

- Up the inner part of your legs
- Up your torso
- Out the inside of your arms and off the fingertips
- Up the outside of your arms
- End with thumping your chest like King Kong.[421]

Be sure to stop and shake the energy off your hands frequently during this exercise. I do this nightly, and it has the immediate effect of making me feel good. This technique is very healthy for your pets, too.

TO FEEL SUPPORTED

Breathe through the back of your heart chakra, to open yourself to Divine support.

Blessings

Everyone has the power to bless; this is not a function reserved for the religious or spiritual elite. In fact, with every thought we have, we could say that we either bless or curse. Intention directs the energy of blessing, but having a "good intention" is not a fool-proof method of doing good; recall the woman's highly religious, well-intentioned aunt who prayed fervently for her niece's conversion and in fact gave her niece blinding headaches (Chapter Eleven). The intention to bless without trying to dictate the outcome may be the safest sort of blessing. The following blessing serves as illustration.

TO SEND THE BLESSING OF GOOD HEALTH

Think of someone who is ill. Part of the problem is that he or she believes the body or the mind *can* be less than perfectly healthy, so without naming or envisioning the illness, concentrate on the person, picturing him or her glowing with good health—walking, dancing, joyful—and surrounded by and infused with light.

> When a brother perceives himself as sick, he is perceiving himself as not whole, and therefore in need. If you, too, see him this way, you are seeing him as if he were absent from the Kingdom or separated from it, thus making the Kingdom itself obscure to both of you. Sickness and separation are not of God.
>
> *A Course in Miracles*

Affirmations, Dreams, and Burning Bowl

Why become irritated, angry, or despondent over a person or situation we cannot control? It's wasted energy. It's wasted time, when we could be feeling good. Asking "How do I want to spend my time?" helps, and using affirmations as simple as "I can feel peaceful instead" reroutes our thinking into a beneficial direction.

We are so much more than we think we are! Affirmations help us remember this, not because we're conning ourselves, but because *we are claiming what is already true.* When we're singing the blues, we are not focusing on what we *choose* to have in our lives. "Make a joyful noise," advises Psalm 101. Why? Because what we sing resonates throughout the body, filling every cell with that music, that vitality. And singing a happy song is one of the ways we move ourselves into the higher frequency emotions. We can do more than merely "watching" our thoughts; we can paint new pictures with our imagination and sing new songs.

Think only the thoughts you choose to materialize.

Affirmations work because they align our thinking with spiritual/quantum truths, broaden our awareness of possibilities, and keep us in an "I can!" mode of living. Below are suggested affirmations. If you like, put them into your own words, using the present tense. Making them into catchy jingles that are easy to remember and fun to repeat often will help them work all the more quickly.

- Spirit is the wind that bears me aloft when I am light-hearted.
- *How hard can it be to be What I already am?* Love. Light. Peace. Kindness. Blessing.
- I am always healthy. (The fact that germs have no power over you takes a while to sink in, but this affirmation—and the new belief that you're creating—really works.)
- Everything I need comes effortlessly to me.
- There's always enough to share.
- I am always safe.
- "Whoever can see through all fear will always be safe." (*Tao Te Ching #46*, and other scriptures)

- I am always supported.
- What I desire is not given or withheld by a Santa Claus God—it's mine for the having!
- I see what I expect; I expect what I invite. I am inviting peace and love and harmony into my life.
- The strain of constantly judging things is what wearies me. I'm going to "judge against" nothing today. (*ACIM*, and below)
- I am more than my ego.
- I am more than my feelings. I am more than my thoughts.
- Nothing has any more power than I give it. I can only be hurt by my own thoughts.
- Seeing myself as nothing more than a body is the only way I can prevent miracles from happening.
- All my suffering comes from believing that I am powerless.
- Today I will touch gently, speak softly, act kindly.
- Everything I touch, I bless.
- When I bless all, I am also blessed.
- I choose _____, and I know it is possible.
- I can choose peace instead.
- My body is my tool, not my master. This is my guarantee that it cannot be sick.
- My body knows how to be healthy.
- I am healing while I sleep.
- I will wake rested and refreshed.
- Today I will only think things that make me feel good about myself.
- Today I will live as if I have no tomorrow.
- I like myself!
- I need not look for love. I only need to break down the barriers I have built around myself.
- The universe supplies everything I need.
- Every day in every way I am getting better and better.
- You know my heart's desires, God, and I know Your goodness; together we are unlimited in our potential.
- Today I will look beyond *what is* to see what is *possible*.
- I choose to live in the state of abundance, where I have faith that all things are working together toward good.
- I will only respond to constructive suggestions.
- I choose to overcome all that is not in my greatest good.
- I refuse to suffer from imagining what is not true.
- Today I will stay centered in peace.
- Every loving remark is true. Anything else is an appeal for my help, no matter what form it takes.
- I need not attack or defend, for I am not weak.

- I am somebody's hero.
- I am good fortune, for God succeeds in me and I in God.
- I am a child of the universe, no less than the trees and the stars; I have a right to be here.
- The universe is unfolding as it should. (From Max Ehrmann's classic "Desiderata.")
- Money comes easily to me.

Rabbi Cooper suggests we say this affirmation when we feel the lack of something (money, time, support, friendship, love or such): "I feel the need for more _____, so I am asking for help to be at peace with what I have."[422] The objective is to re-center in peace, and we may indeed find that what we needed does come to us once we release the feeling of not having it and feel grateful for what we do have.

Think as if each thought will instantly manifest.

Dreams can be used in a variety of ways. Just before falling asleep, suggest that you will use your sleeping time . . .

1. To heal.
2. To meet loved ones.
3. To gain wisdom from a cosmic library, historical figures, or the Divine.
4. To rest peacefully and to wake refreshed.
5. To bring about reconciliations.
6. To hasten manifestation, by suggesting that you dream about what you choose to come true in your life.
7. To restore good spirits and vitality.
8. To try out certain solutions or actions you might take.
9. To become aware of inner problems.
10. To gain inspiration and intuitions and to solve problems.
11. To unite fragmented parts of the self.
12. To connect with mass consciousness.

Dreams may also temporarily correct chemical and hormonal imbalances in the body, and release tension and inhibitions.[423]

Burning Bowl for Things We Wish to Release from our Lives

1. Write on a piece of paper that from which you would be free.
2. Burn the paper in a fireplace, firepit, or any safe place.
3. Give thanks for a new beginning.
4. Claim what you choose with a new affirmation.

Problem Solving

When we have a problem, we slip into a trance and slip out of the present moment. We must be mindful enough to return to the present moment. Then we redirect our attention, which provides an interruption of the "deep trance" state, and this shift provides access to other resources.

When we identify with our problems, they grow so large that we can't see beyond them. To stop identifying with the problem, imagine the problem as a circle, and step *outside* the circle. By allowing your attention to shrink down to this one "particle" and assume that's all you are, you create your own problem or symptom, and then you feel overwhelmed. As long as we label our problem as something bad that we shouldn't be experiencing, we will keep it in our lives. [424]

A guideline I use sometimes is asking myself, "Am I doing this out of fear or out of love and growth?" And I am learning to look at options, to broaden my mindset to think about what might just be possible.

Walter Chrysler (of the Chrysler Corporation) had a habit of jotting down what he was worrying about. He then dropped the "worry" note in a box and forgot about it until his weekly review of the box's contents. At that time, he would find that most of his worries had not been in his control and had resolved themselves without his help or fuss—and then he laughed at himself. [425]

We can create a "worry box," or we can follow the guidelines:

- Immediately return to the present moment.
- Refuse to worry.
- When your thoughts stray to the problem, *imagine the best possible outcome.*
- Counteract any feelings of distress by doing pleasant activities.
- Refuse to think about *anything* that is wrong.
- Imagine telling a friend in the future about the problem that is now over and done with.
- Remember that *any situation can change for the better.*
- Remember that the *best outcome is at least as possible* as the worst solution. [426]

My own prescription for worry: If you *can* do something, do it! If you *can't* do anything, stop worrying. If you can't stop worrying, do something nice for someone else. The final step is best to come *first* in *all* situations: Imagine the *best* possible thing happening.

The Universal Golden Rule

Buddhism	One should seek for others the happiness one desires for oneself. Hurt not others with that which pains yourself.
Christianity	Do unto others as you would have them do unto you.
Hinduism	This is the sum of duty: Do naught to others which if done to thee would cause thee pain. Guard and do by the things of others as they would do by their own.
Islam	Let none of you treat his brother in a way he would himself dislike to be treated. No one of you is a believer until he loves for his brother what he loves for himself.
Judaism	What is hurtful to yourself, do not do to your fellow man. Do not do unto others that which you would not have done to yourself.
Sikhism	I am stranger to no one, and no one is a stranger to me. Indeed, I am a friend to all.
Sufism	The sun never says to the earth, "You owe me." (Hafiz)
Taoism	Regard your neighbor's gain as your own gain, and your neighbor's loss as your own.
Zoroastrianism	Do as you would be done by.[427]

Native American Ten Commandments

The Earth is our Mother—care for her.

Honor all your relations.

Open your heart and soul to the Great Spirit.

All life is sacred; treat all with respect.

Take from the Earth what is needed and nothing more.

Do what needs to be done for the good of all.

Give constant thanks to the Great Spirit for each new day.

Speak the truth—but *only* the good in others.

Follow the rhythms of nature; rise and retire with the sun.

Enjoy this journey, but leave no tracks.

Traditional Indian Code of Ethics

Give thanks to the Creator each morning on rising and each evening before sleeping. Seek courage and strength to be a better person.

Showing respect is a basic law of life.

Respect the wisdom of people in council. Once you give an idea it no longer belongs to you, it belongs to everybody.

Be truthful at all times.

Always treat your guests with honour and consideration. Give your best food and comforts to your guests.

The hurt of one is the hurt of all. The honour of one is the honour of all.

Receive strangers and outsiders kindly.

All races are children of the Creator and must be respected.

To serve others, to be of some use to family, community, or nation is one of the main purposes for which people are created. True happiness comes to those who dedicate their lives to the service of others.

Observe moderation and balance in all things.

Know these things that lead to your well-being and those things that lead to your destruction.

Listen and follow the guidance given to your heart. Expect guidance to come in many forms; in prayer, in dreams, in solitude and in the words and actions of elders and friends.

Ω

Quiz:
Are Science and Spirituality Really Worlds Apart?

Quantum physics has turned our world inside out; today's science is keeping company with spirituality, and quantum physics and string theory are expanding our knowledge of the nature of God. In fact, the Chinese word for "physics" also means "enlightenment."[428] Just as external communications (e-mail and Internet) now range worldwide, so too are the formerly divided hemispheres of philosophy connecting: the Eastern school of thought, which mostly concerns inner workings of life and good health, with the West's "modern" medical science, which has long involved a treat-what-is-sick approach to health and to life itself.

If we took a survey of scientists, we would find that a great number of them believe in a Designer or Power that exists beyond our physical universe—a kind of Quantum God. Let's see if we can, in fact, tell which of the following passages have been expressed by scientists and which are statements made by theologians, philosophers, or swamis.

∞

1. "In allowing the tension of opposites to persist, we must also recognize that in every endeavor to know or solve we depend upon factors which are outside our control, and which religious language has always entitled 'grace'."

2. ". . . when searching for harmony in life one must never forget that in the drama of existence we are ourselves both actors and spectators."

3. "Religion and natural science are fighting a joint battle in a second, never-ending crusade against skepticism and dogmatism, and against superstition. The rallying cry for this crusade has always been and always will be "On to God!""

4. ". . . the mystics of many centuries, independently, yet in perfect harmony with each other . . . have described, each of them, the unique experience of his or her life in terms that can be condensed in the phrase: DEUS FACTUS SUM (I have become God.)."

5. "Thus you can throw yourself flat on the ground, stretched out upon Mother Earth, with the certain conviction that you are one with her and she with you."

6. "Kepler compared the revolutions of the planets around the sun with the vibrations of a string and spoke of a harmonious concord of the different planetary orbits, of a harmony of the spheres. At the end of his work on the harmony of the universe, he broke out into this cry of joy: 'I thank thee, Lord God our Creator, that thou allowest me to see the beauty in thy work of creation.'"

7. ". . . the great Unity—the One of Paremides—of which we all somehow form a part, to which we belong. The most popular name for it in our time is God."

8. "What humanity owes to personalities like Buddha, Moses, and Jesus stands for me higher than all the achievements of the enquiring and constructive mind."

9. "Not once in the dim past, but continuously by conscious mind is the miracle of the Creation wrought."

10. "You could define God as the edge of the universe, as the agent who was responsible for setting all this into motion."

11. "There can never be any real opposition between religion and science; for one is the complement of the other. Every serious and reflective person realizes, I think, that the religious element in nature must be recognized and cultivated if all the powers of the human soul are to act together in perfect balance and harmony. And indeed it was not by any accident that the greatest thinkers of all ages were also deeply religious souls, even though they made no public show of their religious feeling. Every advance in knowledge brings us face to face with the mystery of our own being . . . [O]ver the entrance to the gates of the temple of science are written the words: *Ye must have faith.*"

12. "The very study of the external world led to the conclusion that the content of the consciousness is the ultimate reality."

13. "There is obviously only one alternative, namely the unification of minds or consciousnesses. Their multiplicity is only apparent, in truth, there is only one mind."

14. "The inmost ego, possessing what I have called the inescapable attribute, can never be part of the physical world unless we alter the meaning of the word 'physical' so as to [be] synonymous with 'spiritual' . . ."

15. "To myself I am only a child playing on the beach, while vast oceans of truth lie undiscovered in me."

16. "In nonmanifest reality it's all interpenetrating, interconnected, ONE. So we say deep down the consciousness of mankind is one. This is a virtual certainty . . . and if we don't see this it's because we are blinding ourselves to it."

17. "Who makes us ignorant? We ourselves. We put our hands over our eyes and weep that it is dark . . . If I am in the dark, let me light a lamp . . . Take your hands away and see the light; you are perfect already."

18. "You can say the drop merges in the ocean, but you can also say the ocean is present in the drop. In the new science, the whole is in the part and the part is in the whole, and that is very important."

19. "If scientists got together and only prayed for inventions, would they get them? No. They have to apply God's laws."

20. "It is very interesting, for instance, that in modern physics the more logical you are, the more wrong you are. This shows very clearly the limits of our logic. Actually, the universe often seems unreasonable to us because we apply our own logic to something which is not of the same category. We never can say where a particle is and what it does, and so we can only guess, or define it as either particle or a wave. Yet it is neither one nor the other, but both."

∞

Key to Quiz: All of the quotes except the last four were made by *scientists*, the founders and Nobel Prize winners of modern physics.

1. Wolfgang Pauli, quoted in *Quantum Questions*, Ken Wilber, editor, Shambhala, Boston, 2001, p. 173.

2. Physicist Niels Bohr, "Discussion with Einstein on Epistemological Problems in Atomic Physics," in P. A. Schilpp, *Einstein*, p. 236, quoted in quoted in *the medium, the mystic, and the physicist: Toward a General Theory of the Paranormal*, Lawrence LeShan, Viking Press, NY, 1974, p. 252.

3. Physicist Max Planck, *Where is Science Going?*, London, George Allen & Unwin, 1933, p. 113, quoted in *ibid.*, p.284.

4. Physicist Erwin Schrödinger, quoted in *Quantum Questions*, Wilber, p. 95.

5. Schrödinger, quoted in *the medium, the mystic, and the physicist*, LeShan, p. 98.

6. Physicist Werner Heisenberg, *ibid.*, pp.61-62.

7. Schrödinger, *Dialogues with Scientists and Sages: The Search for Unity*, Renee Weber, Routledge & Kegan Paul, London and NY. 1986, p. xv.

8. Albert Einstein, *ibid.*, p. 215.

9. Physicist Sir Arthur Eddington, quoted in *Margins of Reality*, Robert G. Jahn, Brenda J. Dunne, Harcourt Brace Jovanovich, 1987, p. 347.

10. Stephen Hawking, *Dialogues with Scientists and Sages*, Weber, p. 209.

11. Physicist Max Planck, *Where is Science Going?*, (1933), as quoted in *Prayer is Good Medicine*, Larry Dossey, M.D., HarperSanFrancisco, San Francisco, 1996, p. 23; and quoted in *Quantum Questions*, Wilber, p. 161-2.

12. Physicist Eugene Wigner, quoted in *Einstein's Cosmos: How Albert Einstein's Vision Transformed Our Understanding of Space and Time*, Michio Kaku, W. W. Norton & Company, New York and London, 2004, p. 205.

13. Schrödinger, quoted in *Quantum Questions*, Wilber, 2001, p. 87.

14. Eddington, quoted in *ibid*, p. 194.

15. Isaac Newton, quoted in *After the Ecstasy, the Laundry: How the Heart Grows Wise on the Spiritual Path*, Jack Kornfield, Bantam Books, NY, Toronto, London, Sydney, Auckland, 2000, p. 85.

16. Physicist David Bohm, *Dialogues with Scientists and Sages*, Weber, p. 41.

17. Swami Vivekananda, *Living at the Source*, Shambhala, 1993, pp. 147; 75; 91.

18. Father Bede Griffiths, *Dialogues with Scientists and Sages*, Weber, p. 172.

19. Paramahansa Yogananda, *In the Sanctuary of the Soul: A Guide to Effective Prayer*, Self-Realization Fellowship, Los Angeles, 1998, p. 35.

20. Lama Anagarika Govinda, *Dialogues with Scientists and Sages*, Weber, p. 63.

Beyond Space-Time

The universe began. Just don't ask when.
Particles abounded, coalesced,
and lights impaled the darkness with a string
of colors, some of which became the planets
that churned with fire and heaved adulterous parts
while poisoned skies wept in their spite until
their tears wrought life, a single cell, a sparse
beginning for that, whose end no one can tell
with any certainty, unless to guess
there really was no start, no Bang, no hell
of nothingness (but what we make ourselves)—
Nor is there any end, for Life endures,
re-creating life beyond our fears.

Michelle Langenberg

AUTHOR'S NOTE: We need only about 8,000 people emitting blessings
at the same time to affect the entire human population of the world.

Bibliography

After the Ecstasy, the Laundry: How the Heart Grows Wise on the Spiritual Path, Jack Kornfield, Bantam Books, NY, Toronto, London, Sydney, Auckland, 2000

All in the Family, "Archie and the Computer," first broadcast 10/27/73. Writers: Lloyd Turner, Gordon Mitchell, Don Nicholl; created by Norman Lear.

All in the Family, "Edith Gets Fired," first broadcast 2/25/79. Writer: Mort Lachman; created by Norman Lear

All in the Family, "End in Sight," first broadcast 10/1/78. Writer: Nate Monaster; created by Norman Lear

Alternate Realities: How Science Shapes Our Vision of the World, Joel Davis, Plenum Press, 1997 http://www.anecdotage.com/browse

Anthony de Mello, William Dych, S. J., ed., Orbis Books, 2002

Autobiography of a Yogi, Paramahansa Yogananda, Self-Realization Fellowship, Los Angeles, 1946, 1974, 1998

Awakening to Zero Point, Gregg Braden, Radio Bookstore Press, Bellevue, WA, 1993, 1994, 1997

"Being in Your Wise Mind, and Your Most Resilient Self," Joan Borysenko, Hay House World Summit, June 7, 2013.

"Being You and Living Your Life with a Sense of Ease," Duke Tufty, Unity Temple on the Plaza, June 19, 2005

Bridging Science and Spirit, Norman Friedman, Living Lake Books, 1990

Children's Letters to God: The New Collection, Stuart Hample and Eric Marshall, Workman Publishing, NY, 1991

A Course in Miracles, Foundation for Inner Peace, 1975, 1985

The Dancing Wu Li Masters: An Overview of the New Physics, Gary Zukav, Perennial Classics, NY, 1979, 2001

Dialogues with Scientists and Sages: The Search for Unity, Renee Weber, Routledge & Kegan Paul, London and NY, 1986

Donne, John, "Meditation XVII: *Nunc lento sonitu dicunt, Morieris.* Now, this Bell tolling softly . . ." downloaded 7/29/05: http://www.luminarium.org/sevenlit/donne/donnebib.htm, which then goes to: www.global-language.com/devotion.html

The Edge, April, 2000

Einstein's Cosmos: How Albert Einstein's Vision Transformed Our Understanding of Space and Time, Michio Kaku, W. W. Norton & Company, New York and London, 2004

The Essence of Zen, Maggie Pinkney, editor, Five Mile Press Pty Ltd, 2005

The Essential Koran: The Heart of Islam, trans. Thomas Cleary, HarperSanFrancisco, San Francisco, 1993

Essential Reiki: A Guide to an Ancient Healing Art, Diane Stein, The Crossing Press, Incorporated, Freedom, CA, 1995

Essential Sufism, James Fadiman and Robert Frager, HarperSanFrancisco, 1997

The Essential Zohar, Rav P. S. Berg, Bell Tower, 2002

Excuse Me, Your Life is Waiting, Lynn Grabhorn, Hampton Roads, Charlottesville, VA, 2000

Eyes Remade for Wonder, Lawrence Kushner, Jewish Lights Publishing, 1998

Finding Joy: A Practical Spiritual Guide to Happiness, Dannel I. Schwartz, with Mark Hass, Jewish Light Publishing, Woodstock, VT, 1996

First You Build a Cloud and other reflections on physics as a way of life, K. C. Cole, Harcourt Brace & Company, 1999

Flawless! The Ten Most Common Character Flaws, Louis Tartaglia, M.D., William Morrow, NY, 1999

"From Muhammed to Grandma Rose," Polly Shulman, *Discover, 1998*

"Gaia Theory: Science of the Living Earth," David Orrell, downloaded 7/13/05: http://www.gaianet.fsbusiness.co.uk/gaiatheory.html

Games Zen Masters Play, Reginald Horace Blyth, Mentor, NY, 1976

God and the New Physics, Paul Davies, Simon & Schuster, Inc. NY, 1983

God is a Verb: Kabbalah and the Practice of Mystical Judaism, Rabbi David Cooper, Riverhead Books, 1997

Gospel of the Essenes, Book of The Teacher of Righteousness, Edmund Bordeaux Szekely, Hillman Printers, England, 1937, 1974

Handbook of Meridian Therapy and More, Robert Matt Ulmer (The Tao Doc), 2000

Hands of Light, Barbara Brennan and Jos. A. Smith, Bantam, 1988

Hasidic Anthology, Louis I. Newman, Schocken Books, NY, 1963

The Hidden Domain: Home of the Quantum Wave Function, Nature's Creative Source, Norman Friedman, The Woodbridge Group, 1997

The Hidden Gospel: Decoding the Spiritual Message of the Aramaic Jesus, Neil Douglas-Klotz, Quest Books, Wheaton IL, 1999

The Hidden Jesus: A New Life, Donald Spoto, St. Martin's Press, New York, 1998

The Hidden Messages in Water, Dr. Masaru Emoto, Beyond Words Publishing, Inc., 2004

The Hole in the Universe: How Scientists Peered over the Edge of Emptiness and Found Everything, K. C. Cole, Harcourt, Inc., NY, San Diego, London, 2001

The Holographic Universe, Michael Talbot, HarperCollins, 1991

How God Changes Your Brain: Breakthrough Findings from a Leading Neuroscientist, Newberg, Andrew, M.D., and Waldman, Mark Robert, Ballantine Books, 2009

"How to Live in Heaven on Earth," Bruce Lipton, Hay House World Summit, June 9, 2013

"How to Make Big Changes in Your Life Fast," Ali Campbell, Hay House World Summit, June 5, 2013.

"How, Then, Shall We Live?" Rev. Karyn Bradley, Unity Temple on the Plaza, 18 January 2004

The Individual and the Nature of Mass Events, Jane Roberts, Amber-Allen Publishing, San Rafael, CA, 1981,1995

Infinite Mind: Science of the Human Vibrations of Consciousness, Valerie Hunt, Malibu, 1996

Integrative Health Guide: Symbolism and Treatment, Michelle Langenberg, 2011

Invisible Lines of Connection: Sacred Stories of the Ordinary, Lawrence Kushner, Jewish Lights Publishing, Woodstock VT, 1996

"The Isaiah Effect," Gregg Braden (Unity Temple, 16 May 2000), and from *The Isaiah Effect*

Jon Kabat-Zinn, Unity Temple of the Plaza, Kansas City, Missouri, 30 January 2005

The Kansas City Star, Poets Corner, November 2, 2003

—, "Why Does God Allow This: Tsunami has theologians and scholars pondering the nature of evil," Bill Tammeus, January 1, 2005

Leven Thumps and the Gateway to Foo, Obert Skye, Snow Mountain, 2005

Lewis, C.S., http://www.brainyquote.com/quotes/authors/c/c s lewis.html; downloaded 3/18/05

Lewis, C.S., *http://en.wikipedia.org/wiki/C._S._Lewis*; downloaded 6/13/05

Living at the Source: Yoga Teachings of Vivekananda, Swami Vivekananda, Shambhala, Boston, 1993

Living Buddha, Living Christ, Thich Nhat Hanh, Riverhead Books, G. P. Putnam's Sons, NY, 1995

Living Energy Universe, Gary Swartz and Linda Russek, Hampton Roads, Charlottesville, VA, 1999

The Lord of the Rings and Philosophy, Gregory Bassham and Eric Bronson, eds., Open Court Publishing Co., 2003

Loser, Jerry Spinelli, Scholastic Inc., NY, 2003

The Maker of Dreams: A Fantasy in One Act, Oliphant Down, Gowans & Gray, Ltd., Glasgow, 1917. First performed by the Scottish Repertory Theatre Company at the Royalty Theatre, Glasgow, 1/20/1911; directed by Alfred Wareing

Man's Search for Meaning, Viktor Frankl, Simon & Schuster, NY, 1959, 1962, 1984

Margins of Reality, Robert G. Jahn, Brenda J. Dunne, Harcourt Brace Jovanovich, 1987

M*A*S*H (1), "Mail Call," first aired February 23, 1974; written by Larry Gelbart and Laurence Marks; directed by Alan Alda

M*A*S*H (2), "Pressure Points," first aired February 15, 1982; written by David Pollock; directed by Charles S. Dubin

The Matter Myth, Paul Davies and John Gribbin, Simon and Schuster, 1992

the medium, the mystic, and the physicist: Toward a General Theory of the Paranormal, Lawrence LeShan, Viking Press, NY, 1974

Milkweed, Jerry Spinelli, Scholastic Inc., NY, 2003

Mind Over Matter, K. C. Cole, Harcourt, Inc., Orlando, 2003

The Miracle of Mindfulness: An Introduction to the Practice of Meditation, Thich Nhat Hanh, Beacon Press, Boston, 1975

Miracles: A Jewish Perspective, Rabbi Ronald H. Isaacs, Jason Aronson, Inc., Northvale and Jerusalem, 1997

Modern Physics and Ancient Faith, Stephen M. Barr, University of Notre Dame, Notre Dame, Indiana, 2003

Mostly Harmless: The Fifth Book in the Increasingly Inaccurately Named Hitchhikers Trilogy, Douglas Adams, Serious Productions, NY, 1992

Mutant Message Downunder, Marlo Morgan, HarperCollins, 1991, 1994, 2001

Native American Myths, Diane Ferguson, Collins and Brown Limited, London, 2001

The Nature of Personal Reality, Jane Roberts, Amber-Allen Publishing, San Rafael, CA, 1974, 1994

The Nature of the Psyche, Jane Roberts, Prentice-Hall, Englewood Cliffs, NJ, 1979

No Ordinary Genius: The Illustrated Richard Feynman, Christopher Sykes, W. W. Norton and Company, NY and London, 1994

Odd Thomas, Dean Koontz, Bantam Books, New York, 2003

"One Path to Heaven, One Path to Hell," Duke Tufty (Unity Temple on the Plaza, Kansas City, Missouri, 28 November 2004)

Parallel Universes, Fred Alan Wolf, Touchstone, NY, 1988

Parallel Worlds: A Journey through Creation, Higher Dimensions, and the Cosmos, Michio Kaku, Doubleday, NY, 2004

Perfect Health: The Complete Mind Body Guide, Deepak Chopra, M.D., Three Rivers Press, NY, 1991, 2000

"The Plants Respond: An Interview with Cleve Backster," Derrick Jensen, found at www.derrickjensen.org/backster.html; published in *The Sun*, July 1997, in *Free Spirit* October 1998, translated into Czech and published in "Baraka"; downloaded 7/3/05

The Power is Within You, Louise Hay, Hay House, Inc., 1991

The Practice of the Presence of God, Brother Lawrence, Whitaker House, New Kensington, PA, 1982

"Prayer as the Human-to-Divine Interface," Gregg Braden, Unity Temple on the Plaza, September 11, 2008

Prayer is Good Medicine, Larry Dossey, M.D., HarperSanFrancisco, San Francisco, 1996

Prayers of the Cosmos: Meditations on the Aramaic Words of Jesus, Neil Douglas-Klotz, HarperCollins, NY, 1990

PEAR—"A Linear Pendulum Experiment: Effects of Operator Intention on Damping Rate," R.D. Nelson, G.J. Bradish, R.G. Jahn, B.J. Dunne (1994)

Princeton Engineering Anomalies Research: Scientific Study of Consciousness-Related Physical Phenomena. http://www.princeton.edu/~pear/2a.html, downloaded 3-23-05.

Quantum Questions, Ken Wilber, ed., Shambhala, Boston, 2001

Quantum Reality, Nick Herbert, Anchor Books, 1985

Quantum Theory and Measurement, John Archibald Wheeler and Wojciech Hubert Zurek, eds., Princeton University Press, NJ, 1983

Reaching to Heaven: A Spiritual Journey Through Life and Death, James van Praagh, Spiritual Horizons, Inc., 1999

A Return to Love: Reflections on the Principles of "A Course in Miracles," Marianne Williamson, HarperCollins Publishers, 1975, 1992

The River of Light, Lawrence Kushner, Harper & Row, San Francisco, 1981

Sai Baba, Man of Miracles, Howard Murphet, Redwood Press Limited, Trowbridge & London, 1971

Saving the World Entire: and 100 Other Beloved Parables from the Talmud, Rabbi Bradley N. Bleefeld and Robert L. Shook, Plume, New York, 1998

"The Science Delusion," Rupert Sheldrake, downloaded 3/15/13: youtube.

The Science of Mind, Ernest Holmes, Wilder Publications, 2010

The Self-Aware Universe: how consciousness creates the material world, Amit Goswami, Richard Reed, Maggie Goswami, G. P. Putnam's Sons, New York, 1993

The Seth Material, Jane Roberts, Prentice-Hall, Englewood Cliffs, NJ, 1970

Seth Speaks: The Eternal Validity of the Soul, Jane Roberts, Amber-Allen, 1972, 1991

Seven Experiments That Could Change the World, Rupert Sheldrake, G. P. Putnam's Sons, 1995

The Seven Spiritual Laws of Success, Deepak Chopra, Harmony Books, NY, 1997

A Short History of Nearly Everything, Bill Bryson, Broadway Books, 2003

The Silmarillion, J. R. R. Tolkien, George Allen & Unwen Ltd., 1997

The Sixth Sense: Unlocking the Power of Your Intuition, Belleruth Naparstek, HarperCollins, 1997

The Song of the Bird, Anthony de Mello, Image/Doubleday, NY, 1982

Souls on Fire: Portraits and Legends of Hasidic Masters, Elie Wiesel, Summit Books, NY, 1972

Space-Time and Beyond: Toward an Explanation of the Unexplainable, Bob Toben, in Conversation with Jack Sarfatti and Fred Wolf, E. P. Dutton (NY), 1975

The Spontaneous Fulfillment of Desire, Deepak Chopra, M.D., Harmony Books, NY, 2003

Star Trek, "Shore Leave," first aired 12/29/66; written by Theodore Sturgeon

Strong Measures: Contemporary American Poetry in Traditional Forms, Philip Dacey and David Jauss, eds., Harper & Row, Publishers, New York, 1986

Subtle Energy, William Collinge, Warner Books, 1998

The Sufi Book of Life: 99 Pathways of the Heart, Neil Douglas-Klotz, Penguin Compass, NY, 2005

Take Off Your Glasses and See: A Mind/Body Approach to Expanding Your Eyesight and Insight, Joseph Liberman, Three Rivers Press, 1995

Taking Flight, Anthony de Mello, Doubleday, 1988

Taking the Quantum Leap, Fred Alan Wolf, Harper & Row, Publishers, NY, 1981

Tao Te Ching, Lao-Tzu, Gai-Fu Feng and Jane English, trans., Vintage Books, NY 1989

Tao Te Ching, Lao-Tzu, Stephen Mitchell, trans., Harper Perennial Classics, NY 2000

The Tao of Abundance, Laurence G. Boldt, Penguin, 1999

"Thanks and Giving," Karyn Bradley (Unity Temple on the Plaza, Kansas City, Missouri, 21 November 2004)

Thank You for Being Such a Pain: Spiritual Guidance for Dealing with Difficult People, Mark Rosen, Three Rivers Press, New York, 1998

Therapeutic Touch, Janet Macrae, Alfred A. Knopf, New York, 1997

To Kill a Mockingbird, Harper Lee, J. B. Lippincott, 1960

Trances People Live: Healing Approaches in Quantum Psychology, Stephen Wolinsky, Ph.D., Bramble Co., 1991

The Twilight Zone Companion, Marc Scott Zicree, Silman-James Press, Los Angeles, 1982, 1989

Tying Rocks to Clouds: Meetings and Conversations with Wise and Spiritual People, William Elliot, Quest Books, Wheaton Il, Madras India, London England, 1995

Uncommon Friends: Life with Thomas Edison, Henry Ford, Harvey Firestone, Alexis Carrel, and Charles Lindbergh, James D. Newton, Harcourt, Inc., Orlando, 1987

Unexpected Miracles, David Richo, Crossroad Publishing, 1999

The Universe That Discovered Itself, John D. Barrow, Oxford University Press, Oxford, NY, 2000

The Unknown Reality, Jane Roberts, Prentice-Hall, Englewood Cliffs, NJ, 1977

The Unobstructed Universe, Stewart E. White, E.P. Dutton, 1949

The Verbally Abusive Relationship, Patricia Evans, Adams Media, Avon MA, 1992, 1996

Vibrational Medicine: New Choices for Healing Ourselves, Richard Gerber, Bear & Company, Santa Fe, 1988

Walking Between the Worlds, Gregg Braden, Radio Bookstore Press, 1997

The Way of the Wizard, Deepak Chopra, Random House, NY, 1995

"The When, What and Why of Meditation," Duke Tufty, Unity Temple on the Plaza, Kansas City, Missouri, 31 August 2003

When Science Meets Religion: Enemies, Strangers, or Partners? Ian G. Barbour, HarperSanFrancisco, 2000

Wherever We Are . . . Unity, Michelle Langenberg, ed., Empty Hands Productions, 2003

Wherever You Go . . . There You Are: Mindfulness Meditation in Everyday Life, Jon Kabat-Zinn, Hyperion Books, NY, 1994

"Wisdom from A Course in Miracles," Marianne Williamson, Hay House World Summit, 6/1/13.

Wise Words, Jessica Gribetz, William Morrow Company, Inc., New York, 1997

Who Needs God, Harold Kushner, Summit Books, NY, 1989

Wolf, Fred Alan, at Unity World Headquarters, May 11, 2005

The World's Wisdom: Sacred Texts of the World's Religions, Philip Novak, HarperCollins, NY, 1994

"You are a Love Song," Rev. Paul Tenaglia, Unity Temple on the Plaza, 6/15/03

You'll See It When You Believe It: The Way to Your Personal Transformation, Dr. Wayne Dyer, HarperCollins, 2001

Your Sixth Sense, Bella Naparstek, HarperSanFrancisco, San Francisco, 1998

Zen and the Beat Way, Alan Watts, Charles E. Tuttle Co., Inc., Boston, Rutland, Tokyo, 1997

Zen Essence: The Science of Freedom, Thomas Cleary, Shambhala, Boston, 1989

Zoo Story, Edward Albee, 1960. First performed in New York City January 14, 1960, at Provincetown Playhouse; directed by Milton Katselas.

Also mentioned:

Alice the Fairy, David Shannon, Blue Sky Press/Scholastic Inc., NY, 2004

Becoming: A Master's Manual, Ramtha

In the Sanctuary of the Soul: A Guide to Effective Prayer, Paramahansa Yogananda, Self-Realization Fellowship, Los Angeles, 1998

Enðnotes

Frontispiece

1   *Tao Te Ching* #32 and 6, Stephen Mitchell, trans., Harper Perennial Classics, NY 2000.

Preface

2   Along those lines, in his book, *The Hidden Gospel*, Neil Douglas-Klotz has pointed out some of the hazards of mistranslation and probable alternate interpretations of key phrases of organized Christianity, such as "I am the way, the truth and the life: No man cometh unto the Father, but by me." (John 14:6 KJV) "The Aramaic word *urha*, usually translated 'way' . . . is the light that uncovers a path. The word *sherara*, usually translated as 'truth' . . . a solution or liberation . . . in harmony with the universe. The word *hayye*, usually translated as 'life,' indicates in both Aramaic and Hebrew the sacred life force, the primal energy that pervades all of nature and the universe." He translates John 14:6 as: "No one comes into rhythm with the breathing life of all, the sound and atmosphere that created the cosmos, except through the breathing, sound, and atmosphere, of another embodied 'I' connected to the ultimate 'I Am.' . . . Through attunement with Jesus' breathing, atmosphere, and way of prayer, they will be led to experience what he experiences." Most importantly, Douglas-Klotz adds, "Focusing on the teacher as a doorway to the divine is a spiritual practice that still exists today in Jewish and Islamic mysticism . . . One could simply say . . . that the phrase "except through [me]" is only valid for those for whom Jesus is the primary guide or touchstone for their spirituality." (pp. 65-66) *A Course in Miracles* explains John 14:6 in tandem with the Matthew 28:20, "I am with you always, even unto the end of the world," saying that because Christ is always with us, we *ourselves* are the truth, the way, and the life (p. 108 text).

3   Donald Spoto, in his book, *The Hidden Jesus*, has also brought to light questionable modern-day meanings and absolute fallacies around which the Church's religious doctrine has burgeoned. As for the immaculate conception, Spoto points out that as passionate as John was over Jesus and what he stood for, he surely would have mentioned such a miracle if it were true. He writes:

"There is, contrary to what several generations had assumed, no biblical basis for belief in this doctrine . . . how would it have been possible for Matthew and Luke (late-first-century evangelists writing in Greek outside of Palestine) to know such intimate details about the life of Mary and Joseph? Nowhere else in the same documents—when it would have been so helpful to their cause—do we read of a virginal conception . . . No one who meets or joins himself to Jesus seems to know anything about his special origins." (p. 23, 27) Spoto tells us that "the Hebrew word for "virgin" in Isaiah is *'alma*—meaning simply a "young woman," with no reference to the fact of virginity" (p. 31).

In *The Gnostic Gospels*, Elaine Pagels says the writer of the Gospel of Philip "ridicules those literal-minded Christians" who fail to understand the symbolic nature of the Bible and argues that "virgin birth refers to that mysterious union of the two divine powers, the Father of All and the Holy Spirit." (Vintage Books, New York, 1979, 1989, pp. 63-64).

4   *Einstein's Cosmos: How Albert Einstein's Vision Transformed Our Understanding of Space and Time*, Michio Kaku, W. W. Norton & Company, New York and London, 2004, p. 168.

5   *Living Buddha, Living Christ*, Thich Nhat Hanh, Riverhead Books, G. P. Putnam's Sons, NY, 1995, p. 151.

6   *The Sufi Book of Life: 99 Pathways of the Heart*, Neil Douglas-Klotz, Penguin Compass, NY, 2005, p. xvii.

Chapter One

7   *The Only Planet of Choice*, Phyllis V. Schlemmer, transceiver, Gateway Books, Bath, England, 1993, p. 90.

8   *Dialogues with Scientists and Sages: The Search for Unity*, Renee Weber, Routledge & Kegan Paul, London and NY, 1986, p. 167.

9   *The Hidden Domain: Home of the Quantum Wave Function, Nature's Creative Source*, Norman Friedman, The Woodbridge Group, 1997, p. 182.

10 *Living at the Source: Yoga Teachings of Vivekananda*, Vivekananda, Shambhala, Boston, 1993, p. 124.

11 *A Course in Miracles*, Foundation for Inner Peace, 1975, 1985, p. 15/text.

12 *The World's Wisdom: Sacred Texts of the World's Religions*, Philip Novak, HarperCollins, NY, 1994, p. 166.

13 "The When, What and Why of Meditation," Duke Tufty, Unity Temple on the Plaza, Kansas City, Missouri, 8/31/03. (*Wherever We Are . . . Unity*, Michelle Langenberg, p. 31).

14 *Quantum Reality*, Nick Herbert, Anchor Books, 1985, p. 124.

15 *Modern Physics and Ancient Faith*, Stephen M. Barr, University of Notre Dame, Notre Dame, Indiana, 2003, p. 177.

16 *The Matter Myth,* Paul Davies and John Gribbin, Simon and Schuster, 1992, p. 220.

17 "Light From the Language of Jesus," Rocco A. Enrico, *Science of the Mind Magazine,* September, 1990.

18 *Mind Over Matter,* K. C. Cole, Harcourt, Inc., Orlando, 2003, p. 78.

19 *Hidden Domain,* Friedman, p. 196.

20 *Seth Speaks: The Eternal Validity of the Soul,* Jane Roberts, Amber-Allen, 1972, 1991, p. 41.

21 Princeton Engineering Anomalies Research: Scientific Study of Consciousness-Related Physical Phenomena. http://www.princeton.edu/~pear/2a.html, downloaded 3-23-05.

22 *The Dancing Wu Li Masters: An Overview of the New Physics,* Gary Zukav, Perennial Classics, NY, 1979, 2001, p. 50.

23 "The Plants Respond: An Interview with Cleve Backster," Derrick Jensen, found at www.derrickjensen.org/backster.html; published in *The Sun,* July 1997, in *Free Spirit* October 1998, translated into Czech and published in "Baraka"; downloaded 7/3/05.

24 Zukav, p. 51.

25 *Autobiography of a Yogi,* Paramahansa Yogananda, Self-Realization Fellowship, Los Angeles, 1946, 1974, 1998, p. 411. In our time, poet Naomi Nye writes: "Since I was a small child I've felt that the little inanimate things were very wise, that they had their own kind of wisdom, something to teach me if I would only pay the right kind of attention to them." (*Word of Mouth: Poems Featured on NPR's All Things Considered*) A few decades ago, Yogananda taught us that "Whoever realizes himself as a son of God . . . can reach any goal by the infinite powers hidden within him. A common stone secretly contains stupendous atomic energies; even so, the lowliest mortal is a powerhouse of divinity." (p. 310) About fifty years earlier, Vivekananda wrote, "When the heart has been opened, it can receive teaching from the brooks or the stones . . . but the unopened heart will see nothing but brooks and rolling stones." Two thousand years ago, Jesus spoke on the same matter, as the Gospel of Thomas states: "Split the timber, and I am there; take up the stone, and you will find me there," and "If you become my disciples, and if you hear my words, these stones will minister to you." (Verses 81 and 21)

26 *A Return to Love: Reflections on the Principles of "A Course in Miracles",* Marianne Williamson, HarperCollins Publishers, 1975, 1992, p. 68.

27 *Man's Search for Meaning,* Viktor Frankl, Simon & Schuster, NY, 1959, 1962, 1984, p. 125.

28 *The Nature of the Physical World,* Sir Arthur Eddington, p. 241. Marianne Williamson, "Wisdom from *A Course in Miracles,*" Hay House World Summit 6/1/13: "Remember, miracles arise from conviction.... But if you want to work a miracle, you meet the limited thinking with unlimited thought...In the

universe of the world, there *is* scarcity, but within the universe of Spirit, there is no scarcity, there is *only* abundance—and the universe is beginning again in this moment."

29   *Mind Over Matter*, K. C. Cole, Harcourt, Inc., Orlando, 2003, p. 43.

30   *Alternate Realities: How Science Shapes Our Vision of the World*, Joel Davis, Plenum Press, 1997, p. 245.

31   *Quantum Theory and Measurement,* John Archibald Wheeler and Wojciech Hubert Zurek, eds., Princeton University Press, NJ, p. 194. Quantum principles have found their way into the pages of fiction and advertising and TV scripts. In the second episode of the CBS offering, *"NUMB3RS,"* the show's resident mathematician cites quantum theory and tells FBI agents, "an act of observation affects what is observed."

32   Wikipedia: http://en.wikipedia.org/wiki/Abracadabra, downloaded 12/21/12: In Aramaic, abracadabra means "creating as speaking," and in Hebrew "It will be according to what is spoken." In Aramaic, J. K. Rowling's killing curse, "avada kedavra," means "What I speak is destroyed."

33   *What Is Life?*, Erwin Schrödinger, p.88.

34   Yogananda, p. 38. Like Yogananda and Plato, Rupert Sheldrake says quantum ideas transcend space and time. "They are not made of matter, energy, fields, space, or time; they are not made of anything. In short, they are immaterial and non-physical." (*Seven Experiments That Could Change the World*, p. 182)

35   Herbert, p. 148.

36   *God and the New Physics*, Paul Davies, Simon & Schuster, Inc. NY, 1983, p. 103.

37   *Taking the Quantum Leap*, Fred Alan Wolf, Harper & Row, Publishers, NY, 1981, p. 214.

38   *Hidden Domain*, Norman Friedman, p. 198.

39   *The Individual and the Nature of Mass Events*, Jane Roberts, Prentice-Hall, 1981, pp. 90-1.

40   Vivekananda, p. 75.

41   Jon Kabat-Zinn, Unity Temple of the Plaza, Kansas City, Missouri, 1/30/05.

42   Rev. Duke Tufty, *Wherever We Are . . . Unity*, Michelle Langenberg, Empty Hands Productions, 2003, p. 28.

Chapter Four

43   Novak, p. 159.

44   Herbert, pp. 60-66.

45   *Parallel Universes*, Fred Alan Wolf, Touchstone, NY, 1988, p.81.

46   Herbert, p. 115.

47 *A Short History of Nearly Everything*, Bill Bryson, Broadway Books, 2003, p. 141.

48 Zukav, p. 232.

49 Charles Krauthammer, "Gone in 60 nanoseconds," *The Washington Post*, October 6, 2011.

50 Davies and Gribbin, p. 217.

51 Davies, p. 27.

52 *Miracles: A Jewish Perspective*, Rabbi Ronald H. Isaacs, Jason Aronson Inc., Northvale NJ and Jerusalem, 1997, p. 1.

53 "Fact or Fiction: The Practical Side of Quantum Mechanics" at http://curiosity. discovery.com/topic/applications-of-quantum-mechanics/practical-side-quantum-mechanics-quiz5.htm?answerId=29034 (downloaded 9/4/2011).

54 Herbert, pp. 52-3.

55 Barr, p. 238.

56 *Mind Over Matter*, Cole, pp. 13, 178.

57 *The Nature of Personal Reality*, Jane Roberts, Amber-Allen Publishing, San Rafael, CA, 1974, 1994, p. 26. Ali Campbell, "How to Make Big Changes in Your Life Fast," Hay House World Summit, June 5, 2013: "You're rarely only one thought away from feeling better...Our thoughts happen—sure they do. The problem isn't that we have them; the problem is that we believe them. Just because you thought it doesn't make it *true*...."

58 *Taking Flight*, Anthony de Mello, Doubleday, 1988, p. 41.

59 *The Hole in the Universe: How Scientists Peered over the Edge of Emptiness and Found Everything*, K. C. Cole, Harcourt, Inc., NY, San Diego, London, 2001, p. 105-6.

60 *First You Build a Cloud and other reflections on physics as a way of life*, K. C. Cole, Harcourt Brace & Company, 1999, p. 108.

61 *Hole in the Universe*, Cole, pp. 216, 218-19, 221.

62 *Take Off Your Glasses and See: A Mind/Body Approach to Expanding Your Eyesight and Insight*, Joseph Liberman, Three Rivers Press, 1995.

63 Talbot, p. 186.

64 *Finding Joy: A Practical Spiritual Guide to Happiness*, Dannel I. Schwartz, with Mark Hass, Jewish Light Publishing, Woodstock, VT, 1996, p. 57.

65 Weber, p. 9.

66 *Hole in the Universe*, Cole, p. 92.

67 *Anthony de Mello*, William Dych, S. J., ed., Orbis Books, 2002, p. 102.

68 *Hole in the Universe*, Cole, p. 179.

69 Davis, p. 168.

70 *Mind Over Matter*, Cole, p. 134.

71 Davies, p. 178-9.

72 *The Universe That Discovered Itself*, John D. Barrow, Oxford University Press, Oxford, NY, 2000, p. 417.

73 Davies, pp. 187-8.
74 *Bridging Science and Spirit*, Norman Friedman, Living Lake Books, p. 59.
75 *First You Build a Cloud*, Cole, p. 187.
76 Weber, pp. 192-3.
77 *Taking the Quantum Leap*, Wolf, p. 6.
78 *Infinite Mind*, Valerie Hunt, Malibu, 1996, p. 52.
79 Davies, p. 65.
80 "Being You and Living Your Life with a Sense of Ease," Duke Tufty, Unity Temple on the Plaza, 6/19/05.
81 *God is a Verb: Kabbalah and the Practice of Mystical Judaism*, Rabbi David Cooper, Riverhead Books, 1997, p. 112.
82 © The Associated Press; written by Rodrique Ngowi.
83 Davies, p. 178.
84 *Essential Sufism*, James Fadiman and Robert Frager, HarperSanFrancisco, 1997, p. 26.
85 *The Essential Zohar*, Rav P. S. Berg, Bell Tower, 2002, p. 105.
86 *The Tao of Abundance*, Laurence G. Boldt, Penguin, 1999, p. xxix.
87 Wolf, Fred Alan, at Unity World Headquarters, 5/11/05.
88 Sioux Indian: Wakan Tanka. Lakota: Great Mystery. Algonquian: Gitchi Manitou. Blackfoot: Old Man. Chickasaw: Ababinili. Hopi: Spider Woman or Grandmother Spider.
89 *The Individual and the Nature of Mass Events*, Roberts, p. 121.
90 *The Hidden Gospel: Decoding the Spiritual Message of the Aramaic Jesus*, Neil Douglas-Klotz, Quest Books, Wheaton IL, 1999, p. 125.
91 *The Hidden Jesus: A New Life*, Donald Spoto, St. Martin's Press, New York, 1998, p. 80.
92 Yogananda, p.170.
93 Cooper, p. 57.
94 Novak, p. 48.
95 Unity Temple on the Plaza, 1/1/06.
96 "All things were made by him [the Word, or *Aum*], and without him was not anything made that was made. *Aum* of the Vedas became the sacred word *Hum* of the Tibetans, *Amin* of the Moslems, and *Amen* of the Egyptians, Greeks, Romans, Jews, and Christians. Its meaning in Hebrew is *sure, faithful.*" [sic italics] *Autobiography of a Yogi*, Yogananda, p.237.
97 "Being You," Duke Tufty, Unity Temple on the Plaza, 6/19/05.
98 *Who Needs God*, Harold Kushner, Summit Books, NY, 1989, p. 205.

Chapter Six

99 Weber, p. 92.

100 *Vibrational Medicine: New Choices for Healing Ourselves*, Richard Gerber, Bear & Company, Santa Fe, 1988, p. 63.

101 Davis, p. 244.

102 *Awakening to Zero Point*, Gregg Braden, Radio Bookstore Press, Bellevue, WA, 1993, 1994, 1997, p. 81.

103 Davies and Gribbin, p. 233.

104 Zukav, p. 329.

105 "From Muhammed to Grandma Rose," Polly Shulman, *Discover, 1998*, pp. 85-89 on "six degrees of separation-or less-and interconnections, © 1998 by Polly Shulman.

106 Davies and Gribbin, pp. 284, 224.

107 Novak, p. 9.

108 Yogananda, p. 73.

109 www.derrickjensen.org/backster.html

110 Hunt, p. 70.

111 *Hidden Gospel*, Douglas-Klotz, pp. 19, 70, 65.

112 It appears that healing takes place in harmonic resonance with our planet and, in fact, "each human cell specifically, strives to maintain a constant resonance, or 'tuning,' with the pulsed heartbeat of Earth." Gregg Braden, *Awakening to Zero Point*, p. 39.

113 Hunt, pp. 63-4, 67, 26, 67, 69, 345.

114 *Autobiography*, Yogananda, p. 358.

115 *From the Mouth of God*, Richard Dupuis, BookPartners, 1998, p. 110.

116 *The Spontaneous Fulfillment of Desire*, Deepak Chopra, M.D., Harmony Books, NY, 2003, p. 89.

117 Herbert, p. 35.

118 *The Maker of Dreams: A Fantasy in One Act*, Oliphant Down, Gowans & Gray, Ltd., Glasgow, 1917, p. 19. First performed by the Scottish Repertory Theatre Company at the Royalty Theatre, Glasgow, 11/20/1911; directed by Alfred Wareing.

119 Bryson, p. 166.

120 *Nature of Personal Reality*, Roberts, p. 270.

121 *Hidden Gospel*, Douglas-Klotz, p. 64.

122 Novak, pp. 322, 339, 345.

123 *Hole in the Universe*, Cole, p. 138.

124 *Parallel Universes*, Fred Alan Wolf, p. 315.

Chapter Seven

125 Isaacs, p. 119.

126 Cooper, p. 35.

127 *Nature of Personal Reality*, Roberts, p. 291.

128 Weber, p. 58.

129 *Seth Speaks*, Roberts, p. 286. Ali Campbell, "How to Make Big Changes in Your Life Fast," Hay House World Summit, June 5, 2013: "The bit we forget is, that thought is just a thought. And exactly the same way as you watch a scary movie and you get scared, it doesn't matter if that movie has been in your collection for 20 years or for 20 minutes, you can throw it out just as quick. And as soon as you do, it stops scaring you."

130 *Seven Experiments That Could Change the World*, Rupert Sheldrake, G. P. Putnam's Sons, 1995, p. 104.

131 *The Song of the Bird*, Anthony de Mello, Image/Doubleday, NY, 1982, p. 61.

132 Fadiman and Frager, p. 16.

Chapter Eight

133 *The Hidden Messages in Water*, Dr. Masaru Emoto, Beyond Words Publishing, Inc., 2004. Samples exposed to "thank you" in many different languages, along with those treated to children's folk songs, master classical works, and scenes of nature produced beautiful crystals in Emoto's laboratory. Emoto himself concluded that "Love and Gratitude" produced the most complete, most intricate crystal of all. *See also* work done by Dr. Alfred Tomatis, who said that sound enters the ear, is changed into electrochemicals that travel to the brain and then through the nervous system to the bones and skin. We are *oozing* with sound!

134 *Trances People Live: Healing Approaches in Quantum Psychology*, Stephen Wolinsky, Ph.D., Bramble Co., 1991, p. 6.

135 *Nature of Personal Reality*, Roberts, p. 88.

136 *The Power is Within You*, Louise Hay, Hay House, Inc., 1991, p. 37-8.

137 Yogananda, *Autobiography*, p. 349. Hunt, p. 139.

Chapter Nine

138 Jon Kabat-Zinn, Unity Temple of the Plaza, Kansas City, Missouri, 1/1/05.

139 *The Self-Aware Universe: how consciousness creates the material world*, Amit Goswami, Richard Reed, Maggie Goswami, G. P. Putnam's Sons, New York, 1993, p. 58. Note: Although Bohr did not believe in superstition, he did nail a horseshow over his front door. He told a visitor, "But you know, they say it brings luck even if you don't believe in it." (Herbert, p. 93)

140 *Prayers of the Cosmos: Meditations on the Aramaic Words of Jesus*, Neil Douglas-Klotz, HarperCollins, NY, 1990, p. 17.

141 *A Course in Miracles*, p. 195/text.

142 Yogananda, *Autobiography*, p. 275.

143 *A Course in Miracles*, p. 45/text.

144 Spoto, p. 81.

145 Weber, p. 24.

146 Mitchell, #2.

147 Elliot, p. 94.

148 Cooper, p. 160.

149 *Hidden Gospel*, Douglas-Klotz, pp. 72-3.

150 *Tying Rocks to Clouds: Meetings and Conversations with Wise and Spiritual People*, William Elliot, Quest Books, Wheaton Il, Madras India, London England, 1995, p. 179.

151 *Hidden Gospel*, Douglas-Klotz, pp. 131-2.

152 *The Sixth Sense: Unlocking the Power of Your Intuition*, Belleruth Naparstek, HarperCollins, 1997, p. 69.

153 Novak, p. 370, 142.

154 *the medium, the mystic, and the physicist: Toward a General Theory of the Paranormal*, Lawrence LeShan, Viking Press, NY, 1974, p. 91.

155 *The Seven Spiritual Laws of Success*, Deepak Chopra, Harmony Books, NY, 1997, p. 53. *The Seven Spiritual Laws of Success*, Deepak Chopra, Harmony Books, NY, 1997, p. 53. Einstein said, "Everyone is a genius. But if you judge a fish on its ability to climb a tree, it will live its whole life believing that it is stupid." In a like manner, Vivekananda said, "Everyone must be judged according to his own ideal, and not by that of anyone else. If you are a strong man, very good! But do not curse others who are not strong enough for you. People are doing all right to the best of their ability and means and knowledge. *Woe unto me that I cannot lift them to where I am!*" (*Living at the Source*, p. 32.)

156 LeShan, p. 162.

157 *The Silmarillion*, J. R. R. Tolkien, George Allen & Unwen Ltd., 1997, pp. 15-17.

158 And we are what we think we *shall* be: "Your body's condition is not so much the result of its own comprehension of its 'past history' as it is the result of its own comprehension of the future; it is precognate. It is truer to say that heredity operates from the future backward into the past than it is to say that it operates from the past into the present . . . your present is a poised balance affected as much by the probable future as the probable past." *The "Unknown" Reality*, Jane Roberts, Prentice Hall, 1977, p. 87.

159 *After the Ecstasy, the Laundry: How the Heart Grows Wise on the Spiritual Path*, Jack Kornfield, Bantam Books, NY, Toronto, London, Sydney, Auckland, 2000, p. 223.

160 *A Course in Miracles*, p. 585/text.

Chapter Ten

161 Novak, p. 316.
162 Schwartz and Hass, p. 116.
163 *A Course in Miracles*, p. 151/text.
164 "One Path to Heaven, One Path to Hell," Duke Tufty, Unity Temple on the Plaza, Kansas City, Missouri, 11/28/04.
165 *Seth Material*, Roberts, p. 157.
166 Hunt, p. 48, 64, 66-67. In fact, meditation and visualizing light in injured tissues cured Hunt's polio-like virus in her leg. For more causes of physical illness, see *Therapeutic Touch* by Janet Macrae, *Hands of Light* by Barbara Brennan, *Your Body Believes Every Word You Say* by Barbara Hoberman Levine, *Vibrational Medicine* by Richard Gerber, *Essential Reiki* by Diane Stein, writings by Louise Hay, and "Seth" books by Jane Roberts.
167 The Fox series, *Touch*, which ran for two seasons in 2012-13 (created by Tim Kring and starring Kieffer Sutherland), revolved around the "36 Righteous Ones," based upon a mystical Jewish (Talmudic) concept: the *lamed-vav tzaddikim*, who feel the suffering of all and keep the world from ending; they are, indeed, potential Messiahs. My broader definition of "angels in disguise" includes, as Rabbi Cooper writes in *God Is a Verb*, "...angels of confusion, destruction, fear, fire, hail, insomnia, reptiles, storms, terror, and thunder": not demons, but people and events whose "purpose is to draw us closer to God." (p. 141)
168 *Hidden Gospel*, Douglas-Klotz, p. 28.
169 *Mind Over Matter*, Cole, p. 119.
170 *The Twilight Zone Companion,* Marc Scott Zicree, Silman-James Press, Los Angeles, 1982, 1989, p. 203.
171 *Flawless! The Ten Most Common Character Flaws*, Louis Tartaglia, M.D., William Morrow, NY, 1999, p. 17.
172 *Thank You for Being Such a Pain: Spiritual Guidance for Dealing with Difficult People*, Mark Rosen, Three Rivers Press, New York, 1998, pp. 252-3.
173 Fadiman and Frager, p. 90: "... the rain—it waters all things, whether it loves them or not."
174 *A Course in Miracles*, pp. 173, 223.
175 *Sufi Book of Life*, Douglas-Klotz, p. 156.
176 Herbert, pp. 19, 169.
177 Zukav, p. 329.
178 *The Way of the Wizard*, Deepak Chopra, Random House, 1998, p. 48.
179 *The Nature of the Psyche*, Jane Roberts, Prentice-Hall, 1979, pp. 99, 96.
180 *Hidden Domain*, Friedman, p. 48.
181 Herbert, p. 121.
182 Gerber, p. 60.

183 Einstein, Albert http://en.wikiquote.org/wiki/Albert_Einstein, downloaded 3/10/05.

184 *Prayer is Good Medicine*, Larry Dossey, M.D., HarperSanFrancisco, San Francisco, 1996, p. 29. Dossey was a battalion surgeon in Vietnam.

185 Cooper, p. 141.

186 Dossey, p. 185.

187 Hunt, p. 56.

188 Yogananda, p. 152.

189 Fadiman and Frager, p. 40.

Chapter Twelve

190 *The Edge*, Doreen Virtue, April, 2000.

191 *Awakening to Zero Point*, Braden, p. 55.

192 *Tao Te Ching*, Lao-Tzu, Gai-Fu Feng and Jane English, trans., Vintage Books, NY 1989, #69.

193 Novak, p. 317.

194 Bryson, pp. 122, 376.

195 *Walking Between the Worlds*, Gregg Braden, Radio Bookstore Press, 1997, p. 38. Bruce Lipton, "How to Live in Heaven on Earth," Hay House World Summit, June 9, 2013: "The new science is called epigenetic control: ... Now we know it's how we respond to the environment. That includes our perceptions, emotions, beliefs and attitudes. *So, as we change how we respond to the environment, we change our genetic expression....We are not victims of our genes, we're masters of our genetics!....We must wake up to the reality that our positive and negative thoughts are profoundly affecting our genetics.*"

196 "Seven Steps to Serenity III: Maintaining Harmony in Relationships," Duke Tufty, Unity Temple, 12/4/05.

197 Herbert, p. 37.

198 *Hidden Gospel*, Douglas-Klotz, p. 50.

199 Kornfield, p. 202.

200 Novak, p. 152.

201 *Hidden Gospel*, Douglas-Klotz, p. 92.

202 Weber, p. 86.

203 Emoto, p. 92.

204 Weber, pp. 51, 39.

205 *Walking Between the Worlds*, Gregg Braden, p. xiv.

206 *Nature of Personal Reality*, Roberts, p. 95.

207 Wiesel, p. 27

208 *The [selves] you are not aware of* yet seem more progressed, [but] you are a part of them now . . . a knowledge of the ideas of multipersonhood could help you realize that you have available many abilities not being used . . . [The bulb

and the flower] exist at once. In *your* terms, however, *it is as if* the flower-to-be, from its "future" calls back to the bulb and tells it how to make the flower. Memory operates backward and forward in time. The flower—calling back to the bulb, urging it ahead and reminding it of its (probable future) development—is like a future self in your terms, or a more highly advanced self, who has the answers and can indeed be practically relied on . . . Larger concepts of personhood will indeed lead you to some glimpse of the truly remarkable gestalts of consciousness from which you constantly emerge. (Jane Roberts, *Unknown Reality*, pp. 79-80.)

209 *Space-Time and Beyond: Toward an Explanation of the Unexplainable,* Bob Toben, in Conversation with Jack Sarfatti and Fred Wolf, E. P. Dutton (NY), 1975, pp. 91, 93-4.

210 *Native American Myths,* Diane Ferguson, Collins and Brown Limited, London, 2001, p.52.

211 Boldt, p. 288.

212 *Excuse Me, Your Life is Waiting,* Lynn Grabhorn, Hampton Roads, Charlottesville VA, 2000, p. 22.

213 In John 16:23-24 (KJV), Jesus said, "Whatsoever ye shall ask the Father in my name, he will give it you. Hitherto have ye asked nothing in my name: ask and ye shall receive, that your joy may be full." Douglas-Klotz says that our limited translation of *in my name* "has led to the shell of Jesus' teaching being honored instead of the kernel." In "Jesus' name" means with his experience, his light, his sound (*vibration*). The word translated as "ask," *detheshaloon*, is a straightforward request, and *tesbwoon*, traditionally translated as "receive," is more like being surrounded by the outcome of the request.

214 "Thanks and Giving," Karyn Bradley, Unity Temple on the Plaza, Kansas City, Missouri, 11/21/04.

215 *The Sufi Book of Life,* Douglas-Klotz, p. xxix.

216 *Mostly Harmless: The Fifth Book in the Increasingly Inaccurately Named Hitchhikers Trilogy,* Douglas Adams, Serious Productions, NY, 1992, pp. 111-2.

217 Cooper, p. 290.

Chapter Fourteen

218 *A Course in Miracles,* p. 274/text.

219 *Hidden Gospel,* Friedman, pp. 69-71.

220 PEAR—"A Linear Pendulum Experiment: Effects of Operator Intention on Damping Rate," R.D. Nelson, G.J. Bradish, R.G. Jahn, B.J. Dunne (1994).

221 Novak, p. 278.

222 Reported in *Science,* June 11, 1993 issue (Vol. 260:1590).

223 *Awakening to Zero Point,* Braden, p. 16.

224 Hunt, p. 198.

225 Yogananda wrote that man and creation were made for the purpose that man "rises up as master of *maya,* knowing his dominion over the cosmos . . . when the self is in communion with a higher power, Nature automatically obeys, without stress or strain, the will of man . . . All scriptures proclaim that the Lord created man in His omnipotent image. Control over the universe appears to be supernatural, but in truth such power is inherent and natural in everyone who attains 'right remembrance' of his divine origin . . . Any man of divine realization could perform miracles because, like Christ, he understands the subtle laws of creation." (*Autobiography of a Yogi*, pp. 328, 218-9) Braden, too, writes: "Destructive weather patterns and storms are related to the unsettled consciousness of people where the storms occur." (*The Isaiah Effect*, pp. 208, 217)

226 *Isaiah Effect*, Braden, pp. 236.

227 Weber, pp. 71, 73.

228 Emoto, p. 95; Rupert Sheldrake, "The Science Delusion," 3/15/13.

229 *First You Build a Cloud*, Cole, p. 164.

230 Gregg Braden, "Prayer as the Human-to-Divine Interface," Unity Temple on the Plaza, 9/11/08.

231 *Subtle Energy*, William Collinge, Warner Books, 1998.

232 Gerber, p. 500.

Chapter Fifteen

233 Weber, p. 207, 134.

234 *Living Energy Universe*, Swartz and Russek, Hampton Roads, Charlottesville, VA, 1999, p. 55-6.

235 Cooper, p. 198.

236 "A Birthday Wish" by Thad Langenberg:

She lived a life of solitude./ She lived a life in pain.
She lived a life in which there was/ A strong, ongoing pain.

She had no friends on which to lean/ And cry her problems to.
She had no friends to give her love/ And hope and kindness, too.

She thought about it day and night;/ She lay upon her bed.
Her mind made up, she grabbed a gun/ And put it to her head.

Just then a ring came from the phone./ She pulled the gun away.
Her mom was on the other end/ And wanted just to say,

"Happy Birthday, my dear girl/ Today is just for you.
I care for you with all my heart,/ I hope you know that's true."

These words ran through her mind so much./ The gun was down for good.
She changed her mind about her life/ And then she changed her mood.

She thought about this special day/ And what her mom had said.
The gift her mom gave her that day/ Was the gift of life, *again*.

237 Weber, p. 129.
238 *First You Build a Cloud*, Cole, pp. 205-7.
239 *The Unknown Reality*, Jane Roberts, Prentice-Hall, Englewood Cliffs, NJ, 1977, p. 107.
240 *Souls on Fire: Portraits and Legends of Hasidic Masters*, Elie Wiesel, Summit Books, NY, 1972, pp. 26-7.
241 *The River of Light*, Lawrence Kushner, Harper & Row, San Francisco, 1981, p. 72.
242 Dupuis, pp. 42, 47.
243 *Uncommon Friends: Life with Thomas Edison, Henry Ford, Harvey Firestone, Alexis Carrel, and Charles Lindbergh*, James D. Newton, Harcourt, Inc., Orlando, 1987, p. 19.
244 Gerber, p. 65, 310.
245 Weber, p. 15.

Chapter Sixteen

246 Weber, p. 19.
247 Marianne Williamson, p. 39.
248 Dupuis, p. 111.
249 Hunt, p. 55.
250 Dych, p. 70.
251 *Mutant Message Downunder*, Marlo Morgan, HarperCollins, 1991, 1994, 2001, pp. 51-2.
252 *Awakening to Zero Point*, Braden, p. 18.
253 *Hidden Gospel*, Douglas-Klotz, p. 65: "Focusing on the teacher as a doorway to the divine is a spiritual practice that still exists today in Jewish and Islamic mysticism . . . One could simply say . . . that the phrase "except through [me]" is only valid for those for whom Jesus is the primary guide or touchstone for their spirituality."
254 *Quantum Theory and Measurement,* Wheeler and Zurek, eds., p. 25, quoted in *Bridging Science and Spirit*, Friedman, p. 25.

255 *Hidden Gospel*, Douglas-Klotz, p. 75.
256 Kornfield, p. 3.

Chapter Seventeen

257 Yogananda, p. 282.
258 Spoto, p. 107.
259 *Einstein's Cosmos*, Kaku, p. 21.
260 Yogananda, p. 282.
261 Toben, p. 143.
262 *A Course in Miracles*, pp. 1-2.
263 Davies, p. 39.
264 *Seth Material*, Roberts, p. 243.
265 Davies and Gribbin, p. 82.
266 *Hidden Domain*, Friedman, pp. 95, 126.
267 Davies and Gribbin, p. 213.
268 *Isaiah Effect*, Braden, p. 100. Braden says, "rather than creating our reality, it may be more accurate to say that we create the conditions into which we attract future outcomes, already established, into the focus of the present. Choosing forgiveness, compassion, and peace attracts futures that reflect" those same qualities. ("The Isaiah Effect," Gregg Braden (Unity Temple, May 16, 2000, and from *The Isaiah Effect*, p. 24.)
269 *Nature of Personal Reality*, Roberts, pp. 278-80. "In much the same way, a strong belief in an ability generated in the present will reach into the past and effect whatever changes would have had to occur *there* in order to now make the ability apparent . . . *You are not at the mercy of a past over which you have no control.*"
270 *Isaiah Effect*, Braden, p. 100.
271 Roberts, *The "Unknown" Reality II*, pp. 319-20, 324, 330. Also: "[I]deas and beliefs . . . give signals to the chromosomes . . . There is, then, a way of introducing 'new' genetic information to a so-called damaged cell in the present . . . First the undesirable information must be erased in the 'past' . . . The body on its own performs this service often, when it automatically rights certain conditions, even though they were genetically imprinted . . . You can literally *choose* between health and illness; between a concentration upon the mental more than the physical . . . Your intent is all important—your [conscious] *intent* to become well . . . 'Miraculous' healings are simply instances of nature unhampered." Roberts, *The "Unknown" Reality II*, pp. 319-20, 324, 330.
272 *Hidden Domain*, Friedman, pp. 73, 196-7.
273 The space-time continuum is not only curved, it also has topographical properties, i.e., it can be connected in crazy ways, like a donut. It can also

twist. Gary Zukav, *The Dancing Wu Li Masters: An Overview of the New Physics*, Perennial Classics, NY, 79, 2001, p. 200.

274 *Mostly Harmless*, Adams, p. 40.

Chapter Eighteen

275 Talbot, p. 253.
276 Cooper, p. 78.
277 Novak, pp. 98-9.
278 *Odd Thomas*, Dean Koontz, Bantam Books, NY, 2003, p. 5.
279 *The Practice of the Presence of God*, Brother Lawrence, Whitaker House, New Kensington, PA, 1982, p. 24.
280 *Living Buddha*, Hanh p. 175.
281 Yogananda, p. 312.
282 *Einstein's Cosmos*, Kaku, p. 240, 180.
283 *All in the Family*, "End in Sight," first broadcast 10/1/78. Writer: Nate Monaster; created by Norman Lear.
284 *A Course in Miracles*, p. 110/text.
285 *Therapeutic Touch*, Janet Macrae, Alfred A. Knopf, New York, 1997, p. 23.
286 *The Fellowship of the Ring*, J.R.R. Tolkien, Bookspan, 1954, 1965, 1982, 2001, p. 386.
287 Yogananda, p. 264.
288 *Sufi Book of Life*, Douglas-Klotz, p. 1.
289 See Endnote #2.

Chapter Nineteen

290 *Einstein's Cosmos*, Kaku, p. 35.
291 Yogananda, p. 358.
292 *Parallel Worlds: A Journey through Creation, Higher Dimensions, and the Cosmos,* Michio Kaku, Doubleday, NY, 2004, p. 18.
293 *Bridging Science and Spirit*, Friedman, p.76.
294 Cooper, pp. 69-70.
295 Toben, p. 98.

Chapter Twenty

296 Kornfield, pp. 133, 282.
297 *River of Light*, Kushner, p. 66.
298 *Seth Material*, p. 271. Also: "There is a portion of All That Is directed and focused within each individual, residing within each consciousness. Each consciousness is, therefore, cherished and individually protected . . . If you

prefer to call this supreme psychic gestalt God, then you must not attempt to objectify him, for he is the nuclei of your cells and more intimate than your breath. You are co-creators." (pp. 271, 269)

299 *Prayers of the Cosmos*, Douglas-Klotz, p. 17: Douglas-Klotz recasts the word traditionally translated as "perfect" as "all-embracing." See also *"Ehyeh asher Ehyeh,"* usually translated as "I Am That I Am," in Part Two: 1.

300 *Strong Measures: Contemporary American Poetry in Traditional Forms*, Philip Dacey and David Jauss, eds., Harper & Row, Publishers, New York, 1986, p. 31.

301 *You'll See It When You Believe It*, Dr. Wayne Dyer, HarperCollins, 2001, p. 169.

302 Weber, p. 94.

303 Kornfield, p. 167.

304 Feng and English, p. 86. Also, as Zen master Xiatang said, "Although gold dust is precious, when it gets in your eyes, it obstructs vision." Obsession, even with becoming enlightened, is not good. Thomas Cleary, *Zen Essence: The Science of Freedom*, Shambhala, 1989, p. 74.

305 Rumi: "O pure people who wander the world, amazed at the idols you see, what are you searching for out there, if you look within, you yourself are it" and "Whatever pearl you seek, look for the pearl within the pearl!" and "Only from the heart can you touch the sky."

306 *Episode Three: Revenge of the Sith.*

307 *The Kansas City Star*, "Why Does God Allow This: Tsunami has theologians and scholars pondering the nature of evil," Bill Tammeus, January 1, 2005.

308 Blyth, p. 97.

309 Hunt, p. 52.

310 LeShan, pp. 248-9.

311 *All in the Family*, "Archie and the Computer," first broadcast 10/27/73. Writers: Lloyd Turner, Gordon Mitchell, Don Nicholl; created by Norman Lear; "Edith Gets Fired," first broadcast 2/25/79. Writers: Mort Lachman, Patt Shea, Harriet Weiss.

312 *Sufi Book of Life*, Neil Douglas-Klotz, p. 166.

313 *The Lord of the Rings and Philosophy*, Gregory Bassham and Eric Bronson, eds., Open Court Publishing Co., 2003, p. 16.

314 Kornfield, p. 43.

315 *Mind Over Matter*, Cole, p. 46.

316 Dych, p. 47.

317 Mitchell, #1.

318 *Mind Over Matter*, Cole, p. 54.

319 Davies and Gribbin, p. 282.

320 *Bridging Science and Spirit*, Friedman, p. 68.

321 Michio Kaku, quoted in *Prophets of Science: George Lucas*, broadcast 3/9/2012.

322 Gregg Braden, "Prayer as the Human-to-Divine Interface," Unity Temple on the Plaza, 9/11/08.

323 *Hidden Gospel*, Douglas-Klotz, p. 33.

324 *A Course in Miracles*, p. 123/text.

325 *The Hidden Gospel*, p.70: Speaking about *shem*, usually translated as "name," Douglas-Klotz says: ". . . all individual name-light-vibrations return in various ways to the one sacred *shem* of the divine . . . All vibration is part of the whole vibration of the universe. In fact, one of the words for 'universe' or 'cosmos' in Hebrew-Aramaic consists of the root *shem* along with the ending -*aya*, which indicates that the divine name-light-vibration is in every particle of existence."

326 Weber, p. 55.

327 Elliot, p. 86.

328 Vivekananda, p. 140.

329 *First You Build a Cloud*, Cole, p. 154.

330 "Seven Steps to Serenity IV: It's All About You," Duke Tufty, Unity Temple on the Plaza, 12/11/05.

331 Williamson, p. 165. Hunt, p. 180: We can no longer entertain beliefs that we are unworthy and inadequate." When you believe this, you have a new awareness and everyday life improves, which occurs because "you are getting out of your own way. You may know about future events or cause things to happen without effort. Experiences may be more intense. Your body enlivens." *Prerequisites for this level of awareness: 1. a secure selfhood/ego; 2. some degree of success and satisfaction in society; 3. some degree of comfort in relationships; 4. enough economic security to satisfy needs and wants; strength of will to direct energy and a sense of self-worth to support it. Otherwise, your energies are diffused and dissipated upon attention for physical existence. So, divert the energy you were directing toward material problems—*know you will be sustained, and be peaceful*—to spiritual problems.

332 *Einstein's Cosmos*, Kaku, p. 182.

333 *River of Light*, Lawrence Kushner, p. 121.

334 Fadiman and Frager, p. 73.

335 Some 20th-century heroes are still alive (Billie Jean King, the Dalai Lama, Bishop Desmond Tutu, Nelson Mandela, Lech Wałęsa and Guenter Schabowski, whose announcement about unrestricted visas ultimately brought down the Berlin Wall), but current leadership and the sports, cinematic, and literary worlds seem less impressive to me than before.

336 *Leven Thumps and the Gateway to Foo*, Obert Skye, Snow Mountain, 2005, pp. xiii, 91.

337 Jahn and Dunne, p. 341.

338 Talbot, p. 237.

339 Zicree, p. 111.

340 Mitchell, #26 and p. 96.

341 *Zoo Story*, Edward Albee, 1960. First performed in New York City January 14, 1960, at Provincetown Playhouse; directed by Milton Katselas, p. 19.

342 *Zen and the Beat Way*, Alan Watts, Charles E. Tuttle Co., Inc., Boston, Rutland, Tokyo, 1997, p. 63.

343 Kornfield, p. 209.

344 *Einstein's Cosmos*, Kaku, p. 34.

345 Langenberg, p. 47. In the autumn of 2002, I *allowed myself* (no blaming it on what my father said) to spiral down into a depression, when all I really wanted to do was to sleep or spend time in a hot bathtub—two "safe" places. I couldn't make even the smallest of decisions, like what to eat for lunch, or even whether I was going to eat. Westlake has a character who couldn't decide whether he was going to the kitchen to make himself a bologna sandwich or take the gun out of the drawer and shoot himself. I was in that spot, without the gun. And I knew I was doing it to myself. Finally I said, "Enough," and meant it, and committed myself to life, just as it was. I wasn't where I wanted to be, doing what I wanted to do, but that did not change what was, and what I had to work with—myself.

346 *The Verbally Abusive Relationship*, Patricia Evans, Adams Media, Avon, MA, 1992, 1996, p. 175.

347 Yogananda, p. 240.

348 Talbot, pp. 153-4 (also mentioned in *Autobiography*, Yogananda, p. 358).

349 *Taking Flight*, de Mello, p. 5.

350 "Mr. Bevis," first aired on April 8, 1960, Zicree, pp. 134-5.

351 Hunt, p. 192.

352 Cooper, pp. 77, 191, 125.

353 *Eyes Remade for Wonder*, Lawrence Kushner, Jewish Lights Publishing, 1998, p. 133.

354 Spoto, p. 149.

355 *Saving the World Entire: and 100 Other Beloved Parables from the Talmud*, Rabbi Bradley N. Bleefeld and Robert L. Shook, Plume, New York, 1998, p. 123.

356 Roberts, *Seth Speaks*, p. 416.

357 *Unexpected Miracles*, David Richo, Crossroad Publishing, 1999.

358 Watts, p. 3.

359 Cooper, p. 209.

360 From the National Library of Medicine's Internet search service at: http://www.ncbi.hih.gov.entrez/query.fcgi?db=pubmed&cmd=Display&dopt=pub med_pubmed&from_uid=15925737, downloaded 8/23/12.

361 *Quantum Questions*, Ken Wilber, ed., Shambhala, Boston, 2001, p. 144; Weber, p. 111.

362 Skye, p. 66.

363 Rev. Duke Tufty, "97,219 Steps to Spiritual Enlightenment," Unity Temple on the Plaza, 11/11/01, and Ilan Shamir, Unity of Denver, 7/11/04.

364 *Einstein's Cosmos*, Kaku, p. 179.

365 Schwartz, with Mark Hass, pp. 43, 85, 47.

366 Kornfield, p. 192.

367 *Milkweed*, Jerry Spinelli, Scholastic Inc., NY (etc.), 2003, p. 158.

368 *Hidden Gospel*, Douglas-Klotz, pp. 33-4.

369 At this writing, Valdi and I are making the shift to "best of friends" and author/editor, and I am practicing Unity's mantra, "This or something better," in my private little hell, remembering that Grace is most likely working a "blessing in disguise" on our behalf via Valdi and his courage, his integrity, his sacrifice (and, perhaps, his foolish "inattentional blindness").

370 Wiesel, p. 38.

371 *The Essential Koran: The Heart of Islam*, trans. Thomas Cleary, HarperSanFrancisco, San Francisco, 1993.

372 *Zen Essence: The Science of Freedom*, Thomas Cleary, Shambhala, Boston, 1989, p. 74.

373 Kabat-Zinn, *Wherever You Go . . . There You Are*, p. 147.

374 Studies have proven that women benefit from *not* wearing bras and, in fact, should take every opportunity to liberate their chests, as the strictures that tight bras place on the lymph nodes can contribute to breast cancer. Women who wear tight-fitting bras 24 hours a day are 125 times more likely to have breast cancer than women who do not wear bras at all. "Dressed to Kill, The Link Between Breast Cancer and Bras," Sydney Ross Singer, Soma Grismaijer.

375 *Hasidic Anthology*, Louis I. Newman, Schocken Books, NY, 1963, p. 95.

376 Schwartz and Hass, p. 26.

377 Fadiman and Frager, p. 163.

378 *Sufi Book*, Douglas-Klotz, p. 4.

379 *No Ordinary Genius: The Illustrated Richard Feynman*, Christopher Sykes, W. W. Norton and Company, NY and London, 1994, p. 225.

380 *Sufi Book*, Douglas-Klotz, p. 178.

381 Also, to name a few: Clara Scott, who blossomed in the life of a lonely gradschooler (1960-3); Mr. Foster, who recommended me for an elite music school (1962); the lady who shared her pork chop dinner when I was an unemployed college grad (1975); Dick Barkalow, who first helped balance my checkbook (1976); the driver who stopped in the blizzard when I slid off the interstate (1975); Dr. Irwin, who put down my sick dog Ashes at no charge (1984); Sue Cannon (and my sister Nancy and Mom) who brought food (1985); Polly and Herman Swafford, who befriended a young author and editor (1991); Dr. Thiergart, Rex Rogers, Dennis Wiggins, Jeff Gray,

and Gene Mitchell, who willingly read and commented on my manuscripts; 16-year-old Sean, who spent half a week's income to buy an impoverished teen new jeans; Tad, who helped an out-of-work family while he was making minimum wage, and Roxie, Matt and Kate, who fed me for months while I was brokenhearted—These are only a few of the kindnesses I still remember, and they still warm my heart.

382 *Mind Over Matter*, Cole, pp. 166-7.

383 John Cleese on "Creativity" at the Hotel Grosvenor House, London, Video Arts, 1991.

384 *Perfect Health: The Complete Mind Body Guide*, Deepak Chopra, M.D., Three Rivers Press, NY, 1991, 2000, pp. 44-56; 266-83, and *Handbook of Meridian Therapy and More*, Robert Matt Ulmer (The Tao Doc), 2000.

385 Ulmer.

386 Boldt.

387 Ulmer.

388 drlwilson.com/articles/yin%20yang%20healing.htm

389 Ulmer.

390 Boldt.

391 Ulmer.

392 Boldt, pp. 318-20.

393 drlwilson.com/articles/yin%20yang%20healing.htm

394 Boldt, pp. 318-20.

395 Ulmer.

396 Boldt, pp. 318-20.

397 drlwilson.com/articles/yin%20yang%20healing.htm

398 Gerber, p. 401.

399 *Perfect Health*, Chopra, pp. 164, 166, 201.

400 Hunt, p. 70.

401 Jon Kabat-Zinn, Unity Temple of the Plaza, Kansas City, Missouri, 1/30/05.

402 Weber, pp. 58-9.

403 Newberg, Andrew, M.D., and Waldman, Mark Robert, *How God Changes Your Brain: Breakthrough Findings from a Leading Neuroscientist*, Ballantine Books, 2009, p. 156.

404 Cooper, p. 182.

405 *Perfect Health*, Chopra, p. 171.

406 Yogananda, p. 158.

407 *Perfect Health*, Chopra, p. 173.

408 *Hidden Gospel*, Douglas-Klotz, p. 106.

409 Cooper, p. 144.

410 *Sufi Book*, Douglas-Klotz, p. 102.

411 The energy of Reiki connects with Mother Earth, Attunement with the Divine. Together, Reiki and Attunement provide maximum access.

412 *A Course in Miracles*, pp. 111-12/text.
413 Kriya Yoga Workshop, Paramahamsa Prajnanananda, Leawood, Kansas, 2000.
414 *Living Buddha*, Hanh, p. 17.
415 Chris Jorgensen, *Love Made Visible* and Attunement meetings.
416 "Meditations and Intuition," *The Edge*, Nirmal Kaur Khalsa, April, 2000.
417 Chris Jorgensen, *Love Made Visible* and Attunement meetings.
418 Yogananda, p. 247.
419 *The Edge*, April, 2000.
420 Joan Borysenko, "Being in Your Wise Mind, and Your Most Resilient Self," Hay House World Summit, June 7, 2013.
421 Ulmer, 2000.
422 Cooper, p. 222.
423 From various "Seth" publications of Jane Roberts.
424 Wolinsky, p. 86.
425 Tartaglia, p. 80.
426 *Nature of Personal Reality*, Roberts, p. 296.
427 "Peace on Earth, Good Will to All, Part Two," Duke Tufty, Unity Temple on the Plaza, 12/7/08.
428 Zukav, p. 7.

About the Author

M ichelle Langenberg is a prize-winning poet, editor, artist, teacher, Alzheimer care provider, and Master Reiki healer. She graduated from the University of Iowa with a degree in Latin, but prefers comic crime, Harry Potter, and Vivekananda to Cicero and Catullus. She loves the song of the sea, and dreams of living in a bungalow that glows with love, laughter, and blessing.

She has been published by *Chicken Soup* and *The Kansas City Star,* and is author of *The Painted Bible; Portraits of a Poet; Wherever We Are . . . Unity; You Won't Always Be Little, Tad* (children's picture book); *The Book of Great Beginnings: Two-hundred First Lines to Give Writers a Running Start,* the manuscripts, *Lessons from the Brick Wall School* and *Integrative Health Guide,* and two screenplays looking for a producer. She is an INFJ who does not have a pet named "Schrödinger's Cat." She lives by the Law of Kindness and believes that "we are so much more than we think we are." Her website address is www.langefinearts.com.